THE BIRDS OF THE PENTLANDS

"Hills of Home"

Blows the wind to-day and the sun and the rain
    are flying,
Blows the wind on the moors to-day and now,
    where about the graves of the martyrs
    the whaups are crying.
My heart remembers how.

Robert Louis Stevenson

THE BIRDS OF THE PENTLAND HILLS

IAN MUNRO

SCOTTISH ACADEMIC PRESS
EDINBURGH
1988

A*

Published by
SCOTTISH ACADEMIC PRESS LTD.
33 Montgomery Street
Edinburgh EH7 5JX

First published 1988
ISBN (Cased) 0 7073 0542 X
ISBN (Paper) 0 7073 0538 1

British Library Cataloguing in Publication Data

Munro, Ian
　　Birds of the Pentland Hills
　　1. Scotland. Pentland Hills. Birds
　　I. Title
　　598.29413'5

　　ISBN (Cased) 0-7073-0542-X
　　ISBN (Paper) 0-7073-0538-1

Typesetting and Printed in Great Britain by
Lindsay & Co. Ltd., Edinburgh

CONTENTS

Page

Illustrations   vi

Foreword   vii

Preface   x

Acknowledgments   xi

THE BIRDS OF THE PENTLAND HILLS

Introduction   1

Historical Survey   4

A Pentland Traverse 1948-49   14

Species List   20

Summary of Census Work 1932-1934   203

Bibliography   205

Species Index   207

ILLUSTRATIONS

Plates   *facing page*

1   Glencorse Reservoir....................   32

2   Bavelaw Reservoir in Summer...........   33

     Bavelaw Reservoir in Autumn...........   33

3   Logan Glen...........................   48

     Green Cleuch.........................   48

4   Middle Threipmuir....................   49

     Threipmuir Reservoir.................   49

5   North Esk Reservoir...................   96

     Baddinsgill Reservoir.................   96

6   Carnethy and Scald Law...............   97

     Near Dunsyre.........................   97

7   West Water Reservoir.................   112

     Crane Loch...........................   112

8   Medwin Water........................   113

FOREWORD

ROBERT LOUIS STEVENSON spent much of his boy-
hood in Colinton. The yew tree upon which he had a
swing and which is mentioned in his *Child's Garden of Verse*
still stands today in the garden of Colinton Manse, where he lived
with his grandparents, the Very Reverend Dr Louis and Mrs
Balfour. The sojourns he made from the leafy dells of the Water of
Leith into the nearby Pentland Hills, left a deep impression which
lasted all his life. Banished by ill-health to the more clement clime
of tropical Samoa, thoughts of his "hills of home" filled his heart
with a longing so poignantly expressed in his poem 'To S. R.
Crockett'. These verses make immortal the "hills of sheep and
homes of the silent, vanished races". Enshrined in that vision of
the dying poet, is the true likeness of the Southern Uplands of
Scotland known to every walker in the Pentland Hills. Nor are
birds omitted, for it is the "wheeple" of the whaup (curlew) and
the cry of the peewit (lapwing) there, which recounts history and
makes time stand still.

Stevenson's need was not unique. Every city dweller needs a
health-giving outrun to quiet and natural places filled with clear
air and running with pure, clear water — places which have a
great pull on people for a variety of reasons. Recreation in the
countryside is seen today, more than ever before, as essential to
the well-being of people who live and work in towns and cities.

To the folk of "Auld Reekie" and the Lothians, the Pentland
Hills offer a freedom in physical and intellectual pursuits of which
hill-walking and natural history have been an attractive
combination for almost two centuries. During the last century,
ornithology has outgrown all other branches of natural history in
Britain and has carried the banner of nature conservation to the
people. All along, Edinburgh has been a centre of national
interest through the University and the Royal Scottish Museum.
Jardine, Macgillivray, Audubon, Harvie-Brown, Clarke and

Ritchie, all played an important part, but it was not until the 1930s that the modern era began with the founding of the Midlothian Ornithologists' Club (MOC) which subsequently grew into the Scottish Ornithologists' Club (SOC) and, in 1959, the Centre for Ornithology in Scotland. Adjuncts were the Bird Observatory on the Isle of May and the publication of *The Birds of Scotland* (Baxter and Rintoul, 1953) and *Birds in Scotland* (Thom, 1986). The Royal Society for the Protection of Birds and the Scottish Wildlife Trust have also established their headquarters in Edinburgh and have stimulated great interest in birds.

In the midst of all the developments in the last sixty years was J. H. B. Munro, known to all as Ian Munro. With other young contemporaries, to whom he makes acknowledgment in this book, he was a founder-member of the MOC and SOC. A career in accountancy did a great deal to whet his appetite for bird watching, applying himself to ornithology with the painstaking accuracy of a Chartered Accountant! As is obvious from his survey of the Pentland Hills in 1948-49, his appetite for "birding" was greatly enhanced by his long wartime absence. His dedication to study and recording has continued throughout his life, stimulating a daily interest in birds where'er he is and particularly in his annual visits to the Isle of May and many sojourns abroad to Europe, Africa and Asia. In this interest he has been accompanied by his wife Bep, who is an accomplished observer of birds in her own right.

The Birds of the Pentland Hills has been long in coming! As an ardent naturalist and walker in the Pentlands, I have often been in need of this book. Every walk is different and part of that difference — which makes every one as fresh as the one before — is in the birds I see. To walk the Pentlands with this book at hand, is to see the hills through new eyes, to anticipate what might be over the next rise and to have the thrill of seeing a rare species or event. Rarity breeds interest, and with the changes which are taking place today in agriculture and forestry, the use of lime, nitrogenous fertilisers and herbicides in crop-production, some species will become rare or locally extinct, while others will become abundant. The changing face of the Pentlands is evident enough in the character and extent of field, wood, moor, stream and loch. However, for the seeing eye of the naturalist, the birds provide a good indication of what is happening to the habitat as a whole and what might be done to correct mistakes.

To those who manage the Pentland Hills, and to those who go there only to find their enjoyment, Ian Munro has given not only a useful and scholarly reference work on the birds, but a deeper insight into the natural beauty of the Hills and the love he (and thousands like him) has for them.

J. Morton Boyd, CBE, DSc, FRSE,
Colinton,
St Andrew's Day, 1987.

PREFACE

FOR many years the history of the birds in the Pentland Hills was written in the game bags of the landed proprietors, and notes about rarities were published in the records of scientific societies in Scotland.

In the twentieth century, however, public interest in the study of birds has increased and the pace quickens daily, helped by clubs such as the Scottish Ornithologists' Club and the Royal Society for the Protection of Birds, whose meetings and publications have brought bird watching from the province of the few to the hobby of many.

The aim of this book is to bring together the historical records of Pentland birds in the hope that they may form a basis for future investigations.

I have divided the content into four parts:

1. An introduction describing the area covered.
2. A historical survey of this area across the centuries.
3. An account of a fifteen mile traverse of the hills made in 1948-49 which covered 780 miles on the same route.
4. A species list. In addition I have given a summary of census work undertaken in 1932-34. This will be found as an appendix to the text.

ACKNOWLEDGMENTS

I AM most grateful to the members of the Inverleith Field Club and the Midlothian Ornithological Club for their involvement in the census work 1932-34. These were: A. G. S. Bryson, H. F. D. Elder, M. K. Hamilton, W. M. Kerr, G. L. Sandeman, P. W. Sandeman, F. H. Simpson, B. A. Stenhouse, J. G. Stewart, V. Van Someran, G. Waterston, A. D. Watson and E. V. Watson. On one occasion we also had the help of P. W. G. Gunn.

The Misses Rintoul and Baxter kindly sent me unpublished notes from their walks in 1934. R. L. Swann let me have his detailed assessment of the status of species at Threipmuir Reservoir as at 1972. Mr Milne of Musselburgh let me see the volumes of David Hamilton's diaries which started early this century and continued for over fifty years.

Through the courtesy of the Royal Scottish Museum, I was able to have access to unpublished notes by Harold Raeburn, and to see also the *Crosswood Migration Schedules* (1908-19). These are records of dates of arrival of certain species at Crosswood Reservoir each year, kept by the waterkeeper there for W. Eagle Clarke.

Several good friends have allowed me to use their photographs, and Ann Gordon has kindly typed my manuscript.

In 1939 the occupiers of twenty farms or houses in the Pentlands very kindly supplied notes on the status of eighteen species with dates of arrival that year if these species were not resident.

In particular I am very grateful to G. L. Sandeman who answered many queries, and let me have details of his many Pentland records over the years.

Finally, I have been given invaluable advice and help by Scottish Academic Press Limited.

THE BIRDS OF
THE PENTLAND HILLS

INTRODUCTION

THE Pentland Hills run south-west from the City of
Edinburgh for a distance of sixteen miles, and have a
breadth of seven miles at their widest point. To the north
lies the fertile plain of the Lothians, and to the south east low
farmland and moorland stretch across to the Moorfoot Hills. For
convenience I have defined the Pentland area as being contained
within the following boundaries: to the north, the Lanark road
from Colinton to Boston Cottage; to the south, the Biggar road
from Fairmilehead to Dolphinton; to the east, the road from
Colinton to Fairmilehead via Hunter's Tryst; and to the west, the
moorland path from Boston Cottage to near Anston Park, and
thence by the road to Dolphinton via Dunsyre and Garvald
House.

Birds, of course, are not limited in their distribution by
terrestrial boundaries, but the Pentland Hills are isolated to some
extent from the surrounding terrain, and form an interesting
ecological area.

It is believed that the hills were thrust up by earth movement
some three hundred million years ago and consisted of volcanic
and carboniferous rocks. Successive ice ages removed nearly all
the six to seven thousand foot covering of these carboniferous
rocks until about 5000 B.C. when most of the ice had melted, and
the hills had taken roughly their present shape. They do not now
form a continuous ridge but are broken up by many intersecting
glens and hollows, the chief being the valley of the Glencorse burn
near the north-east end. At the east end of the Pentlands,
Caerketton, Allermuir, Capelaw and Castlelaw stand out,
separated from the main chain by Den's Cleuch and the

1

Glencorse valley. To the south of this group, the hills rise to the splendid summits of Carnethy, Scald Law (the highest at 1898 feet), the South Black Hill and the West Kip, whose sharp peak is such a feature of the Pentland range. The other main group consists of the East and West Cairn hills facing the Lanark road.

The hills are crossed by paths, many of which were kirk and market or drove roads in the old days, and these enable one to savour the freedom and ever-changing beauty of the hills. Covered as they are today by rough grass with considerable areas of heather, and with farmland on the lower slopes, views are extensive. Grouse, a relic of more arctic conditions, and Curlew are common, and where the grass is short, Lapwing too. Golden Plover and Dunlin nest in some parts, and where bracken grows one may expect to find Whinchats. The Glencorse valley is particularly rewarding, for here the Ring Ousel is the most common, and Common Sandpipers and Grey Wagtails come to nest. The Water of Leith, which rises beyond Harperrig Reservoir, flows along the Pentlands to reach the sea at Leith; at one time its water was used by many mills, each of which had its dam and lade beloved of Dippers and Grey Wagtails. Nearly all these mills have now gone and the water is cleaner as a result; perhaps the Kingfishers may return one day.

The Lyne Water flowing out of Baddinsgill Reservoir and the North Esk River flowing from the North Esk Reservoir also attract birds. The Peeblesshire West Water which joins the Clyde is a delightful burn with many mossy pools.

The only natural loch in the Pentlands is the Crane Loch lying in a desolate stretch of moorland a mile from the Lanark road, but it has Golden Plover and Dunlin nesting nearby. It seems likely that its name derives from the presence long ago of Herons and not Cranes, a name often given to the Heron in Scotland. Slipperfield Loch at West Linton attracts duck and other water birds.

The ten reservoirs formed between 1822 and 1868 have now been joined by those at Baddinsgill and West Water; all attract birds, and Threipmuir is particularly good as the marshy area of Bavelaw at its west end gives nesting places for duck and grebes. There is also a Black-headed gullery there in most years, while Herons have nested either in Redford Wood (now felled) or

among the pine trees growing near or in the water. The islands at
West Water and Harperrig Reservoirs have attracted Common
Terns and Black-headed Gulls to nest.

There is little woodland within the Pentlands now, and such as
there is largely consists of coniferous shelter belts on sheep walks,
with some deciduous amenity planting at lowland habitations or
along the Water of Leith and other waters. A large recent
afforestation scheme, again of coniferous trees, has been planted
along the Lanark road between Harperrig and Crosswood
Reservoirs, and this has already attracted Short-eared Owls and
Hen Harriers among other species.

HISTORICAL SURVEY

DURING the centuries that followed the last ice age an arctic flora, with its associated animals and birds, spread into the Lothians; for example in 1886 bones of the Horse, Wolf, Fox, Lemming and Reindeer were found in the so-called Reindeer cave on the Dreghorn estate in the Pentlands. It is not unreasonable to suppose that bird species now present in arctic Scandinavia bred on the Pentlands, and included Ptarmigan, Willow Grouse and Brambling. Wading birds such as Wood Sandpiper, Ruff, Spotted Redshank, Whimbrel and Turnstone may also have been common.

As the glaciers slowly receded, large areas of water and marsh were left in the Forth valley right up to the northern flank of the hills: to the south lay an extensive deciduous forest.

When man ventured north into Scotland he was greeted by a rich fauna. Reindeer were common, there were still wild Horses, and the giant Irish Elk may have been present. The great Wild Ox spread through the land. Among smaller animals, the Mountain Hare, which still betrays its former arctic association by its spring and autumn colour change, lived in the hills. Elk were common in the forests; Red Deer, sometimes bearing twenty-two points, were abundant. Roe Deer, while present, were however scarce. Wild Boar were plentiful, as were Badgers and Otters; European Beavers and Lynx still lingered on. The Brown Bear had a wide distribution, and Wolves, because of their abundance, were the most dangerous beast of prey.

About A.D. 80 the Romans swept into the Lothians and later founded large forts at Pathhead and Inveresk, along with a base at Cramond, which were intended to house field armies of tens of thousands of men. Communications to the south were by Dere Street, and another Roman road which ran along the south-east side of the Pentlands. Stretches of this road can still be seen between Nine Mile Burn and Carlops; and at Fairmilehead. The Roman troops and civilian settlements no doubt got much of their

4

food locally, including game from the Pentlands The marshes resounded to the boom of the Bittern, and the plains to the breeding calls of the Crane and Great Bustard.

In the fourteenth century the hills and valleys of the central lowlands were still clothed in the remnants of the ancient forest: this was a vast, little inhabited tract of deciduous woodland, consisting of oak, birch, and thorn, mingling with alder and willow in the swampy valleys that swathed the country, particularly from Peeblesshire to the English border. This forest no doubt formed a safe refuge for birds of prey such as the Buzzard and Kite, and for many passerines (the Black Douglas also found it a safe harbourage).

There were still extensive lochs and marshes near Edinburgh as late as the sixteenth century when the south or Burgh Loch extended to sixty-three acres. Near Sciennes it became a marsh in dry weather, when the copious reeds were the resort of wildfowl and other birds. From 1581 onwards the civic authorities issued edicts against women who in cutting reeds for their cattle harried the birds. The first order proclaimed: "That na gyrs (rushes) women or utheris pas within the South Loch to sheir the gyrs thereof, hary the burdis nestis, tak away the egges of the saming before Midsymer nixt under the payne of skurgein (whipping)," *Historic South Edinburgh*, C. J. Smith.

The extensive Corstorphine Loch with associated marshes lay to the north of the Pentlands, and a lantern burned on the outside wall of the parish church to light travellers crossing this dangerous area. Ducks and waders were no doubt common in the marshes.

Tradition still speaks of the existence of forest in many a district where it is now known only by name. An old jingle goes:

> Calder wood was fair to see
> When it went to Cameltrie
> Calder wood was fairer still
> When it went o'er Crosswood hill.

We must of course remember that "forest" was an area given over to hunting, but may also have contained some woodland and covert along with open areas of browsing pasture.

There was, over the centuries, considerable loss of forest, partly due to climatic change, but much in the Lothians due to man's demands for fuel and housing. The need for fuel must have been great, for even in the fifteenth century coal was extensively used in place of wood, which was scarce. Next in importance was the use of wood for housing: timbered houses were characteristic of Edinburgh even later than 1666, when the great fire destroyed timber built London. In 1508 the Edinburgh magistrates encouraged the citizens to begin clearing the Burgh Muir of its great trees, and many timber wrights were employed. Citizens willing to remove the felled timber were allowed to use it to extend their frontages in the old town by seven feet. Even before this the Romans and later invaders levelled great tracts of forest which might harbour enemies or highwaymen who lurked in remote or closely wooded areas: Thieves Road in Colinton, a name now regrettably renamed Wester Hailes Road, commemorated a favourite place for robbing coach travellers on the road to Lanark. Predatory animals such as the Wolf were mercilessly hunted in the remaining forest areas. The name Wolf Craigs on Baddinsgill Burn suggests that the species occurred on the Pentlands. Birds also suffered. The Kite and Osprey, once common in Scotland, became scarce; while the Raven, which along with the Kite was encouraged as a scavenger on the Edinburgh streets in the sixteenth century, was later mercilessly persecuted.

King Robert the Bruce is reputed to have followed the chase on the Pentlands. Sir Walter Scott relates how Sir William St Clair of Roslin wagered his head that his hounds would kill a white stag, which had always escaped from the King's hounds, before it crossed the March Burn. Luckily for him, his hounds managed to turn the stag at the critical point, and kill it on the near side, gaining for their master the lands of Kirkton, Loganhouse and Earncraig "in free forestrie". Lennox Tower and Bavelaw were traditional hunting seats of James VI, and Mary Queen of Scots also lived in Lennox Tower from time to time, no doubt for hunting or hawking.

Game was getting scarce by the middle of the sixteenth century; in the reign of Queen Mary a statute was passed stating that "deare, rae or other wild beasts and wild fowels are clean exiled and banished by schutting with half-hag, culvering and pistolet", and laying down the death penalty and confiscation of all goods for transgressors. With the troubles and lawlessness of the seventeenth century, and the steady growth of agriculture, the days of many wild animals and predatory birds were numbered. By Act of Parliament of May 1599 it was ordained that "since wyld foule has become so scarce, and since hawking is necessary to keep the lieges from becoming effeminate in times of peace", the sale of certain birds should be prohibited. The Tufted Duck is among the species listed.

I have found no record of the Pentlands having been afforested in historical times, but amenity planting of trees no doubt took place at some great houses such as Bonaly Castle, Dreghorn Castle (originally seventeenth century), and Woodhouselee which was the site of a fourteenth century fortalice. At Woodhouselee, a silver fir was planted about 1700, as well as a considerable number of laburnums.

When we get to the time of the *Statistical Accounts of Scotland* (1791 and 1845), we get a clearer impression of the counties in which the Pentlands lie. In 1791 the report from Dunsyre parish was "there is not much wood. It is chiefly fir, ash, and a few limes". At Kirknewton however we learn that "the appearance of the ground particularly towards the south side of the parish, which was formerly bare and barren, is now greatly altered, both in soil and climate, by means of the improvements and thriving wood plantations that shelter and adorn the higher parts". In Linton parish it was said that "any large plantations are yet in their infancy; the natural wood is hazel, birch, mountain ash and willows. Birch is generally found in the mosses, but no oak has occurred, except once a large one in a moss near the top of Mendick hill. Farmers are now planting trees for shelter belts on the 57 years leases recently granted, for the sheep prevent the growth of natural wood."

In 1791 Calder Wood was still said to be of considerable extent, but it seems to have been formerly six or seven miles in length: the wooding consisted chiefly of oaks, birches, scotch fir and larches. In Currie parish it was recorded that "in the higher grounds to the south where shelter is most needed it is very bare".

One can only guess at what birdlife existed on the Pentlands at this time, but the parish minister for Linton reported in the *Statistical Account* for 1791 that "Goldcrest and Bullfinch are but lately come" and that "migratory birds were Corncrake,

Lapwing, Curlew, Redshank and Swallows''; he also said "The Earn Eagle is sometimes but rarely seen on the heights", and "in winter the Huppoe sometimes visits us". This last record seems suspect, but the Sea Eagle could well have visited the Pentlands as late as 1791, and we know about the grant of Earncraig to St Clair of Roslin as one of the lands won by his wager. The following birds were listed for Mid Calder parish at the same time: Red Grouse, Partridge, Snipe, Woodcock, Skylark, Blackbird, and Linnet. The Goldfinch was recorded but was rare, and Bullfinches were fairly numerous in Calder Wood but uncommon in the neighbourhood.

Changes in agricultural methods were also taking place. The large four horse plough was being replaced by the more modern two horse plough, which enabled more ground to be cultivated in the same time, but in Glencorse parish oxen were still being used. Animal husbandry was being increasingly employed; for example in 1791 Colinton parish had the following stock:

Work Horses	171	Cows	127
Saddle Horses	31	Carriage Horses	10
Breeding Sows	6		

Sheep had been introduced in some numbers, and in 1791 parish totals were:

| Colinton | 4000 | West Calder | 6000 |
| Linton | about 10000 | Currie | a good many |

At Currie, too, considerable numbers of black cattle and also some horses were reared on the pasture ground. These cattle were folded nightly (to prevent them damaging the growing crops) between Whitsunday and the end of September or early October; the folds were constructed on a part of the outfield grass — the enclosure being made of sod dykes — and whins were inserted below the coping sod to make the fence more formidable. These sod dykes were levelled after harvest and the land ploughed. A succession of three or four crops of oats was taken before the field reverted to grass.

Such changes must have had a considerable effect on bird life: passerines no doubt took advantage of the increased insects and seed harvest, while raptors and corvids would benefit from the increase of domestic animals. Wild animals certainly did, foxes were numerous and George Robertson in his *Agriculture of Midlothian* 1794 records "the greatest hardship is the almost impracticability of keeping sheep in the vicinity of Edinburgh, as they are so liable to be destroyed by the ravenous troops of dogs which are so frequently sallying out upon them from the town, often killing scores at a time". Predatory birds no doubt took advantage of this state of affairs. There were rabbits too in the sandhills of Linton parish by 1802 and they would form an additional source of food.

Means of communication were primitive until about 1750: hay and straw in trusses were carried to market on horseback, and dung in bags was brought back in the same way. The public roads were narrow, and often dressed up like avenues or private approaches with tall hedges and woodland plantations which would give shelter and food to an increasing population of finches, buntings, and corvids. Such changes continued and accelerated until in 1845 the *Statistical Account Report for Penicuik* read "its natural and but recent wilderness is everywhere relieved by stripes of planting, dykes or hedgerows".

The *Colinton Statistical Account Report* for 1845 said "there are plantations on the bank of the river belonging to Woodhall, Spylaw, above Swanston (planted by Mr Trotter of Mortonhall in 1766), and on the lands of Mr Trotter of Dreghorn".

In both Mid Calder and West Calder parishes too, where trees were rare about sixty or seventy years before 1845, they were now abundant. In Glencorse parish, a great deal of wood had been planted within the last forty years prior to 1845, and being regularly thinned, had grown to a considerable size: this would provide nesting sites for pigeons, tits, goldcrests and woodpeckers, as well as other passerines and raptors.

It is perhaps worth being reminded of the bareness of the counties surrounding the Pentlands as late as 1802 when Findlater wrote in his *Agriculture of Peeblesshire*, "the variety of hill and dale and water, might furnish scenes of great natural beauty, or even grandeur, were it not for the almost total want of natural wood, for although tradition reports that a great deal of wood once grew in the county, at present few traces of it remain, and where any are found upon the banks of the waters and skirts of the hills, it is mere brushwood, consisting chiefly of birch miserably stunted in growth, some species of grey willow, and a few mountain ashes, with sometimes a fringe of dwarfish alders marking the courses of the rivulets. It may be no doubt reckoned unfair to judge what the natural wood might have been by the remnant that now appears. The former wood may have been grubbed out for fuel, or to make room for pasture or the plough, and what remains may have been stunted in its growth by the repeated croppings of the sheep. The trees however found in the mosses . . . are generally, it must be confessed, of diminutive size. The wood most commonly found in our peat mosses is birch of hazel. Oak is sometimes though rarely found.''

A hundred years earlier (in 1705) Taylor in "a journey to Edinborough" wrote "we travelled the indifferent country to Linton . . . there is no wood in all the country except a few shrubs growing on the sides of the mountains". Taylor saw "but few houses which were more like hog styes". Even about 1750 many of the Scots day-labourers' cottages were built of turf with stone buttresses or wooden posts built into the wall supporting the heavy timbers of the roof. Bird life must have been poor also, certainly so far as number of species was concerned.

In 1794 Johnston in his *Agriculture of Tweeddale* wrote "around Linton there is a considerable quantity of croft land . . . upon which they raise luxuriant crops of turnip and clover for which the soil is peculiarly adapted; none of this land is inclosed". The report from Midlothian for the same year was "enclosing appears to have been but lately introduced, and to have followed . . . the other improvements here, even as late as thirty years ago there was hardly a farm enclosed in the whole county". There were many weeds; wild radish, wild mustard, thistle, dockweed and couch grass are listed, and seed eating birds would benefit.

Findlater reports in 1802 that in Peeblesshire "a considerable number of arable farms were mostly enclosed with hedge and ditch, which by constant repairs with paling, makes a tolerable fence". He also notes "near a great town such as Edinburgh, there is always such high demand for pasture for milk cows and horses, that no mode of culture . . . can compete with pasture in point of profit".

By 1845 it had been found possible to plough higher lands; in

Colinton parish for example this had been done at Swanston at a height of some seven hundred feet above sea level. At Currie a great amount of drainage had been carried out during the previous twenty years: the south west or upland district of the parish consisted of a thin moorish clay, and farmers depended chiefly on growing oats, the rearing of cattle and dairy produce; agriculture was however described as "now in a state of great advancement". There is an interesting social comment on the times: "in consequence of the vicinity of Edinburgh, a number of idle and disorderly persons frequently invade to commit depredations, and besides the great abundance of game, both on the cultivated fields, and on the adjoining moors of the Pentlands, present temptations often too strong for the young and profligate to resist, poaching is consequently no uncommon crime". No detail is given of the nature of the "game", but no doubt it consisted of Hares, Rabbits, Partridge and Grouse, with Blackcock in places. Glencorse Parish too had progressed, for all kinds of grain were being raised, potatoes were planted, and turnips for the winter feed of cattle. Draining was widespread, and the whins which covered many of the fields had been rooted out. Such measures would encourage seed eating birds but reduce the population of Linnets, Yellow-hammers and Stonechats, and also Snipe and Redshank from the marshes.

By 1845 the conditions of the inhabitants had changed. It was reported from Currie that "a great improvement has recently been introduced here as elsewhere into the construction of cottages, which instead of the wretched pig stye like huts that have so long disgraced the character, and deformed the appearance of the county . . . are neat houses with slated roofs and divided into two apartments with other appurtenances". At this time the food of the "peasants" consisted of the various preparations of oatmeal, potatoes, wheaten bread, tea and sugar.

There were Trout and Eels in the waters, and Perch and Pike at Slipperfield Loch, and these no doubt augmented the diet.

What has gone before has I hope painted the backcloth for the historical records of Pentland birds. An arctic fauna gradually disappeared with climate amelioration. After this the hills with low scrub on their sides were surrounded, to the north by lochs and marshes, and to the south by extensive deciduous forest with scope for a richer fauna until the forest was cut down and the marshes drained. It seems likely that at this time the bird population consisted of comparatively few species compared with the present day.

Later the great development of agriculture, the enclosing of fields and the amenity planting of trees and hedges, would have encouraged the spread of finches and woodland species. Corncrakes were regular breeders in the fields until modern farming methods contributed to their extinction.

The maximum variety and species population was probably reached immediately after the 1939-1945 war, during which little interference by man took place. The last thirty years have seen many changes instituted by the greatest predator — man. Woods have been felled, hedges grubbed up, and the stranglehold of increasing housing schemes grows ever tighter. The hope that the Edinburgh ring road might limit the encroachment of the town seems doomed, for there are schemes afoot to "develop" the Swanston and Woodhall farm areas. The hills are increasingly used for recreation, with a successful ski lift at Hillend, fishing facilities at the reservoirs (where considerable poaching goes on), and boating at Harperrig and Threipmuir. All these activities are splendid for humans but detrimental to breeding birds. Mink have been allowed to escape from mink farms and are reported to be devastating wild life, and against which there seems little remedy.

In spite of all the changes that have altered the face of the Pentlands, particularly in recent years, the hills still retain their deep appeal which I have felt over some sixty years of walking for many miles through the glens, and over the crests. One is privileged to become a part of one's natural environment, and to share in its life, with a vivid enjoyment, and sense of belonging. David Hamilton also felt this keenly. On 3rd March 1907 he wrote in his diary: "As I went up by Bonaly Hill I saw several Lapwing wheeling about and a Curlew and also some Golden Plover. It is strange what a delight it gives anyone interested in nature to see certain birds back at their accustomed haunts for the first time after a long absence, especially if you have been in the habit of going over the same ground through the winter when all is lonely and quiet, as the hills are in winter, till one day you are greeted with the well known cries. It does not matter how often you experience this it still gives the same pleasure year after year. At least that is how I feel it.''

A PENTLAND TRAVERSE 1948-49

IT seemed appropriate after six years in the army, when Hitler had interrupted my study of Pentland birds, that I might celebrate my freedom by filling my lungs with good Pentland air, and by finding out something about the pattern of the bird populations, movements, and migration as seen during a fifteen mile traverse through the hills.

The traverse began at Nine Mile Burn, crossed the 1500 feet contour west of the Kips, went through the shelter plantations which then existed south-west of Bavelaw Castle, turned east to pass Bavelaw, Threipmuir, Harelaw, Clubbiedean and Torduff Reservoirs, and so on to Colinton where one could at that time enjoy an excellent high tea.

The first weekly traverse took place on 15th February 1948, and the last (described here) on 31st January 1949. Fifty-two crossings of the hills were made in all, and over 780 miles walked, all on the same route. Ninety-seven bird species were seen.

It soon became evident that the bird population of an area like the Pentlands is never static. In winter, weather conditions may determine distribution, in the breeding season attachment to nesting sites may limit movement, but for the rest of the year the population ebbs and flows like the tides.

Birds were quiet on 15th February 1948, for the skies were overcast and there was some mist and drizzle. There was a little 30 foot Lark song at Nine Mile Burn, but no passerines were seen on the hills apart from a few brave Chaffinches singing in Braid Law Wood at 1250 feet. Other high woods were deserted. Next week when light dry snow fell all day, these Chaffinches had fled, and no birds sang, but there was an infux of Mallard, Tufted Duck, and Goldeneye to Threipmuir. On the 29th, thirty Lapwing appeared on a low field. The reservoirs were frozen and the duck had been driven out. There was little bird song, but Larks were chasing over low stubble, and there were 200 Common Gulls on Threipmuir.

The warm sunshine of 7th March brought big changes. Black-headed Gulls, Golden Plover and Curlew appeared on low ground. The wintering duck population was dropping, but Pochard and Goosander were seen. The first Pied Wagtail of the season flew over Nine Mile Burn. On the 14th there was warm to very warm sunshine all day, and a grand feeling of spring. Chaffinches and Greenfinches were singing, spread out in Braid Law Wood; Curlew were still mostly in flocks on the low ground; but some bold individuals had appeared on territories higher up. The first Redshanks and Coots appeared and Black-headed Gulls were back in their Bavelaw breeding colony. Lark flocks had broken up and there was quite a lot of song. The first Meadow Pipit flew west at Harelaw, and a Mistle Thrush was found in Braid Law Wood.

Next week, however, high wind and lashing rain from the west froze colonisation. Lark flocks were seen once more, no Chaffinches sang, and the high woods seemed deserted. A few Meadow Pipits, Little Grebes and a Dipper were recorded. At East Kenleith two Lesser Black-backed Gulls were down on plough.

The 28th of March was a perfect day of bright sun shining from a cloudless sky. The tempo of colonisation had increased very noticeably. The first returning Starling was reported back at West Bavelaw Farm (on the 25th) — the species is a summer visitor to high farms. Chaffinches had occupied all the high woods except Cap Law at 1400 feet. Neither Larks nor Meadow Pipits had reached the highest moors, but were frequent on lower ground. There was an increase of Coots and Tufted Duck on Bavelaw. Lapwings had occupied territories on low ground, but were not common. There was still a flock of Curlew present. Woodpigeons had reached the low woods on the Kitchen Moss and turned up in Braid Law Wood. Several hundred Common Gulls had come in.

When the next traverse was made on 11th April, complete occupation of breeding areas had been made by Chaffinches, Reed Buntings, Skylarks, Meadow Pipits, Redshanks, Curlews, Lapwings, and Woodpigeons. Blackbirds were as high as Westside Farm at 1200 feet. Jackdaws appeared on grass moorland, but no Mistle or Song Thrushes were seen. Common

Gull flocks were still about, but duck numbers had greatly decreased.

By 25th April summer had come in, for Willow Warblers were found even in the highest woods. Tree Pipit, Whinchat and Common Sandpiper were seen. All the mature Common Gulls had gone. Winter returned briefly on 2nd May when a blinding snowshower arrived at 1 p.m. to be followed by a warm clear period. Sandpipers were common, and a few Swallows and Sand Martins were hawking for flies over the reservoirs. A Shoveler was seen on Bavelaw, to which Tufted Duck had moved from Threipmuir, and where Black-headed Gulls had increased at the breeding colony.

On 9th May breeding birds were still coming in and there were more Meadow Pipits and Whinchats. Snipe were drumming freely. A pair of Black Grouse were in Cap Law Wood and a migrant Green Sandpiper turned up at Bavelaw. On the 16th Chaffinches had left the stack-yards; a young Robin was seen at Westside Farm. Cap Law Wood held a Dunnock and three Greyhens, while Swifts were recorded at Bavelaw Castle.

By 30th May breeding was at its height. Cap Law, the highest wood, had Chaffinches singing freely, and a Robin was also there. There were Mallard broods on Bavelaw and eggs in the Black-headed Gull colony. Three Spotted Flycatchers were seen, and a Wood Warbler was singing at Bavelaw Castle. Rooks and Jackdaws were feeding on hillsides up to 1200 feet for the first time that year. The breeding intensity continued into June. On the 6th loose flocks of Starlings appeared on pasture. Siskins were thought to be nesting in Braid Law Wood. A Tree Pipit sang in Cap Law Wood and a Sedge Warbler at Bavelaw where broods of Little Grebes were seen. There was a flock of Woodpigeons at Bavelaw, but no Common Gulls were present.

Next week Rooks and Jackdaws were foraging up to 1700 feet. There were several Redpolls in Redford Wood. Whinchats were recorded up to 1500 feet. Wheatears were feeding young, and two Goldfinches were at Nine Mile Burn, but Willow Warbler song was decreasing. By the 20th Lark song was also decreasing, and a week later Rooks had ceased to feed on high ground, where there were also fewer Curlews about. This decline in breeding activity continued on 4th July when there was less Chaffinch song. The

Cuckoo ceased to be heard and there were fewer Coots. By the 11th there was no Chaffinch song, and Willow Warblers sang less frequently. Lapwings were flocking.

On 18th July the gradual withdrawal from the open hills had started: only two Larks and just the odd Meadow Pipit were recorded. Lower down there were Rook flocks on rough hillsides, potato fields and cut hayfields, but not on high ground. There was a Starling flock on heather on Hare Hill summit at 1470 feet, and Blue Tits were seen in Cap Law Wood at 1500 feet. No Redshanks were seen.

By 1st August the autumn had set in. Only one flock of Starlings was seen — on Pillar Knowe — and there were small flocks of Meadow Pipits and a pack of eighty plus Woodpigeons at Bavelaw Castle. Curlew were scarce, but there was a noticeable increase in Snipe. The Gull colony at Bavelaw was deserted, and two parties of Oystercatchers flew south-west over Threipmuir. Despite the 15th August being a warm, almost windless day, birds were noticeably absent. Spotted Flycatchers, Mistle Thrushes, Blackbirds, Swifts, Teal, Tufted Duck, Common Sandpipers, Golden Plover, Lapwings and Black-headed Gulls were not seen, but as a makeweight a fine Buzzard appeared over Torduff. This decrease in species numbers continued on 22nd August when no Yellowhammers, Reed Buntings, Pied Wagtails, Song Thrushes nor Curlews were seen, and no Rook flocks. Chaffinches were still in the high woods but in reduced numbers. Larks were commoner, being perhaps on migration, while on the 29th Meadow Pipits were even more common, presumably as migrants. Goldcrests were much more noticeable. The only Swallows seen were at their nesting sites.

Autumn gathered momentum by 5th September when there was a small flock of Greenfinches at Bavelaw Mill along with Chaffinches. Wheatears and Larks appeared to be migrating, while Swallows and House Martins were moving south-west over the reservoirs. Parties of duck (twenty Mallard, thirty Teal, five Wigeon, and three Tufted Duck) were on Bavelaw. On the 12th there were flocks of Greenfinches (fifty plus in total), and fifteen to twenty Mistle Thrushes at Bavelaw Mill. Fifteen to twenty Wigeon had arrived on Bavelaw. There were large flocks of Common Gulls in the Clubbiedean area, where the first migrant

Lesser Black-backed Gulls of the autumn were seen. On the 26th a force 5-6 wind from the south west lashed heavy showers over the route, making the hearing of bird sounds and the use of binoculars almost impossible, but Meadow Pipits appeared to be migrating south-west over low ground, and Teal had increased. October 3rd was by contrast a magnificent day of bright sunshine. The Meadow Pipit migration appeared to be over. Two Lark flocks were seen on stubble but only a single Lark was seen elsewhere. There was a slight increase in Mallard numbers although Teal had decreased. There were Grouse packs on stubble and oat stooks.

October 10th saw an increase in Chaffinch flocks, and breeding Chaffinches had almost deserted the woods. The first Bramblings of the autumn appeared at Braid Law Wood, and among finch flocks at Bavelaw Mill. Mallard had increased markedly but no Teal were seen. It was curious to record Swallow and Snowbunting on the same day. Song Thrushes were migrating south-west.

Bad weather both on 17th and 24th October made observation rather unsatisfactory, but on the 17th there was a flock of seventeen Magpies at Fernilaw Avenue in Colinton. Six Greylag Geese arrived on Threipmuir on the 17th and there were twenty-three on the 27th. There were eight Whooper Swans on Threipmuir on the 17th, and on the 24th the first Goldeneye of the winter arrived.

Despite bright weather on 7th November, the species distribution had become wintry. Skylarks and Meadow Pipits were almost absent. Chaffinches had deserted the high woods, and I felt that winter had descended on the hills. During the next three traverses (14th, 21st and 28th November) the high ground was almost completely deserted, but on low ground, and at the reservoirs, there was a constant ebb and flow of bird life. Yellowhammers were distinctly commoner on the 14th, and included a spartan individual in Cap Law Wood — but it was possibly attracted by the stubble field nearby. Meadow Pipits appeared to be shifting ground. Mallard and Teal had increased and there was a surprisingly large pack of at least twenty-six Shoveler on Threipmuir. Wigeon however had dropped by twenty per cent.

On the 21st there was a very large flock of finches on the West Rig fields, and a few Redwing and Fieldfares were in. The 28th saw an increase in Snow Buntings (first seen on 10th October) to a flock of eighty. There were no Chaffinches in any of the isolated woods and no birds at all in Cap Law Wood. December 12th saw a further contraction in the number of species seen. There were no Larks nor Meadow Pipits, but Snow Buntings and Reed Bunting numbers had increased. By the 19th both Braid Law and Cap Law Woods were completely deserted. A flock of twenty Lapwing arrived at Threipmuir, possibly moving because of a change of weather.

Boxing Day was a beautiful day of light variable wind, bright warm sunshine and hard frost. Bavelaw was icebound, and here only ten Teal were seen, but two Pintail turned up on Threipmuir. No Wrens at all were seen.

On 2nd January there were six inches of snow in the high woods. The hard frost had closed the reservoirs, where duck were much reduced. Two Goldfinches were seen at Harelaw and a flock of eighty Fieldfares at Bavelaw Castle. Ten Fieldfares were seen moving west over the Kitchen Moss, and 300 plus Snow Buntings flew west at Harelaw. On the 9th January, despite the cold north-west wind and patches of frozen snow on the hills, Chaffinches were prospecting in the Braid and Cap Law Woods. Snow Bunting flocks were recorded in five different places.

On 16th January the west wind blowing with a strength of 6 to 7 forced birds to lie low, but duck had moved up to Bavelaw. High winds on 23rd January again made conditions unsatisfactory for observation, but a Goosander arrived on Threipmuir, the first since the spring. The 30th January was a beautiful day of bright sunshine. Larks, surely feeling the pulse of spring, were seen in quite a number of places on low ground and some sang. Woodpigeons were moving into the higher woods, where they were cooing in anticipation of what lay before them.

The tide of life was again flowing into the hills.

SPECIES LIST

DIVERS

Great Northern Diver. *Gavia immer.* Rare visitor.

An apparently undamaged bird was diving in the Water of Leith at Currie from 3rd to 5th January 1935. There is another record of a single bird at the same spot from 3rd to 8th January 1966.

Black-throated Diver. *Gavia arctica.* Rare visitor.

A single bird was seen on Torduff on 25th and 29th December 1930.

Red-throated Diver. *Gavia stellata.* Rare visitor.

One slightly oiled bird was seen on Torduff Reservoir on 4th and 5th February 1987. It was then seen on Glencorse Reservoir on about 7th February and on into March.

GREBES

Great Crested Grebe. *Podiceps cristatus.* Breeds. Occasional winter visitor.

Apart from some records in October the species is purely a summer visitor, arriving during March and leaving early in September. Pairs attempt to nest each year with varying success; this is largely dependent on the water level in the reservoirs. In a dry spring, for example, Bavelaw dries up too early to allow the Grebes to hatch their eggs.

The Misses Rintoul and Baxter recorded (British Birds 1933) that the species appeared to have colonised Threipmuir about 1910, and Bavelaw in 1916, and that nesting continued in both places. In 1931 a pair managed to rear one chick on Bavelaw, while in the same year single adults were seen on Crosswood and Harperrig in October. In the following year a pair was again successful in rearing a single chick, but had to move down to

Threipmuir to avoid being stranded. In 1933 a pair was again present at Bavelaw during the nesting season. In 1934 an attempt was made to nest at Harperrig, where three nests were built by two pairs; by 4th August one nest was almost on dry land but contained three eggs. On 8th August, however, the eggs had gone and nesting was abandoned. 1932-34 census totals were March 4, September and December nil. 1935 and 1936 were both bad years, no young being reared. In 1938 a pair with a young bird were seen at Harperrig on 15th August.

R. L. Swann told me that one pair bred regularly at Bavelaw until 1958, when numbers began to increase. G. L. Sandeman has records of a pair breeding at Bavelaw/Threipmuir in 1972, 1974 and 1975, but although birds were seen on Harperrig in 1970, 1973 and 1974 they did not breed. He saw one bird at Crosswood on 30th April 1970, and two on 22nd May 1973. Two were seen on Glencorse on 14th June 1973, and one on 17th June 1974.

At Bavelaw only one young bird was reared in 1980, but in 1981 three pairs had four young and in 1982 there were five or six pairs. This increase continued in 1984 when five broods were raised, and for a short time in July there were nine pairs present.

The 1984 numbers were held in 1985 and 1986

Red-necked Grebe. *Podiceps grisegena.* Rare visitor.

In 1980 a pair arrived at the east narrows of Threipmuir, and built a nest on which they sat for some weeks. Unfortunately there appears to be no record as to whether eggs were laid or not, and the pair disappeared. In more recent years three birds frequented Bavelaw in the breeding season but there was no confirmation of breeding. It seems that one was seen on Harperrig on 7th April 1979.

Slavonian Grebe. *Podiceps auritus.* Rare visitor.

There are records of one having been seen at Threipmuir on 18th October 1964, and one on Glencorse on 24th December 1967.

Black-necked Grebe. *Podiceps nigricollis.* Rare visitor.

A pair was seen at Bavelaw in 1934 and another pair on Threipmuir on 28th April 1945. There were two records in 1979, one bird being seen on Threipmuir on 27th August and another on Crosswood from 28th September to 15th October. In 1983 one was recorded from West Water Reservoir on 30th April.

Little Grebe. *Tachybaptus ruficollis*. Breeds. Occasional winter visitor.

As a rule the Little Grebe appears on the reservoirs during March, and by early April the full breeding stock is established. Bavelaw is the main breeding area, and here the species is common; but nests have been found at East Threipmuir, Clubbiedean, Bonaly and Harperrig. Normally only one pair breeds on Bonaly, and probably no more than this at Harperrig. In dry weather some nests built near the water edges are left high and dry in June, but a good stock of young is reared each year. During August the families from Bavelaw and East Threipmuir move to Threipmuir. The species then becomes common here, as many as seventeen birds having been seen together in a loose group.

The Grebes generally leave during September, not to return until the following spring; but there are odd records during mild winters from Glencorse, Torduff and Clubbiedean.

David Hamilton saw a pair of Bavelaw on 31st May 1903, but it was 1910 before he recorded the species from Glencorse, and this was a late bird on 20th November. Census totals 1932-34 were March 9, September 27, December 1.

Recent records (1979-84) show an increase in breeding numbers at Bavelaw and Threipmuir from two pairs in 1979 to nine or ten in 1984, when a pair was present on North Esk Reservoir as well.

Breeding numbers continue to increase. There were fifteen to eighteen pairs in 1985 and sixteen to seventeen pairs in 1986.

PETRELS

Fulmar. *Fulmaris glacialis*. Summer visitor. Breeds.

On 30th May 1972, G. L. Sandeman saw one flying over Bonaly Tower, and in the following year one was flying over Torduff on 21st June. Birds have been seen flying over Colinton on several occasions in more recent years. Several pairs have been seen on the quarry face at Torphin and breed there.

During the late 1960s and early 1970s there were occasional reports of Fulmars flying inland over the Edinburgh area. Observations were mainly of single birds from January to July at Torphin. The first evidence of birds occupying a potential breeding site was in 1971, when three were seen for several months on ledges at Torphin Quarry at the north corner of the Pentland Hills 10 km from the sea. In August 1978 one fully grown chick was reported from Torphin Quarry, with four to five sites occupied.

The following records show the progress of this successful colony:

1980	May	27th	Twenty birds
1981	February	26th	Eight birds. Seven sites
	July	7th	Twenty one birds
1982	May	20th	Sixteen birds. One young in August
1983	July	5th	Twenty one birds. No young seen
1984	April	29th	Sixteen birds
	June	19th	Twenty birds
	August	15th	Two young
1985	June	28th	Sixteen sites. One big juv. 4th August
1986	April	2nd	Thirteen sites. Thirty-one birds
	July	1st	Twenty sites. Three sites with possibly six young on 4th August

Storm Petrel. *Hydrobates pelagicus.* Vagrant.

In 1884 William Evans recorded on 19th April that he had heard of one having been caught in an exhausted condition by a shepherd near Harperrig, after one of the severe gales of the last winter.

Manx Shearwater. *Puffinus puffinus.* Rare wanderer.

There are records of the species flying south over Colinton on 18th March 1974 and west over Juniper Green on 4th March

1979. One was seen at West Water Reservoir on 7th September 1980.

CORMORANTS

Cormorant. *Phalacrocorax carbo.* Occasional visitor.

The Cormorant visits the reservoirs occasionally, particularly the larger sheets of water (Threipmuir, Harperrig, Glencorse and Baddinsgill) where the fishing may be expected to be better, but there are records from Torduff and Crosswood. Most of the records are in September and October, and these are usually of single birds which often appear to be immature. Exceptional records are from Crosswood in April, Threipmuir in May, and Glencorse in January. Three were seen together on Glencorse during the winter of 1955, and G. L. Sandeman saw five at Harperrig on 30th October 1973.

There are several recent records in spring. In 1985 three were seen on Threipmuir from 5th to 16th March and three on Harperrig on 9th April. In 1986 there were eight on Threipmuir on 27th April.

GANNETS

Gannet. *Sula bassana.* Vagrant.

Iain Ogilvie of Bonaly Tower told me that during the summer of 1932 an immature bird in starving condition was found on Torphin golf course. It was fed by hand and kept for two months, when it became very tame, coming when called. It eventually learned to take off from flat ground and flew off. The species was seen at Harperrig on 3rd October 1954.

HERONS AND BITTERNS

Grey Heron. *Ardea cinerea.* Resident. Breeds in small numbers when allowed to do so.

Although most often seen at the reservoirs, the Heron is sometimes seen well up the hill burns in all parts of the area, usually singly and throughout the year. It is tempting to link the name Crane Loch — the only natural loch in the Pentlands — with the Crane, but this name was often given in Scotland to the Heron, and it seems more likely that Herons frequented this lonely tarn. No Cranes were mentioned in either Statistical Survey of Scotland (1791 and 1845) as far as the Pentlands were concerned.

David Hamilton saw two at the side of Glencorse on 22nd April 1900 and three there on 24th August 1901, saying "This is the most I have seen there yet". However he saw five standing together at Listonshiels on 25th May 1902, and three at Glencorse on 5th February 1905. On 12th April 1906 William Evans recorded five to six on a tall tree in Redford Wood, and said that they had been there for a week or so; he also mentioned that a number of years earlier R. Lind counted thirteen in the same wood in spring. J. Kirke Nash saw seven wading at the head of Threipmuir on 6th April 1907, and had seen the nest within recent years in the neighbourhood of Threipmuir.

No heronries were recorded in the Pentlands by H. Boyd Watt in 1910, but on 19th April 1913 a nest was found on a small tree growing out of the water at Bavelaw. From 1930 to 1932 nests were found in a wood (now cut down) to the south-east of Bavelaw Mill, and in 1933 a heronry of six to eight nests was found at Buteland Mill: in 1934 this had dropped to two nests. About three or four pairs bred at Bavelaw in 1974 and 1975, but the species is persecuted. One gamekeeper admitted having shot over thirty during the winter of 1932-33. Census totals 1932-34 were March 18, September 46 and December 18.

In 1979 thirty Herons were seen at Bavelaw in the autumn, which suggests the presence of a nearby heronry.

In 1980 there was a maximum of nine at Threipmuir in August to December, and in 1984 a count of eight there on 30th October. Glencorse had counts of eight on 14th January 1982 and seven on 8th December 1984.

A pair bred at Glencorse Reservoir in 1985 and counts of eleven at Threipmuir on 12th April and seven at Harperrig were made. In 1986 there was a maximum of ten at Threipmuir/ Bavelaw on 1st August.

Bittern. *Botaurus stellaris.* Formerly vagrant.
   J. Kirke Nash gives these records:

5th December 1855	A male shot on Mr Cowan's ground on the Pentlands.
24th January 1857	Male shot at Balerno.
19th June 1867	Bittern shot on Pentlands received by Small for preservation on this date.

SWANS

Mute Swan. *Cygnus olor.* A few pairs try to breed.
   The species arrives on some of the reservoirs in spring, and remains until frost or severe weather drives it away.
   J. Kirke Nash said (1935) that it was first introduced to Duddingston Loch in 1678, and that it existed in a state of perfect freedom on such reservoirs as Threipmuir.
   Prior to the 1939-45 war single pairs nested with some regularity at Bavelaw, Harmeny Reservoir, and occasionally on the Water of Leith. R. L. Swann told me that a pair nested at Threipmuir in 1964, 1967 and 1968. G. L. Sandeman said that between 1934 and 1975 he only recorded the bird twice from Glencorse and Loganlee, but that he had breeding records from Bavelaw in 1931, 1932, 1933, 1937, 1939 and 1946. Census totals were March 9, September 13, and December 8.
   In the Mute Swan census of 1981 covering the whole of Britain the only successful breeding place in the Pentlands was at Bavelaw where a pair reared two young. In 1982 there was a pair at Bavelaw but these held territory only.
   In 1985 none bred in the Pentlands. In 1986 two birds were seen on Loganlee Reservoir on 21st April.

Bewick's Swan. *Cygnus columbianus.* Rare vagrant.
   On 18th February 1955 there were two on Bavelaw, along with eight Whoopers and a Mute: these birds had been on the reservoir for at least four days before this. A. J. Smith saw them on the 26th. On 21st February 1956 G. L. Sandeman saw two on Bavelaw, and on 25th April 1960 J. Berry recorded five on Harperrig.

Whooper Swan. *Cygnus cygnus.* Regular visitor in early winter and again in spring.

I have not been able to find any records before 1928, but the species now normally arrives on Bavelaw each year during November in numbers of up to fifty birds, and remains until frozen out in December or January. It has also been recorded at Glencorse, Crosswood, and Harperrig where nineteen were seen on 19th February 1973. In 1953 a few spent the winter at Harperrig and Threipmuir. When Bavelaw is frozen the swans sometimes move down to Threipmuir until this also freezes. In some years they return as soon as the water is again open, but as a rule it is February before the species is again seen.

In spring, numbers are apt to be greater than in autumn. Whoopers usually leave in April, although in 1933 a single bird remained until 2nd May. If they attempt to linger on Bavelaw the cob of the Mute Swan pair which tries to nest there chivvies them relentlessly, which no doubt hastens their departure.

Census totals in 1932-34 were March 7, September nil, and December 8.

The number of Whoopers visiting the Pentlands has increased over 1979 to 1984 as the following records from Bavelaw show:

1980   November 28th   Bavelaw   50

	Jan.	Feb.	Mar.	Apr.	Oct.	Nov.	Dec.
1981	32	31	22	13	16	30	38
1982	4	21	24	9	—	25	20
1983	25	—	2	—	2	20	17

In 1982 there were records from other reservoirs as below:

January 28th, Crosswood ten, April 9th, Harperrig four, November 28th, Crosswood twelve, and December 13th, Harperrig nine.

In 1984 Harperrig had six on January 15th and twelve on November 15th. Other records then were:

Crosswood	February 12th	Eight
	November 8th to 17th	Fourteen
	December 31st	Eight

Threipmuir	December 23rd	Eleven
	April 16th	Last two for spring
Clubbiedean	November 19th	Six flew over

In 1985 the records were:

Crosswood	February 6th	Five
	December 2nd	Two
Threipmuir	March 2nd to 5th	
	April	Up to five adults
	November 23rd	Six
Harperrig	February 26th	Five
	October 30th	Four

In 1986 there were records at:

Threipmuir	March 2nd, April 2nd, November 6th, December 10th
Harperrig	January 14th, March 2nd, November 9th
Crosswood	January 2nd, March 6th

GEESE

Bean Goose. *Anser fabalis.* Vagrant in winter.

There are pre 1939-45 war records for Threipmuir: 1933 October 4th eleven, October 10th eight (a doubtful record), and seven on October 22nd. During the census (1932-34) one Bean Goose was seen in March 1932 and one in December 1933.

A single bird was first seen on Harperrig on 18th November 1933, and it remained there at least until 21st April 1934. It became quite tame, even feeding with domestic geese in Mr Hamilton's garage at Cairns Castle. During the following winter a single bird, possibly the same one, spent a day or two on Harperrig. In 1935 the Misses Rintoul and Baxter recorded "Mr Serle informs us that in recent years this goose has been shot in the Harperrig district".

On 3rd February 1957 one was seen on Glencorse by a number of observers.

Pink-footed Goose. *Anser brachyrhynchus.* Winter visitor, Passage migrant.

This is the commonest Goose in the Pentlands. Flocks arrive early in September and spread out over suitable feeding areas during the winter before leaving again in April. There are recent records from Harperrig and from Baddinsgill Reservoir where the species roosts at night, but the main roost is at West Water Reservoir where large numbers congregate. Here there were 18000 on 6th December 1980 and an astonishing total of 19200 on 16th October 1984, only to be exceeded by 24610 being there on 11th October 1986.

J. Kirke Nash quotes from "Notes" by W. Evans as follows:

1899 December 1st	Saw 25 fly west over Lothian Burn
1901 December 11th	Saw 24 flying over Comiston from the Pentlands
13th-14th	Flock feeding on grass field at Oxgangs
1902 January 12th	Gaggle of 51 flying over Oxgangs at midday
1904 October	One shot at Threipmuir

Last century W. Evans said that it may almost be considered the only member of the group which is found in Midlothian.

In 1946 Mr Prentice, gamekeeper at Baddinsgill, told me that geese believed to be Pinkfeet had started to roost on Baddinsgill reservoir.

White-fronted Goose. *Anser albifrons.* Rare vagrant.

R. L. Swann saw one on Threipmuir on 8th November 1964. Fifteen were seen at Threipmuir on 30th December 1978.

One of the Greenland race was seen at West Linton on 20th October 1986.

Greylag Goose. *Anser anser.* Winter visitor. Passage migrant.

The general pattern is that numbers build up during October and are at a peak in November, with roughly 800 at Harperrig/Threipmuir. During December numbers drop to a very variable wintering population. This decrease seems to coincide with the first onset of really hard weather.

The *Crosswood Migration Schedules* (1909-19) recorded geese flying over on only nine occasions, without specific identification. It seems likely that geese were generally uncommon at that time; even in 1931 when the Midlothian Ornithological Club records began, records of Greylag in the Pentlands were infrequent. Mr Prentice, the keeper at Baddinsgill, told me that one had frequented the reservoir in 1938 since the fishing started that year. I myself saw this bird on 27th August 1938. Dr John Berry writing in 1939 could still describe the species as scarce in the Lothians except in Aberlady Bay. On 9th November 1947 twenty-six were resting on a muddy point at Threipmuir, and on 8th February there were ten at the same place. The species first came to Threipmuir in numbers during the winter of 1949-50. R. L. Swann told me that before this it was unusual to see a Greylag here. Additional figures for Threipmuir are about 200 each November from 1950-54, 1000 in 1964 and 800 in 1968. R. L. Swann says that after winter storms numbers usually rise steeply, reaching up to 3000.

Greylags were recorded on Harperrig in 1952 where peak numbers occur in November, and in the winter of 1952-53 600 were seen. On 29th November 1952 about 500 came in to roost mainly from a westerly or north-westerly direction. None roosted on the other Pentland reservoirs as ice had closed them.

In the *Edinburgh Bird Bulletin* it was reported that since John Berry wrote in 1939 it had become an abundant passage migrant and winter visitor with its inland headquarters at Gladhouse, Threipmuir and Harperrig.

1954 was remarkable in producing some exceptionally large numbers; at Threipmuir there were unusual numbers on two occasions in December, and the continued presence of unusual numbers well into January. Two hundred was the usual roosting population for Threipmuir, but 650 were counted on 28th November and on 11th December F. D. Hamilton estimated 1500-2000 to be on the water, and on the 29th R. Ewing got an accurate count of 1700 in a field by the reservoir. Four visits between 4th and 9th January 1955 produced 500-700 each time. Unfortunately the only records from Harperrig in the winter of 1954-55 were 600 on 7th November (normal for this time of year) and 125 (a day count, so possibly incomplete). On 2nd January

when 550 were roosting at Threipmuir many fields of corn were abandoned after or even before cutting. There were several such fields round Threipmuir, and this may account for the concentration of geese in that area. T. Boyd suggested that excessive shooting at Harperrig may also have driven the geese away to Threipmuir.

Numbers have been studied in detail in recent years, and these results are given below:

1979	December 19th	Harperrig	600	
1980	January 20th	Harperrig	470	Roosting
1981	January 30th	Crosswood	400	
	September 25th	Harperrig	28	
	October 29th	Harperrig	2000	
	November 7th	Crosswood	160	
	November 7th	Harperrig	1950	

Peak counts:

	Feb.	Mar.	Apr.	Aug.	Sept.	Oct.	Nov.	Dec.
1982								
Harperrig	160	—	100	—	—	180	675	—
1983								
Harperrig	—	200	200	—	—	1000	1500	
Threipmuir	—	—	—	—	—	60	300	
1984								
Harperrig	—	—	—	—	—	800	580	8
Threipmuir	—	17	—	38	50	188	150	16
1985								
Threipmuir	29	35	29	24	55	50	170	122
Glencorse	10	17	16	—	—	—	—	—

130 arrived at Crosswood on 12th October and 84 at Harperrig on the same day. On 7th April 91 were seen over Threipmuir.

In 1986 there were peak counts at Harperrig of 750 in January, 800 in March and 800 in November.

There is a feral population at Duddingston Loch in Edinburgh and offshoots from here are starting to colonise the Lothians in increasing numbers. Recent Pentland records are:

1981	Bavelaw	Two pairs
	Glencorse	One or two pairs
1982	Threipmuir	Two breeding pairs
	Glencorse	Two pairs
1983	Threipmuir/ Bavelaw	Two pairs
	Glencorse	One pair
1984	Threipmuir/ Bavelaw	Three pairs
	Glencorse	Three pairs
1985	Threipmuir	Perhaps seven pairs by early May. One pair nested unsuccessfully
1986	Threipmuir	Five-six pairs, one brood.
	Glencorse	One brood

Snow Goose. *Anser caerulescens.* Rare vagrant.

A white-phase bird was seen on Bavelaw on 16th January 1986, and there were two on West Water Reservoir on the 5th October and one there on 11th October.

Canada Goose. *Branta canadensis.* Vagrant.

R. L. Swann saw one on Threipmuir on 25th June 1966. On 31st May 1978 a flock of twenty-five was seen on North Esk Reservoir, and on 4th June 1968 twenty-seven turned up on the West Water Reservoir.

Recent records suggest that the species is becoming more common.

1979	August 24th	Threipmuir	5
	August 27th to September 2nd		11
1980	August 22nd	Threipmuir	2
1981	May 23rd to September 8th	Crosswood and Harperrig	singles
1982	June 13th	Harperrig	10
1983	August 31st	Crosswood	15

Plate 1

Glencorse Reservoir

Plate 2

Bavelaw Reservoir in Summer

Bavelaw Reservoir in Autumn

1984	September 4th	Harperrig	39
	September 17th	Harperrig	17
1985	March 20th	Glencorse	2
	May 11th	Threipmuir	4
	June 18th	Threipmuir	5

Barnacle Goose. *Branta leucopsis.* Vagrant.

On 11th March 1951 there was one at Threipmuir in a mixed flock of Greylags and Pinkfeet. On 24th October 1975 G. L. Sandeman recorded one on Harperrig.

Recent records are:

1982	September 26th	Threipmuir	60
	October 12th	West Water Reservoir	40
	October 21st	Threipmuir/Bavelaw	7
1983	November 13th	Threipmuir	8
	September 30th	Harperrig	80

Brent Goose. *Branta bernicla.* Rare vagrant.

Wedderburn is reported as having seen one on Glencorse in 1863. In February 1912 a bird frequented grass fields on a farm near West Linton, and a day or two later it was shot on the Meadows at Drochil about four miles from the place where it was first seen. The bird was a male in very good condition.

Three were seen on Threipmuir on 9th January 1987.

DUCKS

Shelduck. *Tadorna tadorna.* Uncommon visitor. May have bred.

W. Evans obtained a clear view with binoculars of one on upper Threipmuir on 26th May 1904, and again got a similar view in 1917 when the species was said to have nested by the Bavelaw burn. On 11th August 1957 Charles Walker recorded four adults and three juveniles at Harperrig. G. L. Sandeman saw three there on 11th June 1975, and in 1977 seven were present on the West Water Reservoir on 24th December. Two were seen at Threipmuir on 23rd April 1984.

Wigeon. *Anas penelope.* Migrant spring and autumn. Occasional winter visitor.

The spring migration normally extends from early March to the end of that month, and the autumn movement is during

October. In 1971 R. L. Swann considered that the species was a common winter visitor to Threipmuir where he had seen flocks of up to 150 birds in January.

W. Evans saw eleven on Bavelaw on 5th April 1884, and about two dozen on Harperrig on the 19th April of that year. In the same year he saw sixteen on Glencorse on 2nd November. Harold Raeburn saw some in heather at Threipmuir on 12th February 1888; whilst W. Evans recorded an adult male swimming and flying about alone on Threipmuir on five dates between 16th and 26th May 1904, and he assumed that the female was sitting on a nest somewhere near. W. Evans recorded the species as being a winter and spring visitor to several of the Pentland reservoirs. W. T. Blackwood records that a male in the collection of D. Laidlaw was obtained at Slipperfield Loch.

David Hamilton made the following observations:

1906	April 6th	Threipmuir	flocks
1907	April 6th	Bavelaw	several
1911	February 25th	Threipmuir	several, mostly males
1915	May 16th	Bavelaw	three

The Misses Rintoul and Baxter saw a pair on Bavelaw on 22nd May 1934 and before that year there are records from Baddinsgill, Crosswood and Bonaly as well. In later years David Hamilton recorded Wigeon in small numbers.

1945	April 2nd	Bavelaw	a pair
1946	February 24th	Glencorse	six
1946	April 22nd	Bavelaw	two pairs

Breeding has been proven at Harperrig and Threipmuir but not since 1948 according to Ian J. Andrews.

From the lack of recent records it would seem that the species is less common than it used to be in the Pentlands. There is however a record of forty-seven at Crosswood on 24th December 1984.

In 1985 there was a pair on Crosswood Reservoir on 16th May and in 1986 two males were on Threipmuir Reservoir on 12th April and a pair there on 27th April which suggest breeding attempts.

There were also winter records as below:

1985	November 20th	Threipmuir	15
	December 18th	Harperrig	16
1986	October 11th	Harperrig	9

Gadwall. *Anas strepera.* Rare visitor. Has bred.

W. Evans saw a pair at the head of upper Threipmuir several times between April and June 1916. He was certain they were breeding in the locality, although he failed to find the nest. He said that there did not appear to be any previous record of the species in Midlothian. In 1933 and 1934 the Misses Rintoul and Baxter saw a duck with small young on Threipmuir. David Hamilton said in 1947 that he had never seen the species in the Pentlands over his fifty years experience. P. Holt saw a male on Threipmuir on 3rd May 1958, and I. Balfour Paul saw a pair on Bavelaw on the 11th and 13th May in the same year. In 1965 C. P. Ross saw a male on a small pond at Currie. R. L. Swann has a few winter records of the species.

There is a record of two having been seen on Threipmuir on 29th August 1979. On 2nd August 1982 one was seen on Threipmuir.

Teal. *Anas Crecca.* Resident. Breeds. Passage migrant.

After the Mallard the Teal is without doubt the commonest breeding duck, but numbers and distribution vary from year to year. Nesting begins in March and the families collect on the reservoirs after breeding. Passage on a relatively considerable scale takes place during the latter half of September. Numbers then tend to fall away until the middle of October, when wintering flocks start arriving, and reach a maximum between then and February.

William Evans had records of breeding in the Bavelaw area between 1881 and 1891, and Harold Raeburn found two broods at East Threipmuir marsh on 3rd June 1889. J. Kirke Nash continued the records of nesting in the Bavelaw area in 1898 and 1904. He also found two pairs on a marsh on the top of Torduff

Hill on 19th March 1896. David Hamilton recorded a pair on Glencorse on 5th May 1900, one or two on Bonaly on 12th April 1902, one or two at Bavelaw on 14th April 1906, a pair on Glencorse on 20th April 1907, about three dozen on Bonaly on 20th December 1914 and two pairs at Loganlee on 24th October 1926.

W. Evans recorded nests in the opener part at the west end of Redford wood until the wood was cut in 1919-20. The Misses Rintoul and Baxter said "During winter small flocks frequent the Pentland reservoirs", and they saw a pair at Bavelaw on 22nd May 1934.

The total figures recorded during the 1932-34 census were March 154, September 214, and December 210.

John Prentice, gamekeeper at Baddinsgill, told me that Teal are resident there. G. L. Sandeman found Teal breeding at the Crane Loch on 11th July 1953. A large flock of over three hundred was seen at Bavelaw on 5th January 1947 turning and twisting like waders. In 1971 R. L. Swann said that the Teal was a common breeder at Threipmuir, where twenty to thirty birds were present.

Monthly peaks:

	Jan.	Feb.	Mar.	Sept.	Oct.	Nov.	Dec.
1981							
Crosswood	—	—	—	200	400	300	—
Threipmuir/ Bavelaw	—	50	81	20	—	—	—
1982							
Crosswood	—	—	—	—	300	200	—
Threipmuir/ Bavelaw	25	27	34	—	—	50	25
1983							
Threipmuir/ Bavelaw	—	50	3	—	100	—	—
1984							
Threipmuir/ Bavelaw	—	20	—	—	134	—	—
Crosswood	—	—	26	80	800	150	200

Breeding:
1983
North Esk
Reservoir   One Brood
West Water
Reservoir   Nine to ten broods

Records:

There were 320 on 7th November 1982 also at West Water and 130 on Harperrig in the middle of October 1984.

In 1985 there was a pair on North Esk Reservoir on 29th May and four birds on Crosswood on 27th June, but there was no sign of breeding on Threipmuir/Bavelaw. In 1986 there was one brood there, and a pair on North Esk Reservoir on 11th May. Counts were made:

1985

Threipmuir	Jan.	Feb.	Mar.	Apr.	July	Oct.	Nov.	Dec.
	—	40	—	12	5	2	25	4

1986

| Threipmuir | 33 | — | — | — | — | 40 | 39 | — |
| Crosswood | — | — | 20 | — | — | — | — | — |

Mallard. *Anas platyrhynchos.* Common resident. Winter visitor. Passage migrant.

In the Pentlands, as in most other parts of the country, the Mallard is the commonest duck at all seasons. It occupies its breeding quarters during March, and is then widely scattered round the reservoirs, along the more rural stretches of the Water of Leith and other waters, and on the low moors and bracken slopes up to 1100 feet at least. In 1936 a nest was found at this height in long heather near the Bore Stane on 6th June. Wintering birds arrive in successive waves about the middle of September, and the stock reaches a maximum of around 600-900 between November and February. The birds are not firmly associated with a particular sheet of water, and on being disturbed, rise in packs which often split up, and parties fly off to other reservoirs. Local weather conditions have considerable effect on the winter distribution, severe wind or frost reducing the number of birds present. The wintering population departs during February and March.

Harold Raeburn found two Mallard high up a burn at Medwin on 26th June 1890. W. Evans recorded the species nesting in the opener parts at the west end of Redford Wood until this was cut down in 1919-20. The Misses Rintoul and Baxter found it breeding plentifully in the Lothians, and said that numbers also wintered on many of the reservoirs. The total numbers recorded during the 1932-34 census figures were March 968, September 344, and December 1598. John Prentice, the Baddinsgill gamekeeper, often found as many as 200 on the reservoir there. G. L. Sandeman found it breeding at the Crane Loch on 11th July 1953.

R. L. Swann told me in 1971 that he found the Mallard to be a common breeder at Threipmuir, and that numbers rise to about 450 in winter, with a maximum of more than 1000 on 13th December 1964.

There are also breeding records as below:

1982	Threipmuir/Bavelaw	8 broods
1983	Threipmuir/Bavelaw	7 broods
1984	Threipmuir/Bavelaw	c15 broods
1985	Threipmuir/Bavelaw	13 broods
1986	Threipmuir/Bavelaw	7 plus broods

Recent peak counts:

	Jan.	Feb.	Mar.	Apr.	May	June	July	Aug.	Sept.	Oct.	Nov.	Dec.
1981												
Threip/Bavelaw	310	294	128	—	—	—	—	—	—	450	1000	—
Harperrig	200	—	—	—	—	—	—	—	—	—	—	—
Glencorse	—	131	—	—	—	—	—	—	—	—	117	—
Crosswood	—	—	—	—	—	—	—	—	—	150	—	—
1982												
Threip/Bavelaw	230	250	100	36	—	—	—	163	40	420	200	220
Harperrig	150	100	50	—	—	—	—	—	50	180	150	150
Glencorse	66	47	38	40	—	—	—	—	—	—	140	186
1983												
Threip/Bavelaw	200	208	120	25	—	—	—	394	350	350	300	400
Harperrig	70	110	30	—	—	—	—	—	—	150	80	100
Glencorse	115	77	58	—	—	—	—	—	28	43	200	281
Crosswood	—	—	—	—	—	—	—	—	—	—	—	175
1984												
Threip/Bavelaw	—	200	40	50	42	12	134	578	250	300	—	64
Harperrig	—	55	50	—	—	—	—	—	55	400	100	350
Glencorse	50	126	54	10	—	—	—	—	65	—	80	114
Crosswood	—	21	30	—	—	—	—	—	70	350	200	35

	Jan	Feb	Mar.	Apr.	May	June	July	Aug	Sept	Oct	Nov	Dec
1985												
Threipmuir	100	53	68	27	37	27	47	28	110	266	434	265
Glencorse	48	124	54	—	—	—	—	—	28	104	114	154
1986												
Threipmuir	220	200	112	40	34	19	34	231	78	154	460	160
Harperrig	400	—	50	1	4	—	—	—	—	160	—	—
Glencorse	128	112	66	2	—	—	—	—	8	52	58	184
Torduff	—	73	—	—	—	—	—	—	—	—	—	—
Loganlee	—	—	—	37	—	—	—	—	—	—	—	—

Pintail. *Asas acuta*. Occasional visitor. May have bred.

Most of the records fall between October and January, but in 1904 W. Evans recorded the species on six occasions at Threipmuir between 22nd April and 20th May. He saw a pair there on 16th May. The local gamekeeper said that a pair was on the upper pond in 1910. W. Evans also recorded that he had been told that a Pintail's nest had been found in 1912 near Listonshiels. A drake was seen on Threipmuir on 23rd January 1938, and another on Bavelaw on 2nd April 1939. Single males were seen on Glencorse in January of 1958 and 1964. In 1966 six Pintail were seen on Threipmuir in April. G. L. Sandeman has the following records:

1971	January 15th	Bavelaw	Two
	December 13th	Harperrig	Three
1973	October 2nd	Harperrig	Female
	October 15th	Harperrig	Male
1974	October 11th	Threipmuir	One

Later records are:

1981	October 28th	Threipmuir	One
1982	January 20th	Threipmuir	One
1985	February 6th	Crosswood	Male

Garganey. *Anas querquedula*. Rare visitor.

In 1963 A. D. K. Ramsay saw a pair on Threipmuir on various dates between 11th and 31st July.

Shoveler. *Anas clypeta*. Summer visitor. Breeds. Occasional winter visitor.

The Shoveler normally arrives at Bavelaw/Threipmuir, which is the main nesting area for the species, in March, and leaves after breeding, but it has been recorded in August and September. The winter birds, if any, are normally seen in November, December or January.

The Misses Rintoul and Baxter said that the Shoveler nested annually in Midlothian before 1902 as recorded by Millais, and Threipmuir seemed to be its headquarters. Mr Evans first saw the species there in December 1898, and a pair which he saw in 1904, also at Threipmuir, were, he considered, obviously nesting. He found Shovelers' nests there in 1910.

David Hamilton saw a pair at Bavelaw on 19th April 1913, and Mr Serle found a nest with nine eggs at Harperrig in 1926. In 1934 the Misses Rintoul and Baxter saw a pair on Bavelaw on 22nd May and said in 1935 that the species had established itself and now bred regularly.

The total figures for the 1932-34 census outings were March 20, September and December nil.

G. L. Sandeman has records during the breeding season from Bavelaw/Threipmuir in 1939, 1946, 1953, 1957, 1958 and 1966.

R. L. Swann told me in 1971 that about five pairs bred at Threipmuir in most years where the species was a summer visitor. He considered the maximum number in spring to be twenty-seven, which he saw on 3rd April 1966. His observation seems to indicate some spring migration.

Twelve arrived at Threipmuir from the north-east on 4th October 1970.

Recent records from 1980 to date seem to indicate that numbers have fallen, the highest count during that time being four at Threipmuir on 29th April 1983. There have been sightings in April, May and June, with one at Harperrig on 30th January, and three at Bavelaw on 17th October.

A single bird was seen in spring 1985 at Threipmuir Reservoir, and a pair there on 29th to 31st March 1986, and later, may have bred. Three were seen on Threipmuir Reservoir on 24th November 1986.

Pochard. *Anthya ferina.* Winter visitor in small numbers. Has bred.

Under normal conditions Pochard may be seen in winter between October and March at Glencorse, Harelaw, Harperrig, and Bavelaw/Threipmuir, but frost drives them to unfrozen water. The majority of the birds are males. Scattered records during August and September suggest autumn passage.

W. T. Blackwood recorded that the species had been seen on Slipperfield Loch, from which a specimen was secured for West Linton School Museum in 1925. On 10th December 1905 David Hamilton saw about fifty ducks on Glencorse, and most of them were Pochard; he saw several on Bavelaw on 1st March 1913, and on 23rd December 1928 he recorded "a number" on Threipmuir and Bavelaw.

The total census figures 1932-34 were March 12, September 2, December 28.

The Misses Rintoul and Baxter said that they had been told that before 1935 the species wintered at the Pentland reservoirs. In 1971 R. L. Swann told me that it was only seen in spring and autumn in small numbers, but that in 1966 two pairs bred at Bavelaw and birds were present in the following winter.

Single pairs nested at Threipmuir/Bavelaw in 1968, 1974-75 and 1980.

Recent peak counts:

	Jan.	Feb.	Mar.	Apr.	May	June	July	Aug.	Sept.	Oct.	Nov.	Dec.
1981												
Threip/Bavelaw	—	35	—	—	—	—	—	—	—	19	—	17
Glencorse	—	—	—	—	—	—	—	—	—	—	—	14
1982												
Threip/Bavelaw	6	26	20	—	—	—	—	—	2	36	23	4
1983												
Threip/Bavelaw	6	10	19	4	—	—	—	—	—	18	10	12
1984												
Threip/Bavelaw	—	—	10	12	—	1	5	7	6	23	33	12

There are in addition these summer records:

1981	Threipmuir	April to June	1-2 drakes
1982	Bavelaw	July 23rd	Two
1983	Bavelaw	May 4th	Male
1984	Threipmuir	June 22nd	Male
		July 4th and 8th	Female

The *Lothian Bird Report* for 1985 records that it is now five years since breeding was proved at Bavelaw.

Tufted Duck. *Anthya fugilula.* Winter visitor. Passage migrant. Breeds.

The wintering population, which is largely confined to Bavelaw/Threipmuir, is very variable in size, ranging from one or two to between fifty and a hundred. In March there is an influx, and in 1971 R. L. Swann told me that as a rule some ten plus pairs remain to breed on the Red Moss at Bavelaw.

The species was unknown in the Pentlands a hundred years ago. W. T. Blackwood notes that the specimens in the West Linton School Museum had been obtained on Slipperfield Loch but does not give a date.

The 1932-34 census totals were March 59, September 53, and December 44.

Forty-two were seen on Glencorse on 1st January 1980, and the following peak counts show the recent distribution:

	Jan.	Feb.	Mar.	Apr.	May	June	July	Aug.	Sept.	Oct.	Nov.	Dec.
1981												
Threip/Bavelaw	34	60	43	50	14	26	90	118	50	16	2	2
Glencorse	—	1	—	—	—	—	—	—	19	89	117	50
1982												
Threip/Bavelaw	—	57	30	30	17	19	86	129	60	40	38	36
Glencorse	1	1	—	—	—	—	—	—	46	48	23	1
1983												
Threip/Harelaw	45	19	53	58	14	26	103	127	26	14	11	29
1984												
Threip/Harelaw	—	—	28	44	33	30	102	113	50	26	10	14
Harperrig	—	—	4	—	—	—	14	60	220	40	25	13
1985												
Threipmuir	6	16	68	44	59	62	152	135	18	33	26	20
Harperrig	—	—	—	—	—	2	—	24	17	6	10	—
North Esk	—	—	—	—	16	—	—	—	—	—	—	—
1986												
Threipmuir	36	1	49	48	55	45	125	126	48	33	44	1

Breeding records during the above period showed four pairs on North Esk Reservoir and some eleven to thirteen pairs on Threipmuir and Bavelaw.

The species now appears casually on Torduff and Clubbiedean.

In 1986 two pairs bred on the North Esk Reservoir and one at Harperrig. In addition twelve were seen on Loganlee Reservoir on 21st April where the species is unusual.

Scaup. *Anthya marila.* Rare.

Seven were seen on Crosswood on 2nd October 1931. Two were present on Threipmuir on 3rd and 10th October 1948, and there was an immature bird there on 17th October. R. L. Swann told me that one was seen on Threipmuir on 3rd April 1954.

The above records show that October is the month during which to look for Scaup in the Pentlands, but on 14th November 1983 three immature females turned up on Crosswood, and on 7th November 1985 a female was seen on the West Water Reservoir.

A female was seen on Harperrig Reservoir on 15th and 26th January 1986, and at Threipmuir Reservoir a female was present on 4th and 20th April 1986.

Long-tailed Duck. *Clangula hyemalis.* Rare.

There is a record of one having been present at Harperrig on 11th-12th December 1983.

A female was seen on Threipmuir Reservoir from 16th to 23rd November 1985.

Common Scoter. *Melanitta Nigra.* Rare.

R. L. Swann told me that one stayed on Threipmuir for two weeks in May 1965.

Goldeneye. *Bucephela clangula.* Winter visitor. Passage migrant. Occasional at other times.

The winter visitors normally arrive in October and leave again in February. There are indications of passage in April and September, and there are some summer records which suggest that perhaps the species may nest some year if suitable sites can be found. In 1932, for example, a pair was seen at Harelaw on 28th and 30th June. The 1932-34 total census figures were March 26, September 6 and December 8.

W. Evans only recorded the Goldeneye on three occasions between 1899 and 1920 in winter and on Clubbiedean and Threipmuir. W. T. Blackwood recorded it as having visited Slipperfield Loch in 1925.

In 1947 David Hamilton told me that Goldeneye could be seen in small numbers on most of the reservoirs. He saw a male on Glencorse on 3rd March 1907.

Numbers have increased since these early days; for example six were seen on Harperrig on 10th December 1945. G. L. Sandeman had records from Glencorse and Loganlee from mid-October to mid-February 1946-49, and he saw fourteen on Harperrig on 12th December 1972.

In 1971 R. L. Swann said that it was seen regularly each winter, when he had seen ten on Threipmuir. G. L. Sandeman had two very interesting records: one on Harelaw on 7th May 1974 and one on Threipmuir on 15th May 1975.

In 1980 there was even one on Threipmuir as late as 31st May. In 1982 thirty were seen on Harperrig on 5th November.

In 1985 there was an immature male on Threipmuir Reservoir on 23rd May, and in 1986 a female was seen on Threipmuir as late as 10th May where the maximum number of birds present was nineteen on 13th April that year.

Smew. *Mergus albellus.* Occasional winter visitor.

The first record I have been able to trace was of a female on Threipmuir on 25th October 1947, and since that date there have been several sightings between then and 3rd April indicating that the species is a winter visitor between October and April. Most of the records are of single birds — females or redheads — but a male was seen on Loganlee on 24th December 1967. Threipmuir is the favourite reservoir, but there is a record from Glencorse in addition to the Loganlee one above.

In 1971 R. L. Swann told me that odd birds turned up on Threipmuir in most years between November and March.

Recent records are:

1980	April 4th	Threipmuir	Redhead
1983	December 11th-31st	Threipmuir	Female
1984	January 7th-8th	Threipmuir	Redhead

Red-breasted Merganser. *Mergus serrator.* Infrequent visitor.

There is an early record of a male on Threipmuir on 20th November 1920, but I have no further records until G. L. Sandeman saw three at Harperrig on 16th September 1971. In 1974 he saw a female on Threipmuir on 28th March and two on

Threipmuir on 16th April. In 1975 he saw a male on Harelaw on 16th April.

One was seen on Harperrig on 11th June 1979.

Goosander. *Mergus merganser.* Irregular winter visitor. Passage migrant in spring.

The Goosander is a winter visitor to the larger reservoirs in variable numbers between November and March, usually fewer than six birds being present. In March, however, a relatively large movement takes place, and back in 1933 no fewer than twenty-one were recorded on one day.

At this time, too, Goosanders occur on some of the larger burns such as Medwin and West Water. W. Evans recorded the species on five occasions between 1884 and 1916 in December and March, and a male was seen on Upper Threipmuir in May 1916. The total 1932-34 census figures were March 38, September nil and December 13.

In 1933 David Hamilton saw two on Threipmuir/Bavelaw on 16th April. The Misses Rintoul and Baxter said "It also winters at numerous Pentland localities".

Between 1934 and 1939 G. L. Sandeman saw single birds on Glencorse in March, while R. L. Swann saw singles on Threipmuir in April 1965 and February 1966 as well as one on Glencorse on 13th November 1965.

G. L. Sandeman said that between 1947 and 1975 the species was a winter visitor to Glencorse between October and March, with a maximum of ten there on 5th November 1973. He also saw one on Threipmuir on 1st January 1947, one at Harelaw on 1st January 1975, and another on Threipmuir on 12th December of that year.

Recent peak counts are:

	Jan.	Feb.	Mar.	Apr.	May	June	July	Aug.	Sept.	Oct.	Nov.	Dec.
1982												
Harperrig	7	3	8	—	—	—	—	—	1	—	—	—
Crosswood	—	5	—	—	—	—	—	—	—	—	—	—
Threipmuir	—	—	—	—	—	—	—	2	—	—	—	—
Bavelaw	—	—	—	—	—	—	—	—	14	—	—	—
Glencorse	—	—	—	—	—	—	—	—	—	—	5	—
1983												
Harperrig	—	—	18	18	1	—	—	—	—	—	—	—
Glencorse	—	—	4	—	—	—	—	—	—	—	7	—

	Jan.	Feb.	Mar.	Apr.	May	June	July	Aug.	Sept.	Oct.	Nov.	Dec.
1984												
Harperrig	—	—	14	—	—	—	—	1	4	3	—	14
Crosswood	—	—	17	—	—	—	—	—	3	—	—	—
1985												
Harperrig	—	—	17	3	—	1	—	—	—	7	5	2
1986												
Crosswood	4	—	—	5	—	—	—	—	—	—	6	5
Harperrig	3	—	8	7	—	—	—	—	1	1	—	—

In 1983 two were seen on Threipmuir on 22nd June, and in 1984 there were two females at the North Esk Reservoir on 4th April and a female on Glencorse on 12th May. Such recent records indicate that Gossanders are becoming commoner in the Pentlands and are extending their visits to include the summer months.

BUZZARDS, EAGLES and HARRIERS

Honey Buzzard. *Pernis spivorus.* Rare.

There is a record of one being seen at Balerno on 24th September 1976.

White-tailed Eagle. *Haliaeetus albicilla.* Formerly rare.

The *Old Statistical Account of Scotland* 1791 records for Linton Parish: "The Earn Eagle is sometimes but rarely seen on the heights". The Earn or Erne Eagle is an old name for the White-tailed Eagle.

Marsh Harrier. *Circus aeruginosus.* Rare.

Singles were recorded by R. L. Swann at Threipmuir in spring 1965 and 1971; and at Bavelaw from 11th July to 25th August 1976.

In 1981 a female frequented Threipmuir/Bavelaw from 13th to 24th May, and one was seen at the West Water Reservoir on 29th May of the same year. In 1982 two immature females were seen at Bavelaw on 14th May and one was seen there on 19th May.

Hen Harrier. *Circus cyaneus.* Occasional winter visitor.

Visits appear to be more frequent in recent years, for David Hamilton despite many Pentland visits never saw the species, nor have I in over fifty years of birdwatching there.

In 1837 Macgillivray recorded: "My son while searching for insects on the Pentland Hills in the summer of 1835 saw a pair, when flying low over the heath started a Red Grouse, which one of them captured after a short chase." In 1910 T. G. Laidlaw said "About the beginning of November two Hen Harriers were seen hunting the moors in the West Linton district, and on the 17th one of the birds, an adult female, was shot on the White Moss at Medwin. Its crop contained the flesh of a Grouse. The Hen Harrier is now a very rare visitor to the district."

In 1911 W. Evans wrote "Saw female in Small's shop shot this date 22nd November 1911".

On 18th October 1964 C. Tait recorded one at Threipmuir, and T. Boyd saw two there on 22nd November. In 1971 R. L. Swann said that it was an occasional winter visitor to Threipmuir. In 1974 G. L. Sandeman saw single birds at Threipmuir on 11th October and Bavelaw on 13th November.

There have been an astonishing number of sightings between 1979 and 1984. Most of these records are of single birds and fall during the winter between August through to February. Loganlee, Threipmuir, Harperrig, Bavelaw, Crosswood and North Esk Reservoirs were all visited during that period. A male was seen at Crosswood on 19th April 1982.

There are further signs of an increase of sightings. In 1985 there were records of single birds at Bavelaw on 1st January, 2nd and 16th March and also of two at Bavelaw on 22nd December. In 1986 there were ringtails at Bavelaw on 4th and 16th January and at Harperrig on 11th October.

Sparrowhawk. *Accipiter nisus*. Resident in varying numbers.

It is perhaps interesting to look back to a status note which I wrote just after the 1939-45 war which reads: "Summer visitor, resident in small numbers, also possibly a post-breeding visitor," and went on to say — "the Sparrowhawk is much less commonly recorded than the Kestrel, possibly partly due to its frequenting the more thickly wooded areas, and its secretive habits. Young birds are however frequently met with after the breeding season, and the gamekeepers report birds shot at this season each year. I have breeding records from Harelaw, Buteland Hill and Bavelaw where the Sparrowhawk was nesting in the pine plantations, in the old nests of other species.

There are not many winter records, suggesting that the area may be largely deserted at this season.'' I have no reason to change this status today.

I have been able to trace records back to 1886 when Harold Raeburn saw a pair in the T Wood above Swanston on 11th April. On 12th May 1901 David Hamilton found a nest (c5) at Glencorse, and in 1915 a nest (c3) in a small Spruce at Cockburnhill. Between 1931 and 1939 the Midlothian Ornithological Club records show that odd birds were seen, but that the species was uncommon or very secretive. David Hamilton however said in February 1947 that Sparrowhawks were not uncommon and had in the past nested at Logan Cottage Wood, Cockburn, and in the wood above Listonshiels.

Our only census records (1932-34) over nine outings were one in December and two in March, whereas during the 1948-49 traverse the species was seen at seven different localities. There is no doubt that the species was commoner after the 1939-45 war during which persecution had dropped.

G. L. Sandeman noted that he had very few records from the Flotterstone to Glencorse and Loganlee district between 1934 and 1975.

In 1971 R. L. Swann gave as the status at Threipmuir "Occasional visitor, one female present during most of May 1966". G. L. Sandeman has records from Crosswood on 3rd August 1973, at Threipmuir on 21st January 1974, at Bavelaw on 11th October of that year, at Crosswood on 23rd April 1975, and a breeding record from Harelaw on 23rd July also in that year.

In 1986 one or two were reported from Bavelaw and Bonaly Tower.

Goshawk. *Accipiter gentilis.* Rare.

On 15th April 1966 N. A. Macdonald and R. L. Swann saw one in Dens Cleuch.

Buzzard. *Buteo buteo.* Occasional visitor.

The Buzzard seems to be more often seen nowadays than before the 1939-45 war. I have not been able to find any records

Plate 3

Logan Glen

Green Cleuch

Plate 4

Middle Threipmuir

Threipmuir Reservoir

earlier than 1938 when one was seen being mobbed by Carrion Crows at Bavelaw on 14th September.

David Hamilton saw only one Buzzard on the Pentlands during his fifty years' experience, and that was at Currie on 5th September 1943.

We saw none during the 1932-34 census work, but on the traverse in 1948 two were seen, one at Braid Law on 15th February, and the other being mobbed by Rooks at Torduff on 15th August. One was seen at Baddinsgill on 29th December 1952 and 1st January 1953. One was seen again at Baddinsgill on 3rd June 1956: it flew towards Crosswood. In 1958 one was seen working the hills around Baddinsgill on 4th November, and in 1962 W. M. Kerr saw one just north of Carlops on 20th October. H. A. Ford saw one at Fairmilehead on 28th and 30th August 1964. R. L. Swann has these records for Threipmuir: one on 9th October 1965, and one on 27th November 1966. G. L. Sandeman saw one on the Lang Whang on 13th January 1975.

There is a record of one at North Esk Reservoir on 13th September 1983 and one at West Bavelaw on 24th February 1985.

In 1986 one was seen at Bavelaw on 12th September.

Rough-legged Buzzard. *Buteo lagopus.* Rare winter visitor.

The Misses Rintoul and Baxter said (*A Vertebrate Fauna of the Forth*) "An occasional winter visitor . . . their favourite quarters are the Lammermuirs and Pentlands". A note is given in the Proceedings of the Royal Physical Society of three specimens being taken in the Pentlands and another two that were in the same district but not captured (9th November 1895). On 25th November 1896 one was killed on the Pentlands according to A. H. Evans (*A Fauna of the Tweed Area*). In October 1903 an astonishingly large influx took place. Three were first noticed about the middle of October on a hillside near Logan House. A few days later four were observed, and then more. One was shot shortly after their first appearance, and a second by 5th November. On 7th November no fewer than eight were seen above Loganlee by one of the keepers, and on the same day a third was shot. On 15th November Mr Eagle Clarke and Mr T. G. Laidlaw saw at least four, that number being in view at the same time hunting the Hillsides on the south side of Glencorse Reservoir.

W. Evans went over to Loganlee on 15th December and saw several, (there were three or five) and heard that another had been shot on 3rd December. He said: "Those frequenting the Pentlands have, I believe, been living largely on moles, which have been very abundant on some of the hillsides there of late, though no doubt a good many rabbits have also been taken. One of the birds dropped a mole when shot at, and I found two partly devoured moles on a grassy slope over which the Buzzards were seen to hunt a good deal. All the specimens examined seemed to be immature birds."

In 1965 A. D. K. Ramsay watched one at close quarters hovering and perching on the Black Hill on 12th December, and in 1966 J. Johnson and R. W. Swann saw one at Glencorse on 30th December.

Golden Eagle. *Aquila chrysaetos.* Rare.

A. C. Cowan in (*Edinburgh Bird Bulletin*) reported details of a Golden Eagle which he saw at the Cauldstane Slap on 19th May 1951. "It flew low over the moss in front of us . . . it was swooped at furiously by a Merlin which looked about the size of a Swallow against the Eagle's impressive span. The Eagle was presumably an adult or near adult."

Osprey. *Pandion haliaetus.* Rare.

Now that Ospreys have recolonised Scotland there is an increasing chance that the species may become a regular migrant through the Pentlands, but it is still rarely met with.

Turnbull in his *Birds of East Lothian* records it as rare, but he said that it was occasionally seen among the Pentland Hills, mostly in autumn. J. Kirke Nash in *Birds of Midlothian* said that this probably refers to a bird captured there in 1841. This was preserved by Dr Carfrae and is in the Scottish Museum. In 1837 Macgillivray said that he had seen one that was shot among the Pentland Hills. On 6th May 1933 a single bird was seen being mobbed by Black-headed Gulls at the West end of Harperrig; the bird flew off in the direction of Cobbinshaw where A. G. S. Bryson saw it a few minutes later.

An adult male was shot by a local gamekeeper at Flotterstone on 1st May 1953. One was seen at Harperrig on 26th August 1984.

FALCONS

Kestrel. *Falco tinnunculus.* Common resident.

The Kestrel is our commonest raptor, resident all the year round. It occurs almost anywhere in the area, but likes the more open country rather than the thick wooding of the low ground. It is normally encountered singly or at most as a family party, no tendency to flock being recorded, but there is an interesting record of some eight to ten seen between the East Cairn Hill and Bavelaw on 30th July 1932. Kestrels nest even in the highest coniferous woods, often in the old nests of other species. They also nest where suitable cliffs exist.

On 12th May 1900 David Hamilton found a nest (c5) at the side of Loganlee waterfall: the eggs were laid on the bare ground without any nesting material. In 1902 he found a nest at Listonshiels (c3) in what he took to be an old Magpie's nest. In 1905 there was a nest with young on 15th July between Balerno and Harperrig. On 7th June 1903 he again found a nest (c5) on the cliff near Loganlee waterfall.

William Evans found nests in the thick tops of pines at Redford wood before 1919-20 when this wood was felled. J. Kirke Nash said in *Birds of Midlothian:* "It is common in the hills, nesting usually takes place in May, although on the Pentlands I have found a nest with fresh eggs at the beginning of June."

The total census figures were March 12, September 8, and December 4.

John Prentice, Keeper at Baddinsgill, told me in 1934 that the species was common at Baddinsgill. In 1947 David Hamilton said that numbers seemed to be increasing. The Kestrel nested on a cliff at Torduff in 1932, and the Misses Rintoul and Baxter saw one at Eastside on 25th May 1934. G. L. Sandeman found nests on Caerketton on 10th July 1937 (five young), and again breeding there on 7th June 1975. R. L. Swann said in 1971 that Kestrels were common at Threipmuir.

Merlin. *Falco columbarius.* Summer visitor. Breeds. Occasional in winter.

The Merlin's status seems to have changed little over the last century. It is still a summer visitor breeding in small numbers, many of the records being between April and July, with some winter records.

Heather moors are favourite breeding haunts, particularly those west of the North Esk Reservoir, but the Black Hill is also used. It seems likely that the breeding birds leave the hills at the same time as the passerines such as the Skylark, Meadow Pipit, and Wheatear in July, and that later Merlins are wanderers or migrants preying on passerine migrants at the reservoirs.

In 1837 Macgillivray said "Among the Pentland Hills . . . it is met with in summer dispersed in pairs at long intervals, but in winter it forsakes the higher grounds and betakes itself to the plains". He had noted it at the Lover's Loup waterfall at Loganlee. Harold Raeburn saw one at the Raven's Cleuch on 26th June 1890, and in 1896 and 1897 a pair nested in an open wood at the base of the Pentlands only to be shot at the nest. In 1901 David Hamilton found a nest (c4) in heather on the slope of the Kirk Road from Bavelaw, and in 1906 he found another nest with three young, again in heather in the Logan House district. In the *Birds of Midlothian* J. Kirke Nash said "It is familiar in the Pentlands. The Merlin nests in the heather. In a nest on 15th May 1915 on the Black Hill there were five newly laid eggs. On 27th May 1906 Mr Sim, the keeper at Loganlee, found a nest with four young."

John Prentice, gamekeeper, told me that two pairs nested on the Baddinsgill ground in 1933, one on the East Cairn Hill, and the other on White Craigs, and that there were two pairs on the ground in 1934. He said that the species was not often recorded except at breeding time.

In 1934 too the Misses Rintoul and Baxter told me that Merlin nest regularly but in small numbers. Other records are:

| 1939 | June 1st | One at Wolf Craigs. G. L. Sandeman |
| 1946 | October 6th | Black Hill. One being mobbed by Carrion Crows. J. K. Adams |

Only two Merlins were seen during the nine census outings 1932-34, one in March 1933 and the other in December 1932, while the traverse 1948-49 turned up two, interestingly enough both in winter: one at Nine Mile Burn on 21st November 1948 and the other at Westside on 12th December.

One was seen mobbing a Golden Eagle at the Cauldstane Slap on 19th May 1951, and on 3rd April 1966 one was seen at Glencorse.

R. W. Swann told me in 1971 that he occasionally saw Merlins at Threipmuir. G. L. Sandeman has the following records:

1970	April 6th	Threipmuir	One
1973	October 30th	Harperrig	One
		Crosswood	One
1974	January 21st	Threipmuir	Female
	November 8th	Crosswood	Female
1975	July 2nd	Harperrig	Female

In 1980 breeding was recorded and in 1985 a survey of the area took place: *Scottish Birds* 1985. Eight known, possible or new sites were checked, most on several occasions. In addition several other areas were surveyed but no sign found. Some signs of occupation were found at six sites but only two definitely reached the egg stage, and only one of them reared three young.

Peregrine. *Falco Peregrinus.* Occasional visitor. Has bred.

Most records are in spring and autumn, which suggests that the species hunts over the hills at these seasons, but finds little prey during the winter and normally nests elsewhere. Recently however, and most excitingly, a pair has nested successfully close to a well used path through the hills.

In 1838 Macgillivray reported that a male and female had been shot on the Pentland Hills in January. William Evans notes:

1898	April 22nd	One has been seen about Bavelaw several times recently
1903	November 16th	One at Habbie's Howe
1904	March 15th	A male and two females rose from Clubbiedean wood and soared to a great height
1905	September 16th	One killed a grouse at Nether Habbie's Howe

In 1933 a Peregrine was seen at Threipmuir on 10th September, 1st October (when it was chasing a Heron) and on 29th November.

Four Peregrines were seen during the 1932-34 census work, one in September and three in March, and Rintoul and Baxter saw one flying over Carnethy on 23rd May 1934. G. L. Sandeman recorded one at the Wolf Craigs on 1st June 1939. In 1946 J. K. Adams saw two playing over East Cairn Hill on 1st October, and on 22nd April of that year one was seen at Harperrig. G. L. Sandeman has Pentland records of two on 15th April 1946, two on 14th September 1946, two at Flotterstone on 15th April 1947, and a male on 24th April 1948. He also notes that he had not seen the Peregrine in the Threipmuir/Bavelaw/Harelaw area between 1931 and 1975. R. L. Swann told me in 1971 that his only record from Threipmuir was on 24th November 1951.

In 1979 single birds visited Threipmuir on 28th August and 29th September, while in 1981 single birds appeared again at Threipmuir on 7th January and 17th February. One was seen at Glencorse on 14th February in that year. In 1983 however the two records were in November; one from the West Water Reservoir on the 6th, and the other at Threipmuir on the 25th. Again these were of single birds.

GROUSE

Red Grouse. *Lagopus lagopus.* Common resident.

The Red Grouse, although subject to population fluctuations as elsewhere in Scotland, is still a common bird on the Pentlands. Numbers fell considerably during the 1939-45 war, and poor bags were obtained in 1945. 1946 results were however better. The species is normally commonest on the heather-clad areas, but is in addition frequently seen on grassy moors. The autumn coveys frequent the higher grain fields, feeding either on the stooks or on stubble, and at other seasons Grouse sometimes visit high arable land.

Farming methods have changed over the years and more use is made of combine harvesters which cut and gather the grain in one operation, so that much less is available for the Grouse. Some large coveys still turn up however, for example, on 12th January

1982 78 were seen on Castlelaw and on 25th January 1984 there were 100 plus on Turnhouse Hill.

The *Old Statistical Account* of 1791 gave "a not inconsiderable number for Midcalder Parish". In 1837 Macgillivray said "On the Pentlands it is still plentiful". Mr Charles Cowan in his *Reminiscences* written later in the century says: "The Grouse from the Pentland Hills in the latter part of the season are particularly plump and large which I attribute to their ready access on both sides to the stubbles. I have often seen hundreds of them packed and in possession of the stooks which in these altitudes remain out till the close of the shooting season. Since that time I regret to say that the disease has in more than one season committed terrible ravages. Despite terrible mortality in 1867 there was no want of birds in 1868."

J. Kirke Nash reported that from 1900 to 1907 the yearly bags on the estate from Capelaw to Cock Rig were more than doubled. During that period a portion of ground near Glencorse Reservoir was under plough. Mr Cowan believes that increase was due to extra exposure of grit. Since 1907 this ground has been under grass and the number of birds has steadily declined. Mr Cowan is also of the opinion that much heather burning for sheep and a great increase of pedestrians has had an adverse effect on population numbers.

Extracts from the *Crosswood Migration Schedules* are:

1908	February 8th	Beginning to pair
1910	May 25th	Young seen
1912	April 22nd	First nests seen (c11, 7 and 5)

On 27th October 1907 David Hamilton found several Grouse in a field at Glencorse Reservoir sitting on the sheaves or ricks of oats eating the seed, and in 1909 he recorded several apparently feeding on a Hawthorn tree on 7th November. He often found nests in the Listonshiels area. For example on 5th May 1912 he found two (both of c9).

In 1934 Rintoul and Baxter noted "On the Pentlands they are common. We often saw them there. Mr Patten tells us that record bags were obtained that year."

R. L. Swann (1971) said of Threipmuir: "Seen all the year

round in the bog at the north-west part of the reservoir. In winter the birds come down onto fields round the reservoir.''

On 2nd March 1986, 150 were seen between Glencorse Reservoir and Loganlee Reservoir.

Black Grouse. *Tetrao tetrix.* Resident in small numbers.

When I was considering the status of the Black Grouse prior to the 1939-45 war I noted ''In the Pentlands the Black Grouse is local in its distribution and appears to be decreasing. Localities at which the species is most often seen are, the pine strips south west of Clubbiedean, Redford Plantation, Bavelaw area, Baddinsgill, Listonshiels, Butelands, Malleny Curling Pond and Dunsyre Burn area. Numbers seen together at one time seldom exceed twelve, but there was a pack of twenty Greyhens at Redford Plantation on 18th February 1932, fifteen cocks at the thorn hedges south of Threipmuir on 3rd December of the same year, and at least twenty cocks in Redford Plantation on 11th December 1933. Although seen occasionally at some distance from trees the species is normally found close to hill wooding, or hedges on moorland. In autumn it frequents in addition stubble fields and stacks. It often perches on trees and hedges. It is probably commoner than the Pheasant.''

Rintoul and Baxter writing in 1927 about the decrease of Black game in Scotland said ''In Midlothian a good many used to breed on the Pentlands 1871-2 and they also used to breed in Bavelaw Wood until it was cut in 1919-20.'' They quoted R. Cowan as saying that a few appeared annually about Penicuik in November, and that they stayed for most of the winter when he thought they went later to the hills to breed. Rintoul and Baxter also reported that Mr Francis Cowan had told them that Black Grouse were not common on the Pentlands, but that when a wood was being replanted about 1926 a fair number of birds appeared.

J. Kirke Nash in *Birds of Midlothian* records: ''I have occasionally seen Black Grouse within the last twenty years in the Bavelaw and Listonshiels district, and Mr W. Donaldson, keeper on that estate, tells me that on average they shoot eight brace every season.'' David Hamilton in his early birdwatching days, pre-1900, saw the species at Malleny Curling Pond, Harperrig and Crosswood. In 1901 he found two nests at Crosswood and also two at Listonshiels. There were several at Listonshiels in August 1904 and a fine pair at Balerno Common in February 1911.

W. Anderson in *The Pentland Hills* published in 1926 said of the Black Grouse "It is very scarce on the Pentlands." In 1933 however John Prentice, Keeper, said of the Baddinsgill district that there were about fifteen nests in the neighbourhood. Rintoul and Baxter saw a female at Fairliehope in May 1934. Records continued from the Bavelaw/Threipmuir area in particular, but there were also birds at Listonshiels, Bonaly Hill, and in the Harperrig/Crosswood district right up to the 1939-45 war.

David Hamilton found a flock of thirty-four including fifteen cocks at Malleny Curling Pond on 23rd December 1934, and eight on a field about a mile west of Harperrig on 27th November 1938.

During the census outings 1932-34, nine birds were seen on the three March outings, ten on the September ones, and eighteen in December. In 1948-49 Black Grouse were seen during the traverse in both Braid Law Wood and Cap Law Wood.

On 26th October 1953 D. C. Anderson found a lek of five cocks displaying on the centre of the Balerno/Carnwath road a few hundred yards inside the Midlothian county boundary.

In 1962 there was a report in *Scottish Birds* to the effect that the species seemed to have virtually disappeared from the Lothians in the last few years. The Pentland population however appeared to be holding on with records from Bavelaw on 16th April 1974, Crosswood on 3rd January 1974, Colzium Plantation on 4th February 1975 and from the Lang Whang on 23rd March 1975; all by G. L. Sandeman. In 1978 ten males were seen at Harperrig on 18th April.

The species is still present in the Pentlands, as the following records show:

1980	September 29th	Bavelaw/West Rig	Male
1983	Spring	Harperrig	Five immatures
1984	January 7th	Threipmuir	One
	December 13th	Threipmuir	One female
	June 17th	Bavelaw	One male

Capercaillie. *Tetrao urogallus.* Some old records.

On 21st April 1885 Mr Morrison, the keeper at Malleny, said that Mr Davidson of Dean Park near Balerno shot two there five or six years ago.

In 1886 Mr Mackenzie of Mortonhall said that a hen shot in Bavelaw Wood had been seen by him. In 1898 Mr Harvie Brown reported that Mr Davidson had told him that an old male Capercaillie came to Dolphinton about nine years ago, while hens apparently followed later, and for several years there were broods on the borders of Peeblesshire though the birds had been shot out when he wrote.

In 1906 J. S. Tait of Bavelaw reported that two Capercaillie had been seen in the woods at Bavelaw at the beginning of August, and that he himself in September had flushed the two birds and saw them quite clearly. Sir Thomas Gibson Carmichael wrote that these two birds had been seen on his property in 1907. In January of that year the Rev. H. N. Bonar recorded two at Bavelaw.

PARTRIDGES, QUAIL AND PHEASANTS

Red-legged Partridge. *Allectoris rufa.* Recently introduced.

The following are recent records:

1980	September 3rd	Loganlee	Bred eleven young
1982	April 19th	Crosswood Burn	One
1983	June 3rd	Crosswood Burn	Two
1986		Boll-o-Bere	One

Grey Partridge. *Perdix perdix.* Resident.

The Partridge is well distributed throughout the lower portions of the area, particularly where rough ground with cover exists; but is nowhere common. It is also recorded on crops of all kinds and along hedgerows. Stubble fields are its main source of food in autumn. Although less common on the higher ground, the Partridge occurs regularly among heather, bracken, grass hillsides and on dry reservoir beds. It has even been recorded on Turnhouse Hill at a height of 1250 feet. It is commoner than the Pheasant.

The *Old Statistical Account* of 1791 records that there was a considerable number in Calder Parish. David Hamilton raised two coveys on the hill above Nine Mile Burn on 16th September 1901, and on 24th May 1903 he found a joint nest with four Pheasant and six Partridge eggs at Listonshiels.

In 1936 Mr A. R. Waterston wrote "Quite recently Mr Alex Cowan of Penicuik sent me the crop and contents of four Partridges shot at an altitude of 800 feet on the east side of the Black Hill on 8th November 1935. In each case the contents consisted almost entirely of heather beetles (*Lochmaea saturalis*)."

During the census work 1932-34 the Partridge was noted as being much commoner than the Pheasant, the total figures being three in March, twenty in September, and seven in December. No large coveys were seen on the 1948-49 traverse, the greatest being twelve at Bavelaw on 26th September 1948 and one of twenty in bracken at the Quarrel Reservoir on 21st November 1948.

There is a recent record of sixteen at Threipmuir on 26th November 1984, and in 1986 there were eleven there on 26th December.

Quail. *Coturnix coturnix.* A few early records.

It was reported in the *Annals of Scottish Natural History* that in 1893 Eagle Clarke heard quail on different parts of Comiston Farm in the last few days of July. He added that "They used to come annually to the neighbouring farm of Oxgangs until about twenty years ago".

In 1919 Bruce Campbell recorded: "On Monday evening 7th July at 7.30 p.m. Major Taylor Cameron of the Ninth Royal Scots and I heard a Quail calling in a field close to the farm of Swanston. We listened to the bird for nearly half an hour, and on repassing the place an hour later for nearly half an hour, and on repassing the place an hour later the bird kept uttering the unmistakable Weet weet for a considerable time."

There have been the following recent records:

1982	August 7th	Threipmuir	One
	April 1st	Currie	Three

Pheasant. *Phasianus colchicus.* Resident in small numbers.

It is doubtful if this species would survive long in the area without the hand rearing of chicks as at present. It is nowhere common but may be seen, mostly along the lower wooded slopes. The bird is most often recorded at Malleny Curling Pond, Boghall, Lymphoy, and the Dunsyre area. It also occurs with some frequency among the willows at Bavelaw Reservoir.

David Hamilton, recalling his experience in the Pentlands of over fifty years, found it uncommon. He had found a nest at Cockburnhill, and on 24th May 1913 found a joint nest with a Pheasant at Listonshiels.

The Pheasant was only recorded on five out of nine census outings in 1932-34, and the total numbers seen on these were March seven, September three and December twelve.

During the 1948-49 traverse the Pheasant was seen on twenty-six occasions out of fifty-two visits; mostly as single birds, but twelve were seen at Malleny Curling Pond on 28th November 1948 and ten at the same place on 3rd January 1949.

There was a maximum of eight at Threipmuir on 29th March 1986.

RAILS AND COOTS

Water Rail. *Rallus aquaticus.* Uncommon. Has bred.

Rintoul and Baxter said that Mr Serle had seen eggs taken at Threipmuir. In 1933 the species was recorded at Bavelaw on 30th July and 6th September. On 11th November 1950 two immatures were seen at the top end of Bavelaw, and in 1952 R. W. J. Smith heard the bird calling from Bavelaw marsh on 14th June. In 1958 P. W. Sandeman saw one in an open ditch on Torphin Hill in February, and again on 6th March. R. L. Swann recorded one at Threipmuir on 3rd March 1961.

G. L. Sandeman has the following records:

1974	March 11th	Bavelaw	One
1975	September 19th	Crosswood	One
	November 5th	Logan Burn	One

There are several recent records:

1981	May 24th, June 9th and 12th	Bavelaw	One calling

1982	December 22nd		
	and 29th	Listonshiels/	
		Bavelaw	One
1984	January 22nd	Threipmuir	One
1986	November	Crosswood	One

Corncrake. *Crex crex.* Once common and breeding. Now absent.

The *Old Statistical Account* of 1791 records for Linton Parish that it was a migratory bird.

The species was recorded at Comiston in 1897, 1899 and 1900 in May. On 24th May 1900 David Hamilton saw one by the roadside between Glencorse Reservoir and Hillend.

Further early records are:

1907	May 12th	Flotterstone
1912	May 12th	Carlops

In 1912 H. G. Alexander in his Corncrake enquiry reported: "Some decrease is taking place in parts of the Lothians at any rate in Midlothian."

In 1915 David Hamilton recorded Corncrakes at both Currie and near Threipmuir on 3rd May. In 1947 he wrote that the species was quite common round the lower slopes of the Pentlands thirty years before that year, and used to nest regularly in fields at Flotterstone. J. Kirke Nash also referred to the decrease. In 1929 he wrote "That the Corncrake is now comparatively rare in the Lothians is a matter of regret. The decrease of the Corncrake has only become apparent within the last fifteen or twenty years" (*Scottish Naturalist* 1929).

Records on a reduced scale continued up to the war:

1932	June 13th	Swanston	One
1934	June 19th	Clubbiedean	
	June 17th and		
	26th	Bowbridge fields	
	July 11th	Harelaw	
1939	June 9th	Shothead	

In February 1948 Wilson wrote that the Corncrake had been heard in recent years behind Boghall, and in 1952 he wrote: "A Corncrake continued calling at Balerno till the field was cut and a

Corncrake was accidentally killed in the process. It appears that a pair was present, for one was heard calling the day after the death of its presumed mate. It has not been heard since.'' In the same year one was heard calling at Haughhead near Balerno on 13th July by W. Handyside.

In 1953 T. Hay recorded one at Swanston on 16th May, and A. D. F. Leishman heard one calling throughout the summer at Mountain Cross, West Linton, in the same year. In 1955 D. G. Andrew recorded one at Colinton on 18th June.

Moorhen. *Gallinula chloropus.* Resident and Partial Migrant.

The Moorhen nests at many of the reservoirs and at small pools such as Malleny Curling Pond, Harmeny, Poet's Glen, Garvald House, North Esk Marsh and East Threipmuir Marsh. It also nests along the Water of Leith between Leithhead Mill and Colinton. Some burns are also used, for example Dunsyre, Medwin Water, Lyne, and Crosswood. Bavelaw is its stronghold, for several pairs nest there, but elsewhere there is usually only one pair on each pond or particular stretch of burn. The species is often seen feeding on fields a little distance from water. After breeding some of the more exposed nesting areas are abandoned for the season, but the Moorhen is largely sedentary.

The *New Statistical Account* of 1845 mentions the Moorhen as being frequent in the streams of Colinton. Harold Raeburn found a nest (c5) in rushes at Malleny Curling Pond on 3rd June 1889. David Hamilton found the following nests:

1899	May 7th	Clubbiedean	(c5)
1902	April 26th	Threipmuir	Two nests each (c4)
1904	May 29th	Harperrig	(c7)

The species was noted as being less common in the December censuses 1932-34 than in those of March and September. In 1934 Rintoul and Baxter saw several pairs at Bavelaw on 22nd May, and one at Clubbiedean on 30th May. In the same year G. L. Sandeman found a nest at Clubbiedean (c5) on 19th June. On 16th July 1951 what appeared to be a recently hatched Moorhen was seen disappearing into some cover at the Crane Loch. No adult birds were to be seen. On 17th September of the same year

T. Boyd and R. W. J. Smith found a flock of seven Moorhens at the same place. These appeared to be a family party. No birds were seen in 1950 or 1952 when the terrain was noted as being quite unsuitable, but the Loch is gradually decreasing in size and by 1982 there were areas of weeds and rushes which could encourage further breeding.

G. L. Sandeman has the following breeding records:

1950	June 24th	Crosswood	Family party
1959	June 20th	Crane Loch	Two nests
1971	June 9th	Clubbiedean	Four or five young
1972	June 14th	Crosswood Reservoir Burn	(c6)
	May 30th	Clubbiedean	(c7)
1974	July 25th	Crosswood Reservoir Burn	Chick seen
1975	August 13th	Crosswood	Adult and empty nest seen

R. L. Swann said of Threipmuir in 1971: "Seen commonly from April to November. Several pairs breed."

Recent breeding records from Bavelaw/Threipmuir are:

1982   Three pairs
1983   Six plus pairs   (four to five broods seen)
1984   Nine pairs   (at least four broods)
1985   Seventeen to twenty-one sites, but no young until one fledged on 2nd July.
1986   Twelve to fifteen pairs with five to six broods.

Coot. *Fulica atra.* Summer visitor. Breeds. Occasional winter visitor.

The duration of the Coot's stay in the area seems to be governed by frost and water levels. It has bred at Bavelaw, Middle Threipmuir, Threipmuir East Marsh and Harperrig, but the great majority nest at Bavelaw. Here the population is about fifteen to thirty pairs, with only an odd pair at the other nesting places.

In a normal year the breeding birds arrive about the beginning of March and nesting is in full swing by early April. A late frost or drought may delay arrival, or a warm spring advance it. In 1931 for example, some Coots were present on Bavelaw on 17th February and remained until nesting started. In 1936 on the other hand, none were seen on 1st March, but about ten had arrived by the 8th; and in 1934 no Coots were seen on 24th March owing to drought. Bavelaw normally dries up during July, and the Coot is driven off by lack of water. Late broods seem to move down to Middle Threipmuir where they may be seen up to the middle of August. At this season Coots appear very exceptionally on the main part of Threipmuir. If Bavelaw does not dry up the species may remain there until September or even later. At Harperrig too, lack of water near the reedbeds appears to drive off the Coots, which are usually away by the end of August. When Bavelaw fills up again, commonly in October, it is not usual for the Coots to return until the spring, but there are winter records of a few birds in all winter months. There are no winter records from Harperrig.

On 3rd June 1889 Harold Raeburn found two nests (c5 and c2) at East Threipmuir marsh. During the census work 1932-34 no Coots were seen during the three September outings, and they were recorded only on one occasion in the December ones. Rintoul and Baxter found several pairs at Bavelaw on 22nd May 1934 and one in the backwater of Harperrig on 29th May of the same year. During the 1948-49 traverse no Coots were seen between 7th November and 28th February. G. L. Sandeman found two at Glencorse between September and November 1970.

R. L. Swann said (1971) of Threipmuir: "Common all year round bar December and January when birds leave. Several pairs breed."

Recent records are:

1981   Some 4-5 pairs bred at Threipmuir/Bavelaw and 23 birds were present on 29th September.

1982   Breeding pairs at Threipmuir/Bavelaw had risen to 8-10.

1983   The breeding pairs had again risen to 16 plus pairs and eight broods were seen. On 26th March a count showed 48 birds present.

1984   There were twenty pairs and nine to ten broods seen, and the following figures show numbers at peak counts:

Mar.	Apr.	May	June	July	Aug.	Sept.	Oct.	Nov.	Dec.
24	36	—	—	28	24	21	8	—	2

In 1985 breeding pairs were seen at twenty-eight to thirty-two sites at Threipmuir/Bavelaw with about ten broods. In 1986 there were eighteen to twenty-one pairs which raised three to four broods.

WADERS

Oystercatcher. *Haematopus ostralegus.* Passage migrant spring and autumn. Breeds.

Early records show that the species was a spring and autumn migrant only. The *Crosswood Migration Schedules* (1908-19) give records of small numbers — a maximum of six being seen at any one time; there are two records in March and seven records in July and August.

There are in addition exceptional records in May and June, and a single bird was seen on 13th November 1909.

Breeding seems to have started between 1960 and 1970 and this now takes place regularly at Threipmuir, Harperrig, Crosswood and along the Glencorse glen.

No Oystercatchers were seen on any of the 1932-34 censuses, and a record from Crosswood on 14th July 1934 was considered to be on early autumn passage. During the traverse of 1948-49 Oystercatchers were only seen on three occasions: there were three at Threipmuir on 7th March, and later in the year two packs flew south west over the Kitchen Moss on 1st August. Two appeared at Bavelaw on 24th April 1949.

R. L. Swann said that in 1966 ten pairs summered at Threipmuir. In 1971 birds arrived early in March and were recorded until July, also at Threipmuir, and breeding took place in 1972 and 1973. In 1974 birds arrived on 25th February and probably bred, and in 1975 breeding was again established.

F

Much the same pattern applies to the Glencorse Glen, where G. L. Sandeman told me that Oystercatchers were not seen during the breeding season until 1970 onwards, when they were regularly seen between March and July. They were recorded breeding there in small numbers in July 1973 and April 1974. He also recorded breeding at Harperrig and Crosswood in these years. In 1975 he had breeding records at Clubbiedean on 3rd July and of another pair at Bavelaw.

Thirty-four were seen flying south from Loganlee on 3rd August 1982 and four pairs were breeding at Threipmuir in 1984. The recent increase in breeding pairs is continuing for at Threipmuir and Bavelaw there were five or six in 1985, and in 1986 there were eight to ten territories.

Stone Curlew. *Burhinus oedicnemus.* Rare.
One was seen at West Linton on 26th October 1972.

Ringed Plover. *Charadrius hiaticula.* Passage migrant in small numbers. Breeds.
As a passage migrant the species is more commonly seen in autumn than in spring. The autumn movement normally takes place between the middle of July and the end of September with the main movement coming during the latter half of August. Spring records from the reservoirs occur during March, April and May.

Ring Plovers now breed at Harperrig, Crosswood and Bonaly Reservoirs in small numbers.

There are very few early records of Ringed Plovers, but in 1920 W. Eagle Clark wrote "For the past two years a pair of these birds have successfully reared their young in a field adjoining Harperrig Reservoir. In 1919 the field was under potatoes. This year it was under turnips, and the eggs had to be removed from their original situation — a proceeding necessitated by the process of cultivation — but the birds accepted the change and the eggs hatched in due course. I saw both the young birds and their parents in June." Apart from the above note there is no evidence that Ringed Plovers nested in the Pentlands prior to the 1939-45 war.

During the 1932-34 census outings the species was seen only in

September when there were small numbers on the mud at Harperrig, Crosswood and Threipmuir; and was not seen at all during the 1948-49 traverse.

In autumn quite large flocks sometimes occur. For example on 18th August 1933 twenty-four were seen at Harperrig, and on 24th August 1935 some fifteen were present again at Harperrig. On 31st August 1936 the boatman there said that he had seen a flock of twenty a few days previously. On the night of 26th August 1936 Ring Plovers were heard passing over Threipmuir Reservoir going south west, and again in the early morning. Two birds were seen circling high over the reservoir at the same time.

Recent breeding records are:

1979	Harperrig	Four pairs
	Crosswood	Four pairs
1981	Crosswood	Three pairs
	Bonaly	One to two pairs
1982	Crosswood	Two pairs
1983	Crosswood	Possibly three pairs
1985	Crosswood	Two or three pairs. One brood seen.
1986	Crosswood	Two pairs
	North Esk	Two birds alarmed. The first there since 1981.

In 1983 there were maximum numbers of eight birds on 14th March, and in 1984 there was a maximum of seven birds on 21st May, both counts at Crosswood.

There was a very interesting paper on breeding records for the Pentlands in the *Lothian Bird Report* for 1984. Here are the records:

Pairs	1973	1974	1975	1976	1977	1978	1979	1980	1981	1982	1983	1984
Baddinsgill	—	—	—	0	0	0	0	0	0	1	1	—
Bonaly	—	—	2	1	—	—	—	1	1-2	0	0	—
Crosswood	1	3	2	1	4-6	4	—	—	3	2	c3	2
Harperrig	—	3	5-6	c9	0	6	4	0	0	0	0	0
North Esk	—	—	1	1	2	1	1	1	1	0	0	—
West Water	—	—	1	1	1	1	3	4	3	4-5	2-4	—

Sites checked in 1984 with nil returns: Bonaly, Glencorse, Harelaw, North Esk, Baddinsgill.

Golden Plover. *Pluvialis apricaria.* Summer visitor. Breeding.
   Passage migrant in spring, autumn and winter.

The spring movement starts early in February when large
flocks are often seen, but it is more usual to see the first birds in
March, depending on weather conditions. At this time these
flocks frequent grassland, particularly at the west ends of
Clubbiedean, Threipmuir, and also at Harperrig. Many birds in
these March flocks are very dark below, with white at the sides of
the breast, and are therefore not likely to be breeding birds,
especially as some local breeders are already on their territories
and are much less brightly plumaged. The spring flocks have
normally moved through by the end of March.

The species nests commonly on wet moorland west of the path
from Bavelaw to the Kips, near Listonshiels, the Crane Loch and
the West Cairn Hill, but a pair or two sometimes nest on the
Black Hill above Threipmuir, and on the higher reaches of the
Logan Burn above Loganlee. I have found the nest as high as
1350 feet above the North Esk Reservoir.

The breeding birds start leaving the hills and collect during
July at the reservoirs — particularly at Harperrig — prior to
autumn migration which is in full swing by August when the
species can be seen on arable land once more, as well as on
muddy reservoirs. This migration continues until the end of
September, but in some years a few birds linger until early
October before leaving the area.

In winter flocks are sometimes seen on grass pasture slopes,
particularly on the south side of the hills between Hillend and
Boghall, and the species is occasional elsewhere, usually in small
flocks. There are several records of movements in November,
presumably due to weather conditions elsewhere: for example on
25th November 1932 a flock of eighty to a hundred flew south
west over Balerno, and on 27th November of the same year a
flock was again seen in this area flying in the same direction.

On 22nd May 1886 Harold Raeburn found a pair nesting close
to the edge of Threipmuir Reservoir, which would be quite
exceptional today. On 12th February 1888 he saw a flock near
Threipmuir again.

David Hamilton found a pair at Bonaly Reservoir on 3rd May
1902 and on 4th April 1903 he saw "plenty between West Linton

and Balerno" — presumably breeding birds. On another walk on
5th May 1929 from Dolphinton to Dunsyre and the Crane Loch,
he said that Golden Plovers were "numerous".

The *Crosswood Migration Schedules* 1909-19 give spring arrival
dates between 1st January and 15th March, and record that an
egg was found on the hill on 26th March 1914.

Some large flocks were found during the three March census
outings 1932-34, when a total of 962 birds were counted. All the
breeding birds had left their territories by September, and only 39
were seen. None was seen in the three December census outings.
During the traverse 1948-49 Golden Plovers were recorded
between March and June, a single bird on 1st August, four on
migration on 10th October, and then nothing until the following
March.

More recent records show the size of the spring migration: on
24th and 25th March in 1981 300 were seen at Threipmuir, and
next year some 300 plus arrived at Harperrig on 9th April. In
1983 there were 200 at Threipmuir on 16th March.

In 1985 there was a flock of 400 at Threipmuir on 8th April
where the last 200 were seen on 1st May and in 1986, 300 were
there on 13th April. Both these flocks were recorded as *Pluvialis
apricaria altifrons*. There were three breeding pairs on the Black
Hill on 4th May 1986.

Grey Plover. *Pluvialis squatarola*. Uncommon autumn migrant.

A single bird was seen at Threipmuir on 26th September 1933
and nearly forty years later G. L. Sandeman had these records:
one at Threipmuir on 25th October 1972, three at Harperrig on
2nd October 1973 and two there on 15th October in the same
year.

Lapwing. *Vanellus vanellus*. Spring migrant. Summer visitor.
    Breeding. Autumn migrant. Winter visitor.

The distribution of the Lapwing in the Pentlands is
complicated by the fact that the species is a spring migrant, a
breeding summer visitor, a non-breeding visitor, an autumn
migrant and a winter visitor within the area. As several of these
circumstances may exist at the same time it is often difficult to
decide on the category into which the individuals observed fall.

In February — often as early as the beginning of the month — passage in a westerly direction takes place, and flocks may be seen at the reservoirs or resting on the fields. March brings the arrival of the breeding birds which proceed to take up territory — usually about the middle of the month — but flocks are still present and passage continues. Breeding birds as a rule do not arrive in full numbers until the end of March. The flocks have passed through or split up by the beginning of April, but there is a record of a flock at Bavelaw on 29th April when some birds were sitting on eggs. The Lapwing breeds in the Pentlands from April to early in July and is very largely restricted to ground below the 1000 feet contour. This restriction is in many districts a natural one caused by the area above this height being unsuitable for nesting, either because of the steepness of the hills, or by heather displacing the fields or pasture on which the species normally nests. For example the south-east slope from Flotterstone to Nine Mile Burn is almost barren of breeding Lapwings, which are confined to the fields and flat areas below 1000 feet; there are however localities at about that height at Rullion Green and Swanston where apparently suitable ground has not been occupied.

Not many Lapwings are found nesting on the hills for the species is essentially a bird of fields and pasture, heather and grass moors being barren except where patches of short green turf occur. Pools and the fringes of reservoirs often have Lapwings breeding round them, for the presence of water seems to be an attraction, and river valleys also provide suitable nesting ground: I made a survey of breeding habitat in May and June 1938 covering Swanston, Balerno to Nine Mile Burn via Bavelaw, Cauldstane Slap, North Esk Reservoir and Spittal; Martyr's Cross to Nine Mile Burn; Balerno to West Linton via John's Burn, West Rig, Thrashie Dene, West Cairn Hill, Wolf Craigs and Byrehope Mount. It was found that the population was less than expected: apparently suitable fields were unoccupied or colonisation was incomplete. A preference for arable land rather than pasture was noted, probably because it afforded more suitable nesting sites, although later in the year when the young are hatched the then dense cover might be a disadvantage. Tree fringed fields were used, but near Cockburnhill where rushes were present, and with them a Curlew population, no Lapwings

were breeding although in the next field which had no rushes
several pairs were present.

Small parties of Lapwings were seen on West Cairn ridge and
Byrehope Mount on 18th June 1938. These birds appeared to be
either non breeding residents or perhaps had lost their eggs. The
birds were above nesting Golden Plover.

Early in July, flocks, consisting mostly of young birds, gather at
the reservoirs, and sometimes in the fields, and passage on a
variable scale extends until late October, with the main body
migrating during August and September. In some years the late
autumn migration is complicated by the arrival of winter visitors
which frequent low-lying fields and pasture, particularly near
Hillend and Oxgangs.

The *Old Statistical Account* of 1791 records the Green Plover as
one of the migratory birds found in Linton parish. David
Hamilton had these spring arrival dates:

1903	February 14th	North Esk. One seen
	March 8th	Threipmuir. Several
1906	March 17th	Bonaly/Glencorse/Threipmuir
		One or two have got up to the
		hills again

He found nests on the following dates:

1900	April 21st	Glencorse — c3
1902	May 3rd	Bonaly — c5 at edge of reservoir
	May 11th	Threipmuir — c3 on almost bare
		ground

He saw Lapwings gathering into flocks at Glencorse on 24th
August 1901.

The *Crosswood Migration Schedules* give the following arrival
dates:

1908	February 10th	
1909	March 17th	(numbers)
1914	February 6th	(a number)
1915	March 4th	(flock arrives)
1916	February 4th	(round edges of loch)
1916	March 15th	(arrival noted)

1916   March 22nd   (large flocks on hill)
1917   February 19th   (seen)

In 1912 a single bird was seen on 20th January, and on 10th April 1908 a nest contained four eggs.

Rintoul and Baxter made the following observations during their walks over the Pentlands in 1934:

May 18th	Carlops to North Esk	A lot everywhere
May 22nd	Harelaw to Threipmuir	Common
May 23rd	Harelaw to Loganlee and Flotterstone	On the lower ground
May 25th	Eastside valley	Common
May 27th	Carlops to Bore Stane	Common grassy fields

Only four Lapwings were seen during the three December outings in the census 1932-34, and during the 1948-49 traverse the species was practically absent between October and January. In 1971 R. L. Swann said of Threipmuir "Arrives at the reservoir in March when flocks of up to fifty are recorded. A few pairs breed each year. Numbers rise again in July when flocks of young birds and adults gather in fields by the reservoir and leave in October." A very large flock of 2450 birds was seen at West Linton on 6th August 1978.

In 1983 there were three records of flocks; the first recorded at Threipmuir on 1st and 24th March may have consisted of breeding birds not yet in their territories; and the second one of 400 birds at Crosswood on 2nd August, of birds on autumn migration. The third, of 300 at Threipmuir on 9th November, seems to indicate a weather movement.

Recent breeding records are:
1984	Threipmuir	34-35
1985	Threipmuir	41-42 breeding pairs
1986	Threipmuir	35-37
	Clubbiedean	4

Dotterel. *Charadrius morinellus.* Very rare.
One was seen on Carnethy on 23rd August 1975.

Knot *Calidris canutus*. Irregular autumn migrant.

It seems likely that the Knot travels south west each year from the Forth, and that we only see the species when it is attracted by the state of the mud at the reservoirs. Records lie between August and October as follows:

1935	August 18th and 24th	Harperrig	Three and five
1936	September 12th	Harperrig	One
1953	October 24th	Threipmuir	Two
1972	September 12th	Harperrig	Two
1974	August 15th	Harperrig	One
	September 17th	Crosswood	One
1978	August 6th	West Water Reservoir	Two

Recent records as below extend the period in which we may expect to see Knots in the Pentlands.

1979	August 20th	Threipmuir	Two
1980	July 27th	West Water	Twenty
1983	November 11th	Glencorse	One
1984	August 16th	Harperrig	Two

SMALL SANDPIPERS

Sanderling. Calidris alba. Occasional autumn migrant.

Like the Knot the Sanderling occurs irregularly in autumn, but rather earlier usually between early July and late September, as the following records show:

1934	September 7th to 9th	Threipmuir	Two
1935	August 17th	Harperrig	One
	September 28th	Threipmuir	One
1975	July 3rd	Harperrig	Two
1977	July 22nd	Crosswood	One

Two were recorded in the September 1934 census outing.

In 1979 a very late bird was seen at Harperrig on 14th January, and on 30th July 1980 a Sanderling was present at West Water Reservoir.

Little Stint. *Calidris minuta.* Irregular autumn migrant.

Records are confined to September with one in October. Pre-war sightings were from Threipmuir and Harperrig between 9th and 29th September. Five were seen at Harperrig on 16th September 1936, along with Dunlin and Curlew Sandpipers, but single birds are more usual.

Post-war records are:

1946	September 7th	Harperrig	One
1953	September 14th and 28th	Threipmuir	One
1953	September 6th	Harperrig	One
1973	September 17th	Harperrig	One
	September 28th	Harperrig	Five
	October 2nd	Harperrig	Three
1974	September 3rd	Harperrig	One
1979	September 4th	Threipmuir	One
1981	September 14th	Harperrig	Eight

Temminck's Stint. *Calidris temminckii.* Rare.

The only early record I have been able to trace comes from Mr Iain Ogilvie of Bonaly Tower who wrote to me in 1930 as follows: "The bird seen at Bonaly Reservoir on 7th and 8th August was very tame and could be approached to within a few feet before flying. I had every chance to examine it with care. I have no doubt as to its identity."

There is a record of one being seen at West Water Reservoir in May 1981.

Curlew Sandpiper. *Calidris ferruginea.* Occasional passage migrant in autumn.

There are several pre-1939-45 war records from Threipmuir and Harperrig between the 3rd and 14th September, usually of single birds, but two were seen at Harperrig on 14th September 1936 with Little Stints and Dunlin.

Post-war records are:

1954	August 30th	Harperrig	Two
1973	September 28th	Threipmuir	One
1975	September 3rd	Harperrig	Four
1983	September 11th	West Water	Two

Dunlin. *Calidris alpina.* Summer visitor breeding. Autumn migrant.

There are a few early spring records, but late in April or early May it may be seen in small numbers at the reservoirs and at its breeding haunts.

I have not found Dunlin nesting east of the path from Bavelaw to Nine Mile Burn, but west of this pairs may be seen nesting on the Kitchen Moss and particularly on the boggy moors near Harperrig and Crosswood. Another favourite area is round the Crane Loch. A wet, fairly level moor suits the Dunlin best for breeding, but I have found a nest on a dry grass slope near Harperrig. In late June and July parties, presumably of breeding birds and their young, may be found at the reservoirs, particularly Threipmuir, Crosswood, and Harperrig. A flock of twenty-two turned up on one occasion at Harperrig on 16th July. This post-breeding movement overlaps the autumn migration to some extent, the latter normally extending from July to the end of September. The condition of the mud at the reservoirs has considerable influence on the number of Dunlin resting there while on migration.

Twenty were seen at Harperrig on 26th July 1952, and astonishingly large numbers were present there during September 1973: there were 56 on the 17th, 194 on the 20th, and 42 on the 28th. While the Dunlin is normally absent from the Pentlands after September each year, in some years there are exceptional records in October and November.

In 1837 Macgillivray recorded that a male was shot in the Pentland Hills. From 1883 to 1919 William Evans saw Dunlin between 12th and 28th June, mostly at Harperrig where he found nests, but also at Threipmuir and Crosswood. The *Crosswood Migration Schedules* give these records:

1908	July 31st	Crosswood — Flock flying south
1909	April 21st	Crosswood — Arrival noted
1911	April 21st	Crosswood — Several

Dunlin were only recorded during September in the 1932-34 census. G. L. Sandeman found five to six pairs probably breeding at the Crane Loch on 3rd June 1939, and on 3rd July 1948 found two pairs almost certainly breeding there.

Recent breeding season records are:

1981	June 29th	Crosswood	Fourteen
1982	June 13th	Crosswood	Six
	June 13th	Harperrig	Two
1983	June 10th and 30th	Crosswood	Four

Ruff. *Philomachus pugnax.* Passage migrant in autumn.

Ruffs occur with some regularity during August and September if the water level is low at the reservoirs, exposing suitable areas of wet mud. There is a record in Jardine's Naturalists' Library of one having been shot in the Pentlands in spring, and in 1859 Dr J. S. Smith exhibited a male and female shot in the neighbourhood of Carnwath in the beginning of September (Proceedings of the Royal Physical Society). Ruffs were seen in September during the 1932-34 census. In 1933 singles were recorded at Threipmuir on 24th August and 26th September, and one at Harperrig on 9th September. On 1st September 1934 a flock of twelve containing both sexes was seen at Harperrig; on being disturbed they flew right away in a south-westerly direction. On 8th September of the same year there were three at Harperrig and one at Crosswood. There are some post-war records:

1953	August 23rd	Harperrig	Two
	August 30th	Harperrig	Three
1956	August 4th	Harperrig	Four
1964	August 16th	Threipmuir	One
1972	September 12th	Harperrig	Three
1974	September 3rd	Harperrig	Eleven
1975	August 13th	Crosswood	Two
1976	August 21st	Westwater Reservoir	Nine
1977	August 19th	Westwater Reservoir	Four
1986	August 25th	Harperrig	Two

There are some recent records from Harperrig and Threipmuir between 10th August and 2nd September.

SNIPE AND WOODCOCK

Jack Snipe. *Lymnocryptes minimus.* Irregular visitor.

Rintoul and Baxter (*A Vertebrate Fauna of the Forth*) said that there were records from Bavelaw (1935), and on 31st March 1884 William Evans noted that the Malleny keeper said that he had shot as many as five in a day round Bavelaw, and had also shot them on Bavelaw Moor.

Additional records are:

1931	October 3rd	Harperrig	One
1948	March 26th	Glencorse Glen	One
1952	April 19th	Bavelaw	One
1964	March	Threipmuir	Recorded
1975	December 8th	Bonaly	Recorded
1976	November 6th	Westwater	
		Reservoir	Recorded

Recent records are from Harperrig, West Water, Crosswood and Threipmuir (1980-84) and lie between 3rd October and 29th December.

In 1986 there was one at Threipmuir on 21st November.

Snipe. *Gallinago gallinago.* Resident. Winter visitor. Autumn migrant.

In winter the Snipe can be found in small numbers at marshy parts of the reservoirs, at moist places along the banks of the Water of Leith, and at the lower parts of the larger burns. Spring drumming normally begins at the end of March or early in April. By this time Snipe are widely distributed, spreading to wet heather moors, high springs and pools, as well as at the reservoirs and the Water of Leith.

The population increases noticeably during the period from June to August. This may be due to young birds hatched locally, but in some years numbers suggest immigration from outside the area. There are records at this time of considerable numbers, for example "large numbers at Harperrig 16th June 1932", "very common at Bavelaw August 7th-11th 1932", "many at Bavelaw 9th July 1934", and on 28th August 1938 "very common at Bavelaw and Middle Threipmuir".

By September, however, numbers normally drop to single

birds at suitable places, but considerable irregularity is characteristic of this autumn movement. In 1946 for example, Snipe were rare at Bavelaw during August, and back in 1933 only one or two birds were flushed during this month.

The *Old Statistical Account* of 1791 for Mid Calder Parish notes "no inconsiderable number" of Snipe. Harold Raeburn saw the species at Medwin on 26th June 1890, and on 22nd April 1900 David Hamilton found a nest (c2) in a grassy field at Glencorse Reservoir. Drumming was heard at Crosswood on 31st March 1906, and again there on 10th February 1908.

During the 1932-34 census outings twice as many were seen in March as in September, and in December only one seventh of the March figures was observed. In the 1948 traverse there was a noticeable increase at Bavelaw and Threipmuir on 1st August.

Some recent records during the breeding season are:

1980		Wester Bavelaw	One to two pairs
1981	May 14th	Bavelaw	Seven drumming
	June 30th	Threipmuir	Sixteen plus
1982	June 10th	Threipmuir	Five
1983		Glencorse	Two sites
1984		Threipmuir/ Bavelaw	Four to five sites
	April 2nd	Bavelaw/Loganlee	Eight drumming
	April 23rd	Glencorse	Two drumming
1985		Threipmuir/ Bavelaw	Six territories
1986		Threipmuir	Four territories

Woodcock. *Scolopax rusticola.* Possibly resident. Breeds in small numbers.

There are insufficient records to indicate whether the Woodcock is resident in the area or not, and no proof of the regular autumn influx which exists elsewhere. It is however well distributed during the breeding season in the woods, but nowhere in any numbers. Boghall, Bavelaw Castle, Slipperfield,

Woodhouselee, and Logan Tower wood are localities where nests have been found or Woodcock have been seen during the breeding season.

In the *Old Statistical Account* of 1791 the status of the Woodcock in Calder Parish was described as "no considerable number". Harold Raeburn put up a Woodcock in the T Wood at Swanston on 22nd March 1883.

In the *Annals of Scottish Ornithology* reports of occurrences in the Pentlands on 28th October 1896 and 20th April 1897 suggest that these were sufficiently unusual to be worthy of note. A single bird was seen at Baddinsgill on 25th April 1901. Dr Eagle Clarke said in 1924: "it nests in all suitable localities in the county (Midlothian)". David Hamilton told me in 1947 that the Woodcock was not a common breeder and that it used to nest along the south side of the Lanark road beyond Balerno. He once saw one at Logan Cottage during the winter.

In the census work of 1932-34 five were seen in March, one in September and none in December. John Prentice, the Baddinsgill keeper, told me however that there had been a large increase there in December 1933, and that a few nested in the woods there and also on the hills.

On 4th May 1940 David Hamilton saw two birds in a wood between Flotterstone and Glencorse acting as if they had young. During the 1948-49 traverse the species was seen only once in each of February, March and April, and on two occasions in November.

In 1980 one to two pairs were recorded as breeding at Bavelaw. In 1981 there was roding at nine sites between Flotterstone and Loganlee, and on 24th March four roding at Threipmuir/Bavelaw and also one or two at the Red Moss. In 1982 five sites of roding were found between Flotterstone and Loganlee. In 1983 two birds were seen at Threipmuir on 6th January, one at Bonaly on 8th February and four at Flotterstone on 13th February.

In 1986 the species was reported at Bavelaw from March to June.

CURLEWS AND GODWITS

Black-tailed Godwit. *Limosa limosa.* Rare.

On 1st May 1937 Tom Spence saw one at the junction of Threipmuir and Harelaw Reservoirs, and another or the same one was disturbed further up on Threipmuir.

There are some recent records:

1979	June 11th	Harperrig	One
	August 10th	Threipmuir	One
1982	June 13th	West Water	Six
1984	August 29th and	Harperrig	One
	September 2nd		
1985	May 26th	Threipmuir	One

Bar-Tailed Godwit. *Limosa lapponica.* Rare.

On 11th May 1929 Kirke Nash saw a pair in full summer dress feeding on a mudbank at Threipmuir. On 6th September 1953 T. Boyd saw one at Harperrig. G. L. Sandeman has these records:

1972	July 7th	Crosswood One
1975	July 10th	One flying between the East and West Cairn Hills

Whimbrel. *Numenius phaeopus.* Autumn migrant. Occasional spring.

These are the only reports I have found:

1939	August 8th	Harperrig	One flying west
1952	August 10th	Harperrig	One
1964	July 19th	Threipmuir	One
1975	July 30th	Harperrig	Two
1980	June 12th	Crosswood	One
1983	August 20th	Bavelaw	One
	September 1st	Harperrig	Three
1984	May 11th	Threipmuir	One
	July 7th	Bavelaw	One

Curlew. *Numenius arquata.* Common summer visitor. Breeds. Passage migrant spring and autumn. Occasional in winter.

During the winter the Curlew is sometimes found in small parties feeding on stubble or pasture fields on the low ground, but is rare on the hills. Immigration of breeding birds starts about the beginning of March, and there is also considerable south-west passage through the area during this month. Colonisation is completed in April when the species is widely distributed, and nests freely on the hills right to the tops. Marshy moors are its favourite nesting habitat.

The birds leave the hills as soon as the young are able to fly, and in a normal year this is complete by the end of July. Small parties are to be found then at the reservoirs or adjacent ground.

The main flow of autumn migration takes place during July, and especially in August, usually in quite small parties of up to thirty birds, both by day and night. For example on 8th August 1936 parties passed over Threipmuir during the night calling, and at 8 a.m. on the 9th two flocks came in from the east and passed on west. Autumn migration continues during September, but the bulk of the species has passed through, leaving only the occasional wanderers to colonise the area until the spring.

I was able in 1939 through the kindness of the owners or occupiers of twenty farms and houses on the Pentlands to have from them the dates on which they first saw eighteen species in the spring. In the case of the Curlew dates varied between 18th February and mid April, but the majority of records lay between the third week of February and the first week of March.

In 1791 the status of the Curlew in Linton Parish was given as "among the migratory birds". In 1837 Macgillivray said "it is very numerous on hills and moors". On 27th February 1886 Harold Raeburn noted one flying south west and calling at Colinton, thus sugesting that the species was not present on the hills in winter. On 11th April of the same year he said that Curlews were very noisy on the hill at Swanston.

The following are extracts from David Hamilton's diary:

| 1900 | March 10th | Glencorse — One seen. The shepherd said that he had not seen anything of them yet |
| | March 23rd | Bonaly — Flock of about twenty at side of reservoir |

G

1900	March 30th	The hills are again covered with snow after a week of very hard frost. Only saw one Curlew. The frost has likely driven most of them back to the sea
1901	March 30th	Listonshiels — Curlews back on moors
1903	March 8th	Threipmuir — Curlews starting to visit breeding haunts

The *Crosswood Migration Schedules* for the years between 1906 and 1919 show that most of the first arrival dates in spring lay in the second half of February, with an exceptionally early date on 11th January and one late arrival on 3rd March.

In 1934 the Misses Rintoul and Baxter said "It nests on the Pentlands where it is very abundant".

The total census figures 1932-34 were 226 in March, 22 in September, and none in December. During my traverse 1948-49 my notes showed that Curlews were scarce on the hills by August and were not fully colonised again until mid April.

In the years from 1946 to 1949 G. L. Sandeman found that Curlews were present in the Glencorse Glen from Flotterstone to Loganlee between mid March and the end of August, and that only odd birds were seen from September to November.

On 29th November 1952 after a spell of hard frost a Curlew was seen to fly south-west from Harperrig in the evening, and was picked up shortly afterwards by other observers at Crosswood still heading in the same direction.

Between 1980 and 1984 there are records of strong immigration in March with numbers at Threipmuir of 120 plus and 130 and at Crosswood of 100. In 1984 the breeding sites at Threipmuir were given as eleven to twelve, and in 1985 the estimate was of fifteen to seventeen breeding sites followed by sixteen to eighteen in 1986.

LARGE SANDPIPERS

Spotted Redshank. *Tringa erythropus*. Occasional in autumn.

A single bird was present at Threipmuir on 29th September and 1st October 1934. It was not seen on 5th October.

Recent records are:

1973	September 17th	Harperrig	One
1974	May 10th	Crosswood	Two
1974	June 1st	Harperrig	One
1975	August 13th	Crosswood	Three
1979	August 20th and 29th	Threipmuir	Two
1983	August 2nd	Threipmuir	One
1984	September 7th and 10th	Harperrig	One

Redshank. *Tringa totanus.* Summer visitor. Breeding. Passage migrant. Irregular winter visitor.

The Redshank first appears during early March in numbers which suggest passage, and by the end of the month breeding birds are fully established on pasture fields and marshy ground surrounding the reservoirs. Elsewhere during the breeding season the Redshank is not often seen at any distance from water, and is not very widely distributed.

Breeding has been recorded at Threipmuir, Harelaw, Clubbiedean, Crosswood, North Esk and Baddinsgill, and less regularly at the west end of Glencorse. It is not very often found breeding along the hill burns, except at marshy patches in the lower reaches, and does not nest on the moors.

During July and August emigration takes place in a south-westerly direction, and by the end of August only an odd Redshank is left at the reservoirs. The species sometimes appears in small numbers during October and November. For example there was a flock of sixteen at Threipmuir on 12th November 1933 where only two had been seen on 10th October. On the 27th November of the same year nine were present at Threipmuir. There have also been striking increases during November in other years. Although Redshanks are not regular visitors in winter there are odd records in December, January and February.

Of the seven farms and houses records of first appearances, three were in early March and four in early to mid April.

In 1791 the *Old Statistical Account for Linton Parish* numbered the Redshank among its migrating birds. In 1885 Harold Raeburn found a probable nest at Harperrig on 23rd April, and in 1889 he saw young birds at East Threipmuir on 3rd June. David Hamilton saw a pair at Bonaly Reservoir on 1st April 1902 and dozens flying about Threipmuir on 26th April. He saw a big flock at Harperrig on 5th April 1903, and plenty at Threipmuir on 26th April of the same year. In 1905 he first recorded Redshanks on 19th March, and on 24th March 1906 he saw Redshanks indulging in love flights at Glencorse. In 1907 he saw eight at Glencorse on 24th March, and the species was noted at Crosswood on 18th March.

The *Crosswood Migration Schedules* subsequently noted:

1908	March 17th	One October 29th Heard
1909	March 22nd	One arrived March 26th Three
1910	March 10th	One March 28th Several
1911	March 9th	Two December 2nd One
1912	March 5th	Heard March 9th Several
1913	March 13th	One
1914	March 12th	Six
1915	March 6th	One
1916	March 19th	One March 21st Four. March 24th Twelve
1917	March 14th	Heard
1919	April 17th	One

The total census figures for the three years 1932-34 were 131 for March, three for September, and seven for December. During the 1948-49 traverse Redshanks were seen from mid March to the end of June, and then were not seen again until 13th March of the following year, except for a single bird on 11th July.

In 1934 Rintoul and Baxter saw one or two by Harperrig on 28th May and a pair in Windy Gowl on 2nd June. In 1945 a pair was at Bonaly on 2nd April.

Recent records 1980 to 1984 indicate spring passage during April. In 1980, for example, there were forty-one at Threipmuir on 22nd April, and in 1981 there were thirty-eight at Threipmuir on 8th April, and thirteen at Glencorse on 15th May.

Greenshank. *Tringa nebularia.* Passage migrant spring and autumn.

This species is more often seen during the autumn migration than in spring, but there are some spring records. The earliest autumn date is 11th June, but this is exceptional as August is the great Greenshank month. Early in the month, in years when good mud exists at the reservoirs, Greenshank can be expected to visit them. The favoured reservoirs are Threipmuir, Bavelaw, Harperrig, Harelaw and Glencorse, but no doubt the species visits other reservoirs if the mud is attractive.

The greatest number observed together at one time in one place has been six. On 8th August 1936 two birds were heard to pass singly over Threipmuir between eleven o'clock and midnight. It was a dark night with rain.

Once arrived, the Greenshank (unlike other waders which rapidly pass on) often lingers until the middle of September, and in 1934 an exceptional late bird stayed at Threipmuir until 14th October. In autumn Bavelaw becomes a marsh with a sluggish burn flowing through it among willows. This burn is a favourite haunt of Greenshanks.

The Misses Rintoul and Baxter in *A Vertebrate Fauna of the Forth* said that William Evans saw two at Crosswood on 13th May 1906, and that the Greenshank is recorded commonly from Threipmuir and Harperrig. The *Crosswood Migration Schedules* only have one record — a single bird on 25th May 1913. In 1935 (*Scottish Naturalist*) it was said that the species had been recorded on a number of occasions during August and September and that the latest record for Threipmuir was on 5th October, but David Hamilton saw one at Bavelaw on 14th October 1934.

Only one was seen during the nine census outings 1932-34 (in September 1934), and none during the 1948-49 traverse.

Green Sandpiper. *Tringa ochropus.* Occasional visitor in autumn.

On 30th August 1884 William Evans had an excellent view of one in company with two Common Sandpipers at Harperrig. In 1910 one was seen at Medwin on 1st August. Later records are:

1948	May 9th	One at Bavelaw
1964	August 10th	One at Glencorse
1965	August 23rd	One at Glencorse
1972	August 14th	One at Harperrig
1972	October 12th	One at Clubbiedean

In 1979 one was seen at Threipmuir on 10th August and

another on 4th September. In 1984 three were seen also at Threipmuir on 4th August.

Wood Sandpiper. *Tringa glareola*. Occasional visitor in autumn.

A single bird was present at Threipmuir from 3rd to 7th August 1934. In 1938 a bird which was thought to belong to this species was seen at Harperrig on 15th August. Later records are:

1939	June 1st	Harperrig	One
1976	September 20th	Threipmuir	One
1978	August 6th	West Water	
		Reservoir	One

In 1979 one was seen at Threipmuir on 1st September, and there was another record also from Threipmuir on the 9th September.

In 1986 one was seen at Threipmuir on 11th August.

Common Sandpiper. *Actitis hypoleucos*. Summer visitor. Breeding. Passage migrant.

Breeding sandpipers normally arrive about the third week of April, and early in May the gravelly burns and reservoir edges are fully occupied, the grassy banks forming ideal nesting localities. The Crane Loch, which is a peat loch with no gravel shores, does not hold breeding pairs. I have also found a nest in the wood at Harelaw, and Sandpipers are common along the Water of Leith even in the wooded stretches.

In late July families are common at the reservoirs, and the hill burns are gradually being drained of their breeding stock. Migration through the area takes place in August. On 8th August 1936 five birds had arrived at Threipmuir overnight, and were recorded at 8 a.m. Numbers at the reservoirs fluctuate from day to day suggesting migration. By the end of August only stragglers remain, and by the middle of September the species has normally left for the year.

Harold Raeburn knew the bird well. On 3rd June 1889 he found several pairs at Bavelaw, and a nest (c4) on the bank at the edge of Middle Threipmuir. In 1890 he found some seven to eight pairs on Medwin on 26th June. In 1902 David Hamilton found a nest (c4) on 10th May on a bank among some fir trees at the side of Glencorse.

Some arrival dates are recorded in the *Annals of Scottish Ornithology:*

1894	April 15th	Loganlee
1897	April 16th	Pentlands
1898	April 17th	Bavelaw
1899	April 21st	Pentlands
1904	April 17th	Glencorse

The *Crosswood Migration Schedules* 1908-19 give these arrival dates:

1908	April 30th	
1909	April 20th	
1910	April 14th	
1911	April 18th	
1912	April 19th	
1913	April 20th	
1914	April 15th	
1915	April 25th	
1916	April 24th and 25th	Large numbers
1917	April 27th	
1919	April 20th	

There is a record from Clubbiedean on 11th April 1922. In 1934 Rintoul and Baxter wrote: "In the Pentlands it is a common bird by the burns and lochs." They found two pairs at North Esk, and said that the species was abundant at the Logan Burn, and numerous at the North Esk Burn up to 1300 ft. They also recorded Sandpipers at the Crosswood Burn and at Glencorse.

In the years immediately preceding the 1939-45 war there are records of arrival in the second half of April for the most part, with the earliest being from Baddinsgill on 18th April, and the latest from North Esk on 4th May.

Only nine were seen during the census outings 1932-34, all in September. Later records of first arrivals are:

1945	May 5th	North Esk	
1958	April 27th	Glencorse	
1962	April 23rd	Balerno	
1967	April 9th	Glencorse	
1968	April 21st	Threipmuir	Seven

In the traverse of 1948-49, first dates were 25th April 1948, and 24th April 1949 (both at Threipmuir). By the end of July only one was seen and none on 15th August, but a late bird was seen at Harelaw on 1st October.

G. L. Sandeman reports that in the Glencorse Valley he has records from 22nd April to 27th July, then fewer until the end of September, while R. L. Swann said of Threipmuir in 1971: "Recorded May to September each year. Three pairs usually nest." Nineteen were seen at the West Water Reservoir on 31st July 1978.

Breeding pairs:

	1979	1980	1981	1982	1983	1984
Glencorse	1	—	2-3	—	—	—
Harelaw	1	—	—	—	—	2
Threipmuir	3	1-2	—	—	—	—
Harperrig	—	—	3	—	—	—
North Esk	—	—	4-5	2	2	3
Crosswood	—	—	—	2	—	1
Loganlee waterfall/ Glencorse	—	—	—	8-9	10	—
Logan Burn	—	—	—	—	—	3

In 1986 twenty were present at Threipmuir Reservoir on 1st August.

Turnstone. *Arenaria interpres.* Irregular visitor.

It would appear from the following records that the Turnstone is an irregular migrant in spring and autumn:

1929	April 12th	Threipmuir	One
1934	July 29th	Harperrig	One
1953	August 23rd	Harperrig	One
		Threipmuir	One
1971	May 15th	Glencorse	Four
1974	September 3rd	Harperrig	One
1978	July 23rd	West Water Reservoir	One

Modern records are;

1983	May 8th	West Water Reservoir	One
	August 25th	Harperrig	Two immatures
1984	September 2nd	Harperrig	One

SKUAS AND GULLS

Arctic Skua. *Stercorarius parasiticus.* Irregular visitor.
   These are the records I have found:

1955	June 15th	Crane Loch — One dark phase being mobbed by Black-headed Gulls
1974	May 24th	Harperrig	One
1977	October 16th	Threipmuir	One

Little Gull. *Larus minutus.* Rare.
   T. Boyd saw an adult at Threipmuir on 16th May 1954.
   There are two recent records as below:

| 1979 | September 9th | Threipmuir | One immature |
| 1984 | May 11th-18th | Bavelaw | One |

Black-headed Gull. *Larus ridibundus.* Summer visitor. Breeding.
   Passage migrant. Winter visitor.
   Black-headed Gulls are nowadays much commoner than in the last century, but their distribution in the Pentlands is much restricted between October and February. An odd bird can sometimes be seen at this time at the reservoirs, but where suitable feeding exists in winter, large flocks of several hundred birds are often present. Where ploughing is taking place the birds follow the plough closely with delightful tameness. In this they are often accompanied by Common Gulls. Newly sown crops and pasture are also often frequented at this season. Small groups may also be found along the Water of Leith where drainpipes discharge into the water or rubbish tips provide succulent fare.
   Signs of spring migration become evident in March, when small parties may be seen drifting west, but the movement does

not gather momentum until well on in the month. Flocks are common then along the lower cultivated slopes, and the breeding colonies are occupied. It seems likely that many of these birds are resting while on migration.

At the breeding colonies numbers are very erratic from year to year, due partly to varying water levels at the nests. For example, on 26th May 1946 when the Bavelaw colony should have been in full swing, some fifty birds were flying about but only ten or so were sitting on nests. It is doubtful if any young were hatched.

Colonies start breaking up about the end of July, and birds then appear at the other reservoirs and on fields, usually near the breeding areas. Shortly after this the majority of birds left in the area are immature and linger on until September or October. In some cases they may winter in the area, and account for the records of odd birds, usually immature, recorded during the winter months.

The start and progress of the breeding colonies is well documented.

Bavelaw

In 1920 W. Evans reported: "The extension of Threipmuir Reservoir to the meadow beyond the pine wood was carried out about 25 years ago (1895?), and as the area of sedges and other marsh vegetation increased in extent, it gradually attracted the attention of Black-headed Gulls in the neighbourhood, and in due course a colony was founded. Eggs were first seen, Mr Davidson (keeper) tells me, in 1905 or 1906, and for some years the colony was small: recently however it has increased greatly." (David Hamilton saw a lot of Black-headed Gulls there on 23rd June 1900 and by 1905 he saw about 100 nests.) Mr Evans continues "In 1916 I noted it as a large colony, and in May 1919 I set it down at 250-300 pairs. In the latter year the keeper lifted 15 dozen fresh eggs on 10th May besides many on other dates. This year (8th May 1920) the birds appear to me to be no less numerous. An interesting fact in connection with this gullery may be mentioned, namely that a few nests occur annually in stunted fir trees at the upper end of the marsh."

By 1934 the colony had decreased to between thirty and forty pairs; possibly due to persistent nest robbing as at other Pentland colonies. In 1947 G. L. Sandeman estimated that there were some 400-500 pairs nesting.

During the 1948-49 traverse birds were noisy at the breeding area by 14th March, and on 11th April the colony was in full swing. On 2nd May they were so numerous as to suggest a population increase over previous years. By the first of August the colony was deserted except for an odd bird flying about.

In 1952, however, G. L. Sandeman found only five or six birds present on 26th April, and felt that there had been no breeding that year. He found a few pairs nesting in 1959. R. L. Swann told me that the colony restarted in 1959 and has increased since, and on 20th April 1964 G. L. Sandeman saw large numbers and recorded some breeding on 30th May 1966.

Now that feral mink have infested Bavelaw the future of the colony may well be uncertain.

In 1985 however this colony was very successful with an estimate of 1770-2000 breeding pairs, and on 19th April, 4450 birds were counted.

Harperrig

William Evans in his *Breeding Colonies of the Black-headed Gull* (1920) wrote: "This reservoir was constructed I understand in 1855-6. The main nesting place of the Gulls is near the head of the reservoir on what is more or less of an island according to the height of the water. How far back the colony dates I cannot say; its existence however has been known to me for forty years (since 1880). My first actual visit to it was made on 20th May 1882. On the 26th May nests were plentiful . . . I feel sure that there were not less than 100 to 150 pairs and visits to the locality in 1890, 1897, 1903, 1905 etc. did not reveal any marked change in the size of the colony. Later there would appear to have been an increase culminating, Mr White the keeper of the reservoir tells me in 1915, when he considers that there were at least 250 pairs. After this protection was suspended owing to war time scarcity of food, with the result that a rapid decrease has since taken place, so rapid indeed that last year (1919) there were scarcely thirty pairs, and this year there are still fewer. When I called on Mr White on 14th May he had not heard of a single nest, and I could only see four or five Gulls anywhere near the reservoir, the water level of which was unusually high and the island in consequence very small. Mr Eagle Clarke who landed on the island three days later, reports about a score of new nests . . . perhaps this decrease has some connection with the increase at Threipmuir.''

In 1933 G. L. Sandeman counted 193 nests with young and eggs at Harperrig, and in 1934 Rintoul and Baxter estimated the number at 50-60 pairs. In 1947 when the water level was high only five or six birds were seen, and in 1952 it was reported that the colony was non productive. However in 1956 there were some young on the islet and in 1959 and 1967 a few pairs were nesting.

In 1985 there were about 50 nests and 70-100 young were seen, while in 1986 there were 1150 pairs.

Bawdy Moss

This colony started about 1916 or 1917 but the birds were so much harried that they all left. They returned however in numbers and it became a very large gullery. G. L. Sandeman estimated their numbers at roughly 1500 to 2000 birds in 1933. In 1934 when there were 500-600 pairs the nests were mostly in heather but some were in rough grass.

Numbers continued to vary considerably from year to year; for example in 1948 there were only fifteen or sixteen pairs breeding; in the following year there were about 700, and this number jumped to 1200-1500 in 1950. The breeding pairs then fell to about 400-500 in 1951, and in 1952 and 1953 the colony was completely deserted. Human interference, especially during the war-time egg shortage, has been a common reason given for the desertion of sites, but there is little doubt that large scale drainage operations have been the main cause at the Bawdy Moss. In the spring of 1952, a few pairs did appear, and some eggs were laid, but the birds left almost immediately.

Crane Loch

In 1933 G. L. Sandeman found 500-600 breeding, but in 1947 there were only some fifteen to twenty empty nests, suggesting that the eggs had been taken. The breeding population was sixty pairs in 1948 and 1949, 150 in 1950 and 450 in 1951. In 1952 however numbers fell to about 150 pairs, and even some of these seemed to leave during the breeding season, almost certainly as a result of human interference. In 1959 the colony stood at about 250 birds.

North Esk

There were three hundred pairs in 1978 but these deserted.

General Notes

According to the *Lothian Bird Report* for 1985 there had been a dramatic recovery where 1525 pairs were nesting in that year.

There are some interesting ringing records from the Pentland colonies. A young bird ringed by G. L. Sandeman at Bawdy Moss in 1950 was recovered at the Crane Loch in May 1952, where it was presumably breeding. Another ringed in 1949 was recovered in June three years later at East Boldon, Northumberland. A Ravensglass bird was found dead in the breeding season on the Harperrig Reservoir gullery one year, eleven months after it had been ringed.

Some very interesting breeding statistics have appeared in recent years. In 1979 the water level at Bavelaw was low and no pairs bred, but 200 pairs managed to do so at Harperrig. In 1980 the Bavelaw level was again low and very few young were reared although some 150 pairs bred at North Esk Reservoir. A full breeding census took place in 1981 when it was found that there was very little evidence of success at Bavelaw and colonies at Crosswood and Harperrig were unsuccessful; on the other hand there were 1100 pairs at North Esk Reservoir and 1500 at West Water Reservoir and many young were fledged at these colonies. It was noted that former important colonies at Bawdy Moss and the Crane Loch had been deserted, but in 1985 Crosswood had about fifty pairs and a new colony of about four nests had started at Black Springs, Threipmuir.

The *Lothian Bird Report* for 1981 said that it was difficult to be specific, but human interference (i.e. egg collecting) and mink predation had all contributed to the redistribution of breeding colonies. Bawdy Moss had been drained, and human interference at both North Esk Reservoir and West Water Reservoir had restricted nesting to the islands. North Esk Reservoir was abandoned in 1978 and 1979 after mink were found breeding on an island in 1978, and in 1981 the waterkeeper at Harperrig

Reservoir reported (per G. L. Sandeman) having seen mink clearing out Black-headed Gulls' eggs.

The species seems however to be very resilient for in 1982 the colony at the West Water Reservoir had 1870 pairs and bred very successfully. There were 1200 pairs at the North Esk Reservoir and smaller numbers bred at Bavelaw and Harperrig. The recovery continued in the following years. In 1983 the colonies both at Bavelaw and North Esk Reservoir were noted as being very successful, and in 1984 the number of breeding pairs at Bavelaw had risen to 1000.

Common Gull. *Larus canus.* Winter visitor. Passage migrant.
    Breeds in small numbers.

I have not been able to come across any early records of Common Gulls. Even in 1934 when the Misses Rintoul and Baxter scoured the hills, they had only one record (of an immature) between Carlops and the Bore Stane on 27th May.

During the census work 1932-34 it was found that numbers could vary very considerably owing to the presence or absence of flocks. The total numbers seen were 466 in March, 186 in September, and 466 plus in December. During the traverse 1948-49 numbers started to build up in early spring when flocks were seen until mid-April, but none was seen on 25th April. Flocks had reappeared by mid-July, and numbers fluctuated from then until the early spring influx again. Once again these had largely departed by mid April.

A small breeding colony started at the Crane Loch about 1945 when some three pairs bred. One pair was again present in 1949 and in 1950 and 1951 a clutch of three eggs was found. In 1952 certainly two and probably three or more pairs nested, two nests (c3 and c2) being found on 17th May, and two (c2 and c1) on the 31st. On 25th May 1958 however there were at least sixteen adults present, and four clutches and several empty scrapes (probably due to the frequent visits of eggers) were found.

One pair bred at the North Esk Reservoir 1983-84 and 1-2 pairs at Harperrig in 1984.

In 1985 a pair bred at North Esk Reservoir, and two to three pairs at Harperrig probably did not breed. There was little change in 1986.

There are several records of large flocks at the West Water Reservoir. These were 5500 on 19th February 1977 and 1300 on 7th September 1978.

The flocks can normally be classed between those in winter and those happening during migration. For example on 3rd January 1981 there were between 2000 and 3000 on Threipmuir and in the following year some 6200 on the West Water Reservoir in January with lesser numbers on the other reservoirs during winter. The spring migration numbers are astonishing. In 1980 there were 20000 on the West Water Reservoir on 10th April; in 1982 16000 on 24th March; and in 1983, 13750 there on 19th March.

Lesser Black-backed Gull. *Larus fuscus.* Passage migrant. Occasional in winter. Lately non-breeding summer resident.

Spring passage begins about the end of March when small numbers, or more often just one to three birds, appear at the reservoirs or are seen flying west over the hills. We had no pre-war records of summering, but in 1946 the species was seen throughout the nesting season on the moor south of Harperrig Reservoir. On the 23rd June of that year a bird on the Hagierae Moss, where there were two pairs, dived at my head as I passed, suggesting that nesting was likely.

Autumn migrants appear in most years about the middle of July, and by early September the migration is over.

David Hamilton saw the species occasionally during the nesting season. For example:

1904	May 29th	Harperrig — A pair about
1905	April 16th	Glencorse — One seen
1933	April 16th	Threipmuir — Recorded

In 1934 when the Misses Rintoul and Baxter explored the Pentlands they saw two adults at Threipmuir on 22nd May, and on 3rd June they found an immature bird in the Glencorse valley.

In 1946 two were seen at Harperrig on 22nd April. Since that date the species has turned up in winter more frequently than before, for example:

1951	February 9th	Glencorse	One
	December 29th	Crane Loch	One
		Baddinsgill	One

On 7th January 1962 T. C. Smout recorded a Scandinavian bird sitting on the ice at Harperrig.

R. L. Swann told me in 1971 that there were a few records at Threipmuir each year between March and October. In 1974 G. L. Sandeman saw two at Threipmuir on 21st January, and he has several other records of adults in winter.

The species was not recorded on any census outing in 1932-34, but I have the following records from the 1948-49 traverse:

1948	March 21st	East Kenleith fields. Two on plough
	April 11th	Bavelaw Two. Threipmuir Four
	April 25th	Bavelaw Two. Threipmuir Five
	May 2nd	Not seen
	June 6th	Bavelaw Mill. One immature
	June 13th	Threipmuir. One immature
	September 12th	Threipmuir. Adult and immature
		Clubbiedean Fields. Two

There was then a gap until 24th April 1949 when two were seen at Bavelaw Mill and one at Threipmuir.

During the years 1980-1984 there were records of spring passage between 4th March and 26th April when groups of up to eighty birds were seen together. There are also autumn records between 22nd August and 7th September where the greatest number was thirty plus. Counts made in 1985 were twenty-seven at West Kenleith on 12th March and thirty-three at Threipmuir on 19th April. In 1986 twenty-eight were seen at Threipmuir on 16th July which is a most unusual date. There was also an example of *Larus fuscus fuscus* at Swanston on 4th April.

A bird of the Scandinavian race was at Flotterstone on 31st March 1982.

Herring Gull. *Larus argentatus*. Post-breeding and winter visitor. Irregular in summer.

Herring Gulls begin to appear at the reservoirs about the middle of July, particularly at Threipmuir and Harperrig where numbers may build up to 600-1000, but such numbers may fluctuate greatly. The time of day can also have considerable

Plate 5

North Esk Reservoir

Baddinsgill Reservoir

Plate 6

Carnethy and Scald Law

Near Dunsyre

effect for there is normally a roost on the hill at Harperrig to which many birds fly at dusk. At Threipmuir however the birds often fly down to the sea to roost. There are many immature birds among these.

Herring Gulls can be seen drifting over the hills in winter as often as over the low ground. Where ploughing is taking place numbers are often seen feeding along the furrows. The winter flocks break up during March, but stragglers may be seen after this through to the July influx. The Harperrig roost has been used as late as 28th May.

On 22nd January 1888 Harold Raeburn saw one or two in the Allermuir district drifting about at a great height, and on 5th February of the same year he saw a great quantity flying west in the Colinton and Dreghorn district.

Rintoul and Baxter saw several, all immatures, flying over in May 1934. In 1946 a flock of 100 to 150 was seen on a field at Threipmuir on 22nd April.

Glaucous Gull. *Larus hyperboreus.* Rare.
On 1st January 1948 G. L. Sandeman saw one at Clubbiedean.

Great Black-backed Gull. *Larus marinus.* Winter visitor in small numbers.

Immatures may be seen at the reservoirs in autumn and winter, particularly Threipmuir and Harperrig where there are usually some in the roosting flocks. As an adolescent or mature bird however, the Great Black-backed Gull usually occurs singly, sometimes in numbers of up to four together, on the larger reservoirs between late August and early February. The species rests more often on the water than other gulls, which may prefer the shores.

There appear to be very few if any early records. During the nine census outings 1932-34 a total of three was seen in September and ten in December, but none in March. On the 1948-49 traverse one bird was seen on 22nd February 1948, and then there were no records until 10th October. After this there were odd records until 13th February 1949.

At Flotterstone from 1946 to 1949 G. L. Sandeman found birds between the end of September and the beginning of March. On

H

20th April 1950 one shot at Bavelaw had been ringed in Russia in the previous June. In 1971 R. L. Swann reported for Threipmuir "Seen mainly in winter in small numbers, maximum fifteen. Few summer records".

Kittiwake. *Rissa tridactyla.* Rare.
In June 1981 one was found dead at the North Esk Reservoir.

TERNS

Sandwich Tern. *Sterna sandvicensis.* Rare.
On 13th July 1979 one was heard at Flotterstone, and on 22nd June 1983 there were three at the West Water Reservoir.

Common Tern. *Sterna hirundo.* Summer visitor. Has bred. Post breeding wanderer. Possibly passage migrant.
    Common Terns arrived at their breeding territory at Harperrig about the end of the first week of May, and the breeding population varied from year to year, from one to six or so pairs, but it seems as though this colony has died out. Here are early nesting records:

1932	Four pairs	Successful
1933	Two pairs	?
1934	Two pairs	Successful
1935	Three pairs	Successful
1936	Only one bird seen	Unsuccessful
1938	Two pairs	?
1948	Four pairs	Successful

Unless the spring has been exceptionally dry, or the level of the water has been artificially lowered at the time the birds start nesting, they normally lay on the rocky island at the south-west end of the reservoir in company with Black-headed Gulls. This island is liable to become a peninsula in a dry summer, and the eggs are then dangerously exposed to pillage. In 1946 when food was short, and not one young Black-headed was reared, the Terns were saved by the low level of the water causing two small rocky islands to emerge well out in the reservoir. Here the Terns nested successfully.

A further note about this colony was reported by T. Boyd in the *Edinburgh Bird Bulletin*. "In 1952 the remnants of the old colony nested successfully this year. Terns were first seen on 19th May when four were present, and by 15th June three pairs appeared to be nesting on a small islet exposed in the middle of the reservoir by the unusually low water level. By 20th July these birds were feeding young which could be seen from the shore. On 10th August I saw one pair of Common Terns with young at the flying stage. A week later all had gone." R. W. Smith took up the story again in the *Edinburgh Bird Bulletin*. He said: "At Harperrig on 27th July 1957 there were at least two and possibly three pairs feeding three fledged young."

Up to 7-8 pairs bred at North Esk Reservoir from 1974 to 1976.

Successful breeders leave the colony for the year about the end of August as a rule.

A new nesting colony has started on the West Water Reservoir. Here on 31st July 1966 there were three adults and two chicks on a small islet, and six pairs were breeding in 1978.

The *Crosswood Migration Schedules* 1908-19 record the presence of up to two birds in most years between 16th May and 12th August.

No Common Terns were recorded during the 1932-34 census, nor in the 1948-49 traverse.

G. L. Sandeman has the following records:

1934	June 4th	Clubbiedean	One
1937	May 18th	Clubbiedean	One
1949	June 25th	Glencorse	One
1970	June 10th	Bavelaw	Two
	July 16th	Glencorse	One
1971	May 24th	Glencorse	One
1972	June 8th	Logan House	One
	July 11th	Glencorse	One
1973	May 23rd	Glencorse	Two
	July 9th	Threipmuir	One
1974	June 17th	Flotterstone/ Glencorse	One

After the breeding season Common Terns sometimes appear between the latter half of July and the middle of September at Harelaw, Threipmuir and Crosswood. These may be post-breeding wanderers, unsuccessful breeders, or passage migrants.

There are records of single birds having been seen at Harperrig, Bavelaw and Threipmuir between 15th June and 20th August (1979-84).

Arctic Tern. *Sterna paradisaea.* Rare.

C. Walker reported in the *Edinburgh Bird Bulletin* 5-77 that about 22nd June 1955 one was picked up dead at Glencorse Reservoir. A Tern had been noticed there in the last week of May, and had been seen around the reservoir for about a week obviously in an ailing condition. Two were seen at Bavelaw on 3rd July 1984.

Black Tern. *Chlidonias niger.* Rare.

Tom Delaney saw eight at Threipmuir on 29th May 1966.

AUKS

Little Auk. *Alle alle.* Rare windblown arrivals.

J. Kirke Nash in his *Birds of Midlothian* reports one alive at Dreghorn on 24th January 1895. In February 1940 Mr Wilson of Boghall reported that one had been found alive on his drive after north-east gales. He kept it for two days before it died and had it identified in the Royal Scottish Museum.

SANDGROUSE

Pallas's Sandgrouse. *Syrrhaptes paradoxus.* Exceptional vagrant.

William Evans wrote in the *Zoologist* of 1888 that on 26th May 1888 at Redford Moor he watched a flock of fifteen for over an hour feeding in a field which had been recently sown with oats and grass. They came from the west and on taking wing again proceeded on their eastward (and coastward) course.

PIGEONS AND DOVES

Stock Dove. *Columba oenas.* Resident in small numbers.

The Stock Dove is well distributed in the Pentlands, but is nowhere numerous. There seems to be little change of habitat during the winter, except that the hill breeding birds frequent lower ground. It can be found nesting in trees especially at

Threipmuir, Dreghorn, Woodhouselee, along the Water of Leith, and elsewhere where suitable old timber exists. It has nested in the ruins of Cairns Castle. It also nests in rabbit burrows, sometimes well away from wooding as high as 1200 feet. The Glencorse-Loganlee valley and the slopes of Mendick are favourite areas for his habit.

William Evans (*Annals of Scottish Ornithology* 1896) traced the history of the Stock Dove in the Pentlands. He said "The Stock Dove now appears to have fairly established itself on the Pentland Hills . . . Eagle Clarke observed one about the rocks at nether Habbie's Howe, in the very heart of the Pentlands on 1st May 1892 . . . one or more pairs have annually returned to breed in this spot, for the bird has been seen there on several subsequent occasions including 15th April 1896 (seen by Mr R. Godfrey leaving nesting hole in the same rocks). In 1893 a pair reared two broods in a rabbit burrow on Torduff Hill; seen again there on 10th March 1896; and a group of seven at a rock in Bonaly glen. On 11th May one was seen in the wooded ravine at Glencorse Reservoir. At Malleny, Balerno, one was shot by the gamekeeper nine or ten years ago (1886 or 1887), and the species was seen there again a year or two later."

David Hamilton had these records:

1908	May 10th	Loganlee — Nest (c1) in hole in earth on face of rocks at waterfall
1915	May 15th	Bavelaw — Several seen
1920	May 26th	Woodhouselee — Nested in hole in tree

He said that the species was rather less common than thirty years ago.

Walter Stewart (*Scottish Naturalist* 1928) said: "In the Biggar and Dolphinton districts we have often in autumn and winter seen flocks amounting to an excess of the breeding stock."

During the census work 1932-34 the total counts were six in March, eight in September and sixteen in December. In May 1934 Rintoul and Baxter found several in the Fairliehope and North Esk woods and two at Bavelaw Castle. John Prentice, the gamekeeper at Baddinsgill, wrote to me in 1934 saying that a few pairs nested in Windy Gowl in rabbit burrows.

Only odd birds were seen during the 1948-49 traverse. There were two records in October, two in January and one in April.

R. L. Swann said of Threipmuir that in 1966 a pair nested in an old beech tree.

G. L. Sandeman has these records:

1974	June 24th	East Rig	Eight
1975	December 12th	West Rig	Flock of thirty plus
		Middle Threipmuir	Two

Counts between 1980 and 1984 give numbers at Bavelaw of 20 to 40 between 12th October and 14th March. In 1984 the breeding stock at Threipmuir/Bavelaw was given as four pairs, and this breeding stock remained the same in 1985 and 1986.

Woodpigeon. *Columba palumbus.* Resident. Winter visitor, sometimes in large numbers.

The Woodpigeon is a common breeding bird in the Pentlands, finding in the many pine shelter belts excellent cover for its nest, and convenient fields nearby for feeding purposes. The birds occupy their breeding sites during March, and may then be heard cooing for the first time in the season. Occupation is sometimes irregular, for example on 8th March 1936 both Braid Law and Cap Law Woods (1250 and 1400 feet) contained cooing Woodpigeons, but on the 15th March of the same year, the woods at Medwin Farm and Medwinhead (900 and 1000 feet) were unoccupied.

After breeding the birds often frequent the stubbles and pasture fields in small parties. On 27th August 1933 two were seen on heather at the Baddinsgill Burn, although the species is not normally found on hill ground at a distance from trees. Many birds leave the high woods after they have nested.

Immigration, sometimes on a considerable scale, takes place during December and January, but sometimes this may be largely a hard weather movement. On 23rd December 1934, and again on 19th January 1935, large flocks came in from the north-east. There is a note of a huge flock at Lymphoy in the winter of 1936. Where beech mast is available in winter it attracts such flocks, and these are often seen at Marchbank and along the Water of Leith immediately west of Balerno.

Harold Raeburn found Woodpigeons nesting in the T Wood over a hundred years ago. Here are his records:

1881	April 20th	Four nests with eggs and young
1883	April 6th	Nest found c2
1884	April 6th	Nest found in thick spruce about 6 feet from the ground. Four nests in all
1885	April 5th	Nest c2 in thick spruce about 5 feet up The birds had been cooing on March 22nd
1886	May 22nd	Great numbers in the wood at the east end of Harelaw

And David Hamilton had these notes:

1899	June 12th	Clubbiedean. Nest c2 in fir tree
1901	April 20th	Glencorse. Nest c2 in wood at side of reservoir

The total figures during the census 1932-34 were 122 in March, 54 in September and 203 in December. In May 1934 Rintoul and Baxter saw the species in woods at Fairliehope, North Esk Reservoir and Saltersyke.

Numbers seen during the 1948-49 traverse were very variable, with notes of scarcity on 29th August, 12th September, 3rd October, 9th January, 27th February and 13th March. In 1971 R. L. Swann said of Threipmuir "Very common. Several pairs breed".

In 1978 1000 flew east in twenty minutes in the Pentlands on 30th December (*Scottish Bird Report* 1978).

Large flocks continue to be seen in winter, for example 1000 plus were at Threipmuir on 10th and 15th January 1981, and there were 400 at Threipmuir on 24th March 1986.

Collared Dove. *Streptopelia decaocto*. Formerly unknown, now common in wooded areas.

The species was first noted in the Pentlands about 1970, and since then has spread considerably. Collared Doves are now regular nesters in Colinton gardens. G. L. Sandeman has these records:

1970	September 3rd	Flotterstone/ Glencorse	One
	October 9th	Water of Leith, Colinton	One
1971	November 29th	Harperrig	Two
1975	June 13th	Harmeny	Two
1980	March 22nd	Water of Leith, Juniper Green	At least eight together

Turtle Dove. *Streptopelia turtur.* Rare.

J. Kirke Nash in his *Birds of Midlothian* recorded that Messrs Small the taxidermists received one from Juniper Green in 1878.

CUCKOOS

Cuckoo. *Cuculus canorus.* Summer visitor. Breeding.

The Cuckoo usually arrives towards the end of April, and may then be heard almost anywhere on the lower portions of the area. It is less common on the low wooded ground, probably due to lack of suitable foster parents. The bulk of the adult birds have left by July, and the young follow them during August or early September.

The *Old Statistical Account for Linton Parish* (1791) listed the Cuckoo among the migratory birds seen there. In 1837 Macgillivray noted it as being ''Not rare on the Pentland Hills''.

Some dates of arrival are:

1897	April 28th	Listonshiels (*Annals of Scottish Ornithology*)
1901	April 30th	Dreghorn (*Annals of Scottish Ornithology*)
	May 4th	Loganlee (David Hamilton)
1905	April 30th	Bonaly Tower (David Hamilton)
1906	May 5th	Torduff (*Annals of Scottish Ornithology*)
1909	April 24th	Crosswood (*Annals of Scottish Ornithology*)

In the *Zoologist* of 1907 J. R. Mc'C. said "At the base of the range of the Pentland Hills Cuckoos are not uncommon. In that locality they place their eggs in the nests of Meadow Pipits."

The earliest recorded dates from the *Crosswood Migration Schedules* 1908-19 lie between 24th April and 5th May.

In 1939 the dates of arrival from the houses and farm returns were: One on 30th April, one on 1st May, two on 3rd May, three on 4th May, six on 6th May, one on 8th May, and one at Cairns Castle on 15th May.

In 1945 J. K. Adams first heard one at Carlops on 5th May. The Cuckoo was not heard during the traverse on 1948 until 9th May when it was recorded in four localities, and was last seen on 26th June.

In 1971 R. L. Swann said of Threipmuir: "Up to five singing birds in May and June each year."

Some recent arrival dates are:

1985	April 25th	Glencorse Reservoir
	May 2nd	Loganlee Reservoir
	May 4th	Bavelaw Reservoir
1986	May 4th	Bavelaw Reservoir

OWLS

Barn Owl. *Tyto alba.* Rare.

J. Kirke Nash in his *Birds of Midlothian* wrote "In Midlothian it is rare in comparison with the Tawny and Long-eared Owls". In a note dated 30th November 1883 Mr W. Evans remarks: "Saw one handed in to Small's (the taxidermist) . . . Small says this used to be the most common Owl sent to him, afterwards the Long-eared became the most frequent, and now the Tawny. He now gets very few Barns but thinks that they are on the increase."

In 1947 David Hamilton told me that he had only seen the Barn Owl once in the Pentlands and that was at Bonaly Farm on 13th November 1921.

In 1934 there was a nest in a hollow tree in Fernilaw Avenue, Colinton, which on 11th July contained three eggs and one chick.

In 1948 one was seen hunting in broad daylight at the north corner of Glencorse Reservoir on 2nd January.

There were two records in 1981, one at Harperrig on 13th July and the other at Currie on 5th September.

Tawny Owl. *Strix aluco*. A well distributed resident.

On 11th April 1886 Harold Raeburn saw one in the T wood, and later David Hamilton had these records:

1906	April 29th	Logan House. Nest in a rabbit burrow about 2 feet from the entrance (c4)
1907	April 21st	Logan House. Nest in same position

William Evans (*Scottish Naturalist* 1924) said that they nested in the thick tops of pine trees in Redford Wood until this was cut in 1919-20.

J. Kirke Nash (*Birds of Midlothian* 1935) said "A hollow tree preferably ivy clad is a favourite situation for the nest, although holes in old buildings and old nests of other birds such as Crows are often chosen, and I know of a pine wood in Loganlea Glen where Tawny Owls nested year after year in rabbit burrows . . . Meadow Pipits and Mice proved to be the principal fare".

John Prentice, the Baddinsgill gamekeeper, said in 1934 that Tawny Owls were numerous there. David Hamilton said that in his long experience this century the Tawny was less common than the Long-eared.

Only three were recorded during the nine 1932-34 census outings, and these were all in March. The species was recorded on six occasions during the 1948-49 traverse with two on 29th February, and single birds on 7th March, 30th May, 6th June and 28th November.

G. L. Sandeman has these records:

1931	October 3rd	Threipmuir	One
1939	August 28th	Threipmuir	One
1939	June 3rd	Crosswoodhill	Two
1972	November 2nd	Crosswood	One
1974	May 24th	Crosswood	One

In 1971 R. L. Swann said of Threipmuir: "Now only occasionally seen."

During the years 1979-84 there were reports of up to five breeding sites in the Flotterstone to Loganlee valley.

Long-eared Owl *Asio otus* Resident. Breeds.

Long-eared Owls nest regularly at Bavelaw Reservoir in most years and also at Harperrig.

In 1910 J. C. Adam wrote in the *Edinburgh Naturalist Field Club Transactions:* "Our experience of the bird . . . had been restricted to the upland firwoods, chiefly those long strips of Scots Fir and Spruce which intersect and shelter the moorland fields on the edge of the Pentland Hills. So frequently had we met the bird there . . . that we had come to regard the Long-eared Owl as an upland bird as much attached to that bleak windswept country as the Curlew or the hill Kestrels with whom he would share a living." Coniferous wood strips continue to be its favourite haunts, and there it finds plenty of old nests in which to breed.

William Evans had many early records:

1884	March 17th	Curling Pond Wood, Currie. Nest with two eggs
1885	April 21st	Curling Pond Wood, Currie. Newly hatched young and one egg in spruce
1888	May 26th	Curling Pond Wood, Currie. Nest in old Magpie's nest 40-50 feet up
1889	March 31st	Clubbiedean. Nest with six eggs in Carrions' nest in small Scotch fir
	April 21st	Clubbiedean. Nest with five eggs in Scotch fir
1890	April 10th	Clubbiedean. Nest with five eggs in old Carrions' nest
1896	May	Balerno. Nest with young in old Magpie's nest
	May 20th	Listonshiels. Nest with three eggs in old Magpie's nest
1900	April 12th	Ravelrig. Nest with two eggs in old Magpies' nest
1904	April	Swanston. Nest with four eggs
1905	April 19th	Clubbiedean. Nest with four young

| 1911 | May 5th | Clubbiedean. Nest with three young and one egg |
| 1922 | April 3rd | Clubbiedean. Owls still here |

David Hamilton had these notes:

1900	April 27th	Listonshiels. Nest (c2) in a tall fir
1907	April 21st	Logan House district. Nest (c5) 25 feet up in a spruce
1913	May 10th	Listonshiels. One seen in a fir
1921	April 21st	Clubbiedean. Nest (c4) in old Carrion Crow's nest
1922	May 14th	Harperrig/Crosswood. Parents and young in small plantation of low firs

In 1924 W. Evans said that the Long-eared Owl nested in the thick tops of pines at Redford wood until this was cut in 1919-20.

John Prentice, the Baddinsgill gamekeeper, reported that in 1924 or 1925 there was a large influx of these birds after a vole plague.

In 1932 G. L. Sandeman saw a pair with a fledgeling at Nine Mile Burn on 10th June, and in 1935 he heard a bird calling at Cairns Castle on 21st August.

We did not record any during the nine census outings in 1932-34 and only once during the 1948-49 traverse (18th July at Cap Law wood).

Short-eared Owl. *Asio flammeus*. Autumn and winter visitor. A few may breed.

Most of the records suggest that the Short-eared Owl is normally only seen in autumn or winter, but on 4th May 1946 a pair was seen quartering the ground over a heather moor in the upper reaches of the West Water, and in 1953 a pair probably bred on the Kitchen Moss.

There are some early records. In 1894 it was recorded in the Pentlands on 23rd September (*Annals of Scottish Ornithology*). In the *Vertebrate Fauna of the Forth* Rintoul and Baxter say "Mr Serle considers it chiefly a passage migrant in the Pentlands and by the reservoirs there, and Mr Hamilton tells us of one which he flushed in the Pentlands, from heather on the moor in December 1911". David Hamilton in his diary describes this as being at Clubbiedean.

Other records are:

1933	September 3rd	Craigenterrie. One. *Scottish Naturalist*
1934	November 24th	Threipmuir. Three. *Scottish Naturalist*
1935	January 19th	West Bavelaw. Two. G. L. Sandeman

In 1946 J. K. Adams writing in the Manchester Guardian of 25th October 1946 said: "While we were crossing the Pentlands on 13th October 1946 we caught sight of a couple of Short-eared Owls quartering a slope in front of us." In 1947 G. L. Sandeman saw one at the head of Glencorse Reservoir on 17th July. R. W. J. Smith recorded (*Edinburgh Bird Bulletin*) "In the autumn of 1949 a number of records were received from the Pentlands. . . . A pair nested in 1950 but the young were later found dead in the nest". A bird was seen on 23rd June 1950 three miles out from Balerno along the Lang Whang. Two birds were reported occasionally near Bavelaw Marsh during the winter of 1950-51, and in 1951 A. C. Cowan watched a pair on several occasions in the spring when display was seen on 15th and 22nd April at Clubbiedean. He last saw a single bird a mile away on 3rd May.

There are a good many post-war records:

1950	January 14th	Nine Mile Burn. Two. G. L. Sandeman
1952	May 14th	Crosswood. One sailing high. *Edinburgh Bird Bulletin*
	August 15th	Bonaly. One. *Edinburgh Bird Bulletin*

In 1955, however, a note in the *Edinburgh Bird Bulletin* said "In . . . the Pentlands it is once again a rare bird". In 1971 R. L. Swann said that he had seen one at Threipmuir on 10th June 1957 and one 19th September 1964; and had other winter records. G. L. Sandeman saw one at West Bavelaw on 1st November 1974, and in 1975 he had several records from the plantation of small conifers along the Lang Whang, and from Harperrig and Crosswood.

Short-eared Owls were not seen either in the 1932-34 census work or during the 1948-49 traverse when the habit of hunting by day might have been expected to produce some records had the species been common then.

But short-eared owls appear to have become somewhat commoner in more recent years.

In 1981 two breeding sites were reported on the Red Moss but there were not many sightings elsewhere. In 1984 singles were seen at Loganlee, Harperrig and Bavelaw.

In 1985 singles were reported during the breeding season at Bavelaw, Loganlee, Red Moss and Threipmuir, and on 25th March two were seen at Harperrig..

NIGHTJARS

Nightjar. *Caprimulgus europaeus*. Rare.

On 2nd November 1884 Mr Wood, keeper at Glencorse Reservoir, showed Mr J. Kirke Nash a specimen which he had shot there last year. The Misses Rintoul and Baxter recorded that one was heard in Dreghorn Loan, Colinton, during the late summer evenings after the first world war. On 21st May 1932 one was flushed from a small coniferous plantation at Harmeny, Balerno. David Hamilton said in 1947 that he had no record of the species. On 15th May 1966 a Nightjar rose from a fern-filled valley at Harelaw Reservoir, flew close past the observer and out across a field (*Scottish Birds*).

SWIFTS

Swift. *Apus apus*. Common summer visitor. Breeds. Passage migrant.

As a breeding species, the Swift is largely confined to the urban parts of the area, with a few nests recorded from isolated buildings on the hills and at Cairns Castle where they breed regularly in the ruins. Breeding birds arrive about the middle of May, and there is also considerable migration through the area in this month.

The main autumn migration takes place during the first half of August when birds can be seen high over the hills as well as over the lower ground. The exodus is complete by the middle of the month except for a few stragglers.

On 26th June 1890 Harold Raeburn saw several above the West Cairn Hill at a height of over 2000 feet. The *Crosswood Migration Schedules* give these records:

1909	May 16th	Several pairs
1915	May 12th	Two

There is an early record from Currie/Clubbiedean on 30th April 1927. John Prentice, gamekeeper at Baddinsgill, told me that there are often large numbers high up on the hills. In 1939 the species was first recorded at Cairns Castle on 10th May and at North Esk Reservoir on 14th May. There were no records during the 1932-34 censuses. During the 1948-49 traverse the species was first seen on 10th May at Bavelaw Castle, and on 30th May there were numbers over the water at Threipmuir migrating west. Autumn migration was first noticed on 1st August in a south-westerly direction, and by 15th August none was recorded.

In 1963 there was another early date when I. M. Ford saw the species in Colinton on 1st May. In 1971 R. L. Swann told me that Swifts are normally present at Threipmuir from May to July.

In 1985 two hundred were seen at Harperrig on 12th and 27th June, and in 1986 there was one hundred at Threipmuir on 4th July, showing heavy migration during June and early July.

KINGFISHERS AND THEIR ALLIES

Kingfisher. *Alcedo atthis.* Formerly frequent resident. Now rare.

The Kingfisher bred at one time on the Water of Leith and possibly on other streams in the area but is now very rare. A pair nested in 1931 and 1932 at Kenleith Mills on the Water of Leith and at that time it is likely that there were nests as well at Juniper Green Station and at Scott's Mill, Colinton. In 1932 an excavation was made at the south-east end of Harelaw Reservoir, and birds were seen there throughout the breeding season. The earth bank however proved too hard and the birds only managed to penetrate to a depth of about two inches. I have also seen the Kingfisher at Clubbiedean during May, but here again it seems likely that the banks are unsuitable for nesting sites.

In 1939 during April, I walked the length of the Water of Leith from Colinton Bridge to beyond Harperrig Reservoir where the West Burn joins it. The only Kingfisher I found was at Scott's Mill, Colinton, on 23rd April.

After the breeding season single birds were sometimes seen at the Reservoirs, or even at some distance from water between August and December. On 12th July 1935 a bird flew out of a pine plantation at John's Burn, and birds at Harelaw Reservoir during the breeding season often perched in the pine trees there.

Kingfishers were not uncommon on the Water of Leith in 1845, but the *New Statistical Account for Colinton* for that year said "It has been much hunted of late years for the sake of its plumage, and has in consequence become very rare". In 1878 a female was shot at a cottage door at Dolphinton at some distance from water on Christmas Day. The species must have been common in those days, for Tom Speedy writing in 1890 said: "The Kingfisher may be found on the banks of almost every stream in the south of Scotland."

In 1922 one was seen at Braeburn, Currie, on 30th July. On 19th July 1930 David Hamilton found a nesting hole at Colinton, and in the previous year the Rev. W. Serle said: "I have seen its nest dug out at Colinton."

David Hamilton had other records in later years:

1931	June 7th	Listonshiels/Water of Leith. One seen flying up burn
1932	January 24th	Colinton. Seen
	May 29th	Listonshiels/Water of Leith. One seen
	July 24th	Flotterstone. One flying upstream towards Glencorse Reservoir
1934	December 23rd	Currie Bridge. One
1937	October 31st	Crosswood/Carnwath. One hovering over burn

Iain Ogilvie of Bonaly Tower told me that before the 1939-45 war he had seen Kingfishers on the Bonaly Burn on a number of occasions. David Hamilton told me that in addition to his records listed above he had seen Kingfishers at Medwin and Lyne.

During the 1932-34 census work there were records of single

Plate 7

West Water Reservoir

Crane Loch

Plate 8

Medwin Water

birds at Threipmuir East Marsh on 10th September 1932 and
from the Water of Leith on 22nd December 1934. G. L.
Sandeman has additional records as below:

1932	August 13th	Bavelaw	One
1935	August 3rd	Bavelaw	One
	August 6th	Bavelaw	Two
1948	January 18th	Flotterstone	One

In 1968 one was seen on the Water of Leith on 24th November
and was still there nearly two months later (*Scottish Birds*).

Modern sightings give hope that the Kingfisher shows signs of
returning to the Pentlands. For example in 1985 a Kingfisher was
seen at Glencorse Reservoir on 3rd and 4th September, and in
1986 one was seen at Flotterstone on 22nd March, another on the
Water of Leith at Juniper Green on 1st September, and a third at
Colinton on 18th September.

Roller. *Coracias garrulus.* Rare.
In 1983 one was seen at Dolphinton on 28th August.

Hoopoe. *Upupa epops.* Rare.
Rather surprisingly, the *Old Statistical Account* (1791) for
Linton Parish said: "In winter the Huppoe . . . sometimes visits
us." In 1917 W. T. Blackwood in the *History of Peeblesshire* (1925)
said "Early summer in 1917 one was obtained from Medwin
Estate near West Linton . . . and passed into the hands of Mr
Cleland, Broughton. This specimen is now in the School
Museum, West Linton." In 1923 J. Kirke Nash in the *Scottish
Naturalist* of 1923 recorded: "On April 15th at Butelands my
friend Mr James Cullen consulted me as to the identity of a rare
bird which had been observed by Mr Alex Morham of Butelands,
Balerno". After a visit to Mr Morham, J. Kirke Nash recorded
that it established the identity of the Hoopoe without a doubt.

WOODPECKERS AND THEIR ALLIES
Wryneck. *Jynx torquilla.* Rare.
One was seen at Loganlee on 16th September 1974, and one at
Glencorse Reservoir on 3rd September 1976 (*Scottish Birds*).

I

Green Woodpecker. *Picus viridus.* Resident in small numbers.

The species was unknown in the Pentlands until after the 1939-45 war. Since then it has become a not uncommon resident in the lower wooded areas. G. L. Sandeman first saw the Green Woodpecker in the Glencorse Valley on 25th October 1952, and recorded it again in 1955, 1956, 1971, 1972, 1973, 1974 and 1975. On 29th April 1956 a pair was seen and heard at Woodhouselee. They were not seen here on 6th May but marks of excavations were found by N. G. Campbell (*Edinburgh Bird Bulletin*). There is also a record from 1958 where birds were seen at Bavelaw on 22nd March, and on 5th December one flew over the moor at Bonaly Reservoir and down to the woods at Bonaly Tower (*Edinburgh Bird Bulletin*). One was seen in the same year at the edge of a conifer wood at Bavelaw Marsh on 11th October.

Other records are:

1973	March 9th	Dreghorn
1975	June 27th	Breeding near Hillend
	October 30th	Dreghorn Polo Field

Between 1980 and 1984 there are records from Threipmuir, Balerno, Flotterstone/Glencorse, Crosswood, Bonaly, Torduff and Loganlee, with possible breeding at Loganlee and between Flotterstone and Glencorse, and in 1985 and 1986 breeding was again recorded in the Glencorse/Loganlee valley and one bird was seen at Red Moss on 25th October.

Great Spotted Woodpecker. *Dendrocopus major.* Resident in small numbers.

Rare before the 1939-45 war, now a breeder in small numbers. In 1837 Macgillivray wrote that the species had been recorded from Speyside, Loch Ness and Braemar, although in other parts of Scotland it was very rarely met with. This status existed in the Pentlands until about fifty years ago. In 1931, however, Iain Ogilvie recorded one at Bonaly Tower in April; and in 1939 B. L. Peel told me that he had heard one drumming at Dreghorn on 17th March, and that it was still there on 26th March. A nest was found there on 13th June of the same year.

The species was not seen during the nine census outings 1932-34, but on the 1948-49 traverse it was recorded seven times between 1st August and 14th November in the high woods of Braid Law, Second Wood on Kitchen Moss and Cap Law. As four of these records were of immatures — one in each case — this suggests some post-breeding dispersal.

David Hamilton had no records of the species up to February 1947, but G. L. Sandeman has a good many occurrences from the Flotterstone to Loganlee area between 1947 and 1971. In 1955 C. Walker saw one at Crosshouse Farm pulling straws out of a stack to hammer out the seeds and eat them.

Between 1970 and 1975 G. L. Sandeman had records from Dreghorn woods (where the species was breeding), Harelaw Dam, a fledgeling at East Rig, Harelaw ravine, Redford plantation and Bavelaw.

Between 1980 and 1984 there are records from Bavelaw, Glencorse, Dreghorn, Loganlee and Threipmuir, and in 1985 one was seen at Harperrig.

LARKS

Skylark. *Alauda arvensis.* Winter visitor. Passage migrant spring and autumn. Summer visitor. Breeding. Post-breeding wanderer.

The status of the Skylark is an intricate one. Wintering birds arrive in flocks from the middle of October onwards to feed in turnip fields, plough, and especially on stubble. Single birds, or exceptionally groups of up to four, can be found at this time near the reservoirs and on the heather and grass moors, but for the most part these areas are deserted in winter. Considerable local weather-related movement also takes place during the winter months. The tide of the first summer visitors begins to flow up the hillsides early in February, and song has been recorded as high up as North Esk (1150 feet) and Baddinsgill (1100 feet) by the end of the first week of the month. Full breeding numbers are however not reached until well into March or early April.

The Skylark is remarkable as being one of the very few species found nesting even to the tops of the hills at 1800 feet. There are breeding records from Castlelaw at 1200 feet, Caerketton at 1100 feet, West Cairn at 1800 feet, Black Hill at 1200 feet, and Bawdy Moss at 1250 feet. March also sees small flocks still in the fields and at the reservoirs. It is difficult to say whether these are the remnants of wintering flocks, passage migrants, or summer visitors prior to occupation of nesting territories.

The ebb tide sets in from early July, when breeding grounds are drained of their birds and small parties are to be found at the reservoirs and in fields where the species does not nest. By the end of the month the breeding population has practically disappeared from the high ground. During late August and September, a considerable influx of migrants is sometimes noted, coming in from the north-east and passing on west or south-west. This migration continues until early October, and it seems possible that it lasts until wintering birds arrive to stay instead of moving further on. Some migrating flocks are large, for example on 24th September 1976 a flock of some 2000 was seen at Threipmuir going south.

The *Old Statistical Account* of 1791 records Skylarks in Mid Calder Parish, and in 1890 Harold Raeburn found Larks "very numerous" on the south side of the hills between Medwin and the Cauldstane Slap. David Hamilton heard one at Listonshiels on 24th May 1904, singing high in the air in the dark before 3 a.m. The following are extracts from the *Crosswood Migration Schedules:*

1908	February 15th	Heard singing for first time
1909	February 22nd	Heard singing for first time
1910	February 27th	Heard singing for first time
1911	February 19th	Heard singing for first time
1915	March 6th	Singing very vigorously
1916	February 5th	Singing
1917	February 19th	Singing

In May 1934 Rintoul and Baxter found the Skylark very common up to 1500 feet at the Kip pass and to the top of the grassy hills, but not on the heather clad hills between Carlops and the Bore Stane.

During the census of 1932-34 total figures were 153 in March, 50 in September and 101 in December. The arrival dates given from the houses' and farms' returns (1939) were mostly during the first fortnight of February. At Flotterstone G. L. Sandeman has found Skylarks from the third week of March to mid-July; but during the period 1946-49 he recorded them from February to

April, and then odd birds until mid-September when there was an influx until mid-October.

The traverse of 1948-49 showed the complexity of the distribution. On 15th February 1948 there was some 30 foot song at Nine Mile Burn, and one was calling high on the Kitchen Moss. There were loose flocks on 29th February. On 7th March one was seen at 1800 feet on the Kitchen Moss, and one was singing at 1200 feet. By 14th March the species was largely in pairs and high song was heard at Nine Mile Burn. By the 13th June I noted "Very common Bavelaw and Threipmuir". "Well distributed elsewhere". By 4th July a falling off of song was noted. On 1st August birds appeared to be largely off high ground and rare on low ground. At the end of the month, however, they were much more noticeable. Migration was seen on 5th September and 10th October, and by 7th November Skylarks were almost absent. There appeared to be another influx on 21st November, but only one bird was seen on 28th November, and on 12th December not a single bird was recorded. A flock was present on 19th December but none elsewhere, and again none on 23rd January. By 30th January however the spring migration showed signs of starting, with further signs on 13th February: and by 6th March Larks were singing freely from low ground. A high and cold wind on 13th March imposed a setback, but by 28th March the species was once again in breeding numbers.

Shore Lark. *Eremophila alpestris*. Rare.

On 11th December 1933 a single bird was seen on the exposed mud flats at Harperrig.

SWALLOWS

Sand Martin. *Riparia riparia*. Summer visitor. Breeding. Passage migrant.

The Sand Martin is a regular summer visitor in small numbers, but owing to lack of suitable nesting banks, it is not a common Pentland breeding bird. For years I searched in vain for a breeding colony; in 1946 however after an intensive search four colonies were discovered in the West Linton-Dolphinton district.

These were:

West Water	Ten plus pairs in a sandbank
Medwinbank	Sixty plus pairs in a sand and gravel bank
Walton Cottage	Ten plus pairs in a sand and earth bank
Dolphinton sand pit	One plus pairs

I noted then: "It is possible that there is another colony on the West Water near Slipperfield, as I have seen birds here during the breeding season, and in my experience the species feeds close to its nesting colony."

There seems to be little or no autumn migration along the north side of the hills, the records being only of occasional birds passing with Swallows and House Martins during July and August.

On 26th June 1890 Harold Raeburn found numbers at Medwin and from these suggested that there must be a colony of long standing about. Nearly fifty years later, in 1946, there was still a colony on the Medwin (at Medwinbank). There was only one record of Sand Martins from the *Crosswood Migration Schedules,* one being seen on 2nd June 1911. We did not see a Sand Martin on census outings 1932-34.

Mr Prentice, the Baddinsgill gamekeeper, said (in 1934) that they used to be very numerous at the sandpit used for the construction of the reservoir dam. After this was filled up the birds nested on the scaur on the burn just below the dam. Only a few pairs managed to breed here in 1933, as the dam was leaking and water seeped out through the scaur.

Miss Rintoul saw a pair at North Esk Reservoir in the breeding season of 1934. In 1936 the first pair of Sand Martins visited the Medwinbank colony on 31st March, but this is an exceptionally early date.

In 1947 David Hamilton said that the Sand Martin was not a common bird at the east end of the hills. He had found it nesting in a bank at Glencorse Reservoir ravine, and on the Water of Leith at Boll-o-Bere, and said that a few could be found along the Water of Leith.

During the 1948-49 traverse Sand Martins were recorded

between 2nd May and 22nd August. In 1971 R. T. Swann said of Threipmuir that the species was seen on spring migration between April and June in small numbers. G. L. Sandeman recorded it at the Glencorse Glen from mid May to the end of August between 1947 and 1971.

During the period 1980-1984 Sand Martins were seen in spring between 9th April and 16th May, and in the autumn between 6th August and 9th September. It was noted in 1980 that a few pairs bred on the Water of Leith.

It is clear that the species continues to be seldom recorded, for in 1985 the only report was of one or two at Bavelaw, and in 1986 there was a record of four at Threipmuir on 29th April.

Swallow. *Hirundo rustica.* Common summer visitor. Breeding. Spring and autumn migrant.

The Swallow is a common summer visitor in rather variable numbers, normally arriving about the third week of April, and departing early in October. Exceptional birds have been seen as early as 30th March and as late as the third week in October. The first wave of immigration is often most noticeable at the reservoirs, where numbers may be seen hawking for flies over the water before occupying their nesting sites. It may be that some of these immigrants are on migration through the area.

Farm buildings and barns are favourite nesting places, but other sites are also occupied. I have seen nests in the boathouse at North Esk Reservoir, in isolated barns, and even in an outside public lavatory at Carlops.

Migration to the west begins as early as the middle of July, when some Swallows still have eggs. This migration is usually most noticeable at the reservoirs, where the species can feed as it migrates. At this season considerable extension of range takes place, and Swallows are often seen flying well out among the hills. This migration reaches a peak during August and September, when the young birds, distinguishable by their short tail streamers, join in. By the end of September only stragglers remain.

Arrivals: Swallows were seen at Colinton on 8th April 1898. The *Crosswood Migration Schedules* (1908-19) show arrivals in April on four occasions, and early May on seven. The earliest was on

18th April and the latest on 6th May. In 1914 a bird was seen at Balerno on 11th April. The returns from the farms' and houses' enquiry (1939) show seven arrivals in April and five in May, the earliest being 17th April and the latest 16th May, but most of the May arrivals were early in the month. J. K. Adams first saw Swallows at Carlops on 5th May 1945. During the 1948-49 traverse, pairs had reached West Bavelaw and West Rig on 2nd May and Bavelaw Mill on the 9th. In 1956 C. Walker saw a very early bird at the Crane Loch on 8th April. A. T. Macmillan has spring records from Colinton on 22nd April 1962 and 18th April 1964.

Breeding: J. Kirke Nash in his *Birds of Midlothian* says: "The Swallow nests throughout the county, the barns and sheds of the hill farms being resorted to almost as readily as those in the lower ground."

David Hamilton said that Swallows used to nest in the shed (now removed) at Bonaly public park. They were nesting at Logan Cottage on 23rd May 1903. G. L. Sandeman has many breeding records from the Flotterstone to Loganlee valley for 1946 to 1974 at Kirkton Farm, Logan Cottage, Waterkeeper's House Glencorse Reservoir, etc. On 17th June 1949 he found nests in barns at East Colzium; and on 8th July 1974 there was a family party at Baad Park, Harperrig. On 16th July 1974 there were two nests in barns at Harperrig Farm and a probable family party at Cairns Castle. He says that in the years 1946-49 he recorded Swallows in the Glencorse glen between mid-April and the end of September, with a peak in September.

R. L. Swann said (1971) of Threipmuir: "Seen April to October, with the maximum numbers being seen in May when about twenty-five birds can be seen. In summer the numbers drop to five to ten and a few pairs breed."

Arrivals: During the 1948-49 traverse, pairs had reached West Bavelaw and West Rig on 2nd May and Bavelaw Mill on the 9th.

Migration and autumn records: In 1897 a flock of thirty to forty was seen at Currie on 4th October. The latest record from the *Crosswood Migration Schedules* (1908-19) was 29th September. In 1914 there is a record of a Swallow at Carlops on 2nd October. During the 1932-34 census work the numbers seen in the three September censuses were 43103 and 49. David Hamilton found

Swallows numerous at Torduff on 4th September 1926. During the 1948-49 traverse, four Swallows were seen at the Kip Col on 22nd August. On 5th September all nesting sites had been abandoned, and migration was in progress, when birds were seen high up in the hills. The last bird was seen over Colinton on 10th October. In 1955 Mrs Dover Wilson saw four late birds at Harelaw on 11th October, and one at Balerno on the same day. In 1959 a very late bird was seen at Colinton on 24th November.

House Martin. *Delichon urbica*. Regular summer visitor. Breeds. Passage migrant.

The House Martin is a regular summer visitor in rather variable numbers, normally arriving later than the Swallow, usually in the last week of April or early in May. The dates of arrival from the farms' and houses' enquiry of 1939 were from the last week of April to early June. The earliest was 20th April and the latest, possibly exceptional, being 4th June: with most of the dates being either late in April or early in May.

Unlike the Swallow, which first appears in numbers at the reservoirs, the House Martin normally colonises its breeding quarters on arrival. In the Pentlands these are all on dwelling houses or commercial buildings, on the outer wall under the eaves. It is remarkable how many House Martin colonies are on isolated buildings some way into the hills. The bulk of the population is on the south side of the range in the Glencorse valley and the West Linton area, but the growth of housing schemes in the Colinton and Swanston areas has given fresh scope for an extension of breeding there.

The colonies at Wakefield and Baddinsgill Cottage are of particular interest, the latter having been known as far back as 1900 at least. James Ritchie in his *Animal Life in Scotland* (1920) commented: "In the spring of 1917 before the year's migrants had arrived I saw the old nests plastered thickly under the eaves, from five to seven being occasionally crowded together between the ends of a couple of rafters."

This colony seems to have held its numbers well during the following thirty years, and more, but in 1934 Mr Prentice, the Baddinsgill keeper told me that recently numbers had dropped because the road leading to Baddinsgill Reservoir had been tarred which reduced the source of mud for nest building.

In 1934 Rintoul and Baxter found House Martins nesting at Fairliehope, Logan Cottage, and Carlops; and they saw many pairs building at the sluices on the waterkeeper's house at Baddinsgill on 3rd June.

Between 1934 and 1975 G. L. Sandeman found House Martins breeding at Logan Cottage, waterkeeper's house Loganlee, waterkeeper's house Glencorse, and Castlelaw Farm.

Records of colonies with the number of nests and the years in which the count was taken are:

Cairns Castle	1932 — 10; 1933 — 10-15; 1935 — some
Baddinsgill	1933 — 20; 1934 — 60; 1935 — 76; 1946 — 30-40
Kenleith Mill	1932 — a small colony
Glencorse waterkeeper's house	1933 — 7; 1935 — 6; 1936 — 6
Loganlee waterkeeper's house	1933 — 20; 1935 — 31; 1936 — 40
Galloways Mill, Balerno	1932 — 10-20
Juniper Green Co-op Store	1932 — 1
Malleny Mills	1932 — 7; 1934 — 10; 1935 — 10
Fairliehope	1933 — 3; 1936 — some
Leithhead Mill	1934 — a few
Wakefield	1938 — 80-90; 1946 — 58
Harperrig water house	1939 — some; 1974 — some
Hillburn Roadhouse, Bowbridge	1949 and 1954 — some
Balerno to Marchbank	1971 — breeding at new houses

The Howe,
Loganlee   1982 — 9; 1983 — 9
Easter Bavelaw
Farm   1984 — 18
Bonaly Tower   1985 — 5

As in the case of the Swallow, the autumn migration starts long before the local breeding birds have fledged their young, and late in July the species may be seen over barren hillsides, and indeed over the summits themselves. I have a record of seeing a House Martin flying south over the Wolf Craigs on 30th July 1932, and of several over the hills between Glencorse Reservoir and Currie on 28th July 1935.

Large gatherings may be seen during August, probably of locally bred birds, but even at the end of the month some young birds are still in the nest. David Hamilton found birds sheltering in the wood at Glencorse Reservoir, perching on the trees during a fierce storm on 11th August 1907.

The species has normally left for the winter by the third week of September but I have known exceptional records as late as 20th October.

PIPITS AND WAGTAILS

Tree Pipit. *Anthus trivialis.* Summer visitor in small numbers. Breeds.

The Tree Pipit usually arrives in the Pentlands about the end of April or early May and colonises deciduous woods.

In 1899 the Tree Pipit was noted at Malleny and Balerno on 29th April and at Dreghorn on 23rd April 1900. David Hamilton told me that in 1914 and 1915 it was common in the Balerno district, and in 1914 Tree Pipits were recorded in Redford Wood at Bavelaw when the wood was young.

There is a record from Comiston on 2nd May 1917. J. Kirke Nash knew it (prior to 1933) as a regular summer visitor, usually appearing about the beginning of May. He occasionally found it nesting in the Balerno district. In 1933 Mrs Greenlees saw a very early pair beside Threipmuir on 24th March. During 1934 Rintoul and Baxter heard singing birds at Glencorse Reservoir and Carlops.

In 1946 J. K. Adams found birds in song at Dreghorn on 12th May, and at Thrashie Dene on 11th May of the same year. David Hamilton told me in 1947 that it used to breed frequently near the Lanark road beyond Balerno, and that he had seen Tree Pipits between Flotterstone and Glencorse Reservoir, but he said that the species was now scarce in the Pentlands.

Tree Pipits were not recorded during the 1932-34 census work. There were only two records from the 1948-49 traverse: at Monks Burn on 25th April and Cap Law Wood on 6th June. In 1952 D. I. M. Wallace saw single birds between Carlops and Loganlee on 29th April.

G. L. Sandeman has these records from the Glencorse Gorge Woods: 30th April 1948, 29th April 1970 and 26th April 1972. In 1974 he saw one at Middle Threipmuir. In 1971 R. L. Swann said Threipmuir had fewer than five pairs.

In addition to the above records I have found it at Fairliehope plantation at 1200 feet, along the West Water, and at Baddinsgill Cottage.

Recent records during the breeding season are as below:

1980	Bavelaw/	
	Threipmuir	Three pairs in territory
	Glencorse	Recorded April 20-26
1981	Red Moss	Probably one pair
1982	Bonaly	One pair breeding
	Glencorse	Recorded
1983	Red Moss	One pair breeding
1984	Flotterstone/	Two singing
	Glencorse	
1985	Crosswood	Singing male, 10th May
	Threipmuir	One, 12th April
		Two, 23rd June
	Bavelaw	Singles, 25th June and 7th July
1986	Loganlee	One, 2nd May
	Threipmuir	Three, 15th May
		One, 1st August

Meadow Pipit. *Anthus pratensis.* Common summer visitor. Breeding. Passage migrant.

The Meadow Pipit is a scarce bird in winter. It sometimes

occurs then, usually singly, but occasionally in small parties of three or four birds, on manured fields, heather and grass glens, near the reservoirs, along burns and on grass moors. There is no evidence of wintering immigration on any scale.

Breeding birds normally arrive towards the end of March or early April, but the full breeding population is not in territory until well on in April. As a breeding species the Meadow Pipit, in some areas at least, has a decided heather association, as may be seen when one passes from grass moorland to areas of heather. The Skylark predominates on grass moorland as a rule, but once the heather is reached the Meadow Pipit becomes much the commoner species. It nests right up to the crests of the hills at 1800 feet, and is also found nesting on the lower moors and higher cultivated areas.

There is some indication of spring passage during May. Breeding birds are mostly away by the end of August. From then until the end of the first week in October (but largely in September) considerable migration in a south-westerly direction takes place, the loose flocks arriving from the north east, sometimes in company with Pied Wagtails, and either feeding round the reservoirs for a short time, or passing on.

David Hamilton had some valuable records indicative of the status of the species at various times of the year. For example, on 9th September 1900 he heard only one on Bonaly Hill, and said that the place seemed quite deserted. On 14th March 1903 he said "Meadow Pipits did not appear to have got up to the high ground yet". On 22nd March 1905 he found that at Balerno and elsewhere at the base of the Pentlands the birds were returning to their breeding grounds. Next year (on 17th March) he found that one or two had got up to the hills again in the Bonaly/Glencorse/Threipmuir area. On 28th March 1908 he said that when he was going over Bonaly Hill there were plenty of Meadow Pipits up in the hills. He saw one at Loganlee on 15th January 1911.

On 26th June 1890 Harold Raeburn found the Meadow Pipit particularly numerous in the Medwin area, and on the same day found a nest on the Harperrig side of the Cauldstane Slap. J. Kirke Nash wrote in his *Birds of Midlothian* (1935) "Sedgy moorlands and pastures in the vicinity of marshes are perhaps its favourite haunts. In winter it leaves the higher moorlands and hill valleys for the lower grounds.''

Rintoul and Baxter said in 1934 that they had found it nesting high up in the Pentlands. The total numbers seen on the 1932-34 census outings were 120 in March, 464 in September and 11 in December.

During the 1948-49 traverse the species was first recorded on 14th March, but even by 11th April there was still very little song on high ground where it was commonest among heather. By 1st August the birds were tending to collect in small parties or loose flocks and by 15th August only eight were recorded, all from low ground. The species was much commoner on 29th August, but there was no visible migration although more than eighty were seen. High ground migration was however in progress on 5th September, with loose flocks of twenty to thirty birds, but by 3rd October the species was very scarce, and on 7th November only one was seen. After this odd birds were present, but none was seen on 12th December, and the species was rarely seen until the next spring.

In 1953 a single bird was seen at Listonshiels on 11th January at a height of just over 1000 feet, and on 8th January 1956 two were seen in heather at the Kips at 1300 feet. This was an extremely cold day with patches of snow here and there.

G. L. Sandeman from records going back to the 1939-45 war tells me that in the Glencorse Glen Meadow Pipits were summer visitors from the end of March to August when flocks appeared. The species continued to be recorded until the end of September. In the spring he noted flocks from the end of March to mid-April.

The following observations give an indication of the scale of movements of Meadow Pipits. Spring records are:

1981	March 31st	Harperrig	100
	April 7th	Threipmuir	47
	April 22nd	Threipmuir	50
1982	March 21st	Flotterstone	26
1983	March 11th	Glencorse	11
	April 1st and 15th	Loganlee	100
1984	April 4th	Glencorse	50
	April 23rd	Threipmuir	32

1985	April 9th	Harperrig	140
	April 12th	Threipmuir	43

Autumn records are:

1980	September 19th	Threipmuir	735
	September 23rd	Threipmuir	585
	September 20th	Caerketton	500
1981	September 1st	Harperrig	60 plus
		Crosswood	50 plus
	September 25th	Harperrig	100
	October 16th	Loganlee	30
1982	September 6th	Harelaw	200
	September 13th	Bonaly	100
1983	August 25th	Harperrig	90
	September 9th	Harperrig	150
1984	August 16th	Harperrig	100 plus
	September 6th	Bore Stane	c200
	September 17th	Harperrig	100
	September 18th	Threipmuir	33
1985	September 16th	Threipmuir	116
1986	August 29th	Threipmuir	81

Rock Pipit. *Anthus spinoletta.* Rare wanderer.

There are two records for Crosswood on 14th March 1973 by G. L. Sandeman, and the other on 26th October 1976 (*Scottish Birds*).

One was seen at Threipmuir on 4th April 1980 and one at Glencorse Reservoir on 11th November 1983.

Water Pipit. *Anthus spinoletta.* Rare wanderer.

G. L. Sandeman has two records, one at Harelaw on 28th December 1972, and one from Threipmuir on 5th December 1973.

Yellow Wagtail. *Motacilla flava.* Uncommon vagrant.

A *flavissima* male was seen on pasture at Threipmuir on 7th May 1933. G. L. Sandeman saw one at Bonaly Tower and another at Harperrig on 10th August 1946. R. L. Swann saw one at Threipmuir during the first week of May 1964, and in 1978 one was seen at Harperrig on 26th April (*Scottish Bird Report* 1978).

David Hamilton never saw the species during his many years experience of birdwatching in the Pentlands.

Three were seen at Threipmuir on 7th September 1980, and one was seen at Bavelaw in 1985.

Grey Wagtail. *Motacilla cinerea.* Summer visitor. Breeds.

The Grey Wagtail is only a summer visitor to many parts of its breeding area. It occurs in winter sparingly along the Water of Leith, and is occasional elsewhere at this season, when single birds are more often seen than larger numbers. It arrives at its nesting quarters sometimes as early as the middle of March, but normally at the end of this month or early in April. It may then be found at the fast running hill burns, and along the Water of Leith. It has been found nesting at these hill burns up to about 1000 feet, especially near waterfalls. The number of nesting pairs each year cannot be very great, perhaps as low as thirty to forty, but it is widely distributed. Along the Water of Leith it frequents stretches bordered by trees. Towards the source, where the river runs through grass moorland or fields, it is seldom seen, possibly owing to the absence of waterfalls of any size. Even where the river runs through villages, and there is still some contamination of the water, the Grey Wagtail nests at the weirs and waterfalls. It is seldom recorded at the reservoirs, except where its nesting site is close at hand.

There is no indication of passage migrants halting in the Pentland area either in spring or autumn. Families appear to leave after the breeding season, for there is no increase along the Water of Leith, where the species sometimes remains all winter.

David Hamilton found a nest (c4) at Torduff Waterfall on 18th June 1899, and on 4th May 1902 he saw a nest (c5) at the side of the burn just below the waterman's house at Loganlee.

The following are extracts from the *Crosswood Migration Schedules:*

1909	April 16th	One arrived
1910	April 8th	One arrived
1912	March 25th	Pair seen
1914	March 26th	Pair seen
1915	March 23rd	Pair seen

During the 1932-34 census outings we saw a total of four during the three March outings, two during the September ones, and two in the December ones. In 1934 Rintoul and Baxter found a nest on the rock opposite the old mill at the North Esk, Carlops. In 1935 J. Kirke Nash wrote in *Birds of Midlothian:* "Brawling hill burns are its favourite haunts . . . rapid flowing streams between well wooded banks are much favoured as the bird perches freely on the overhanging branches". Rintoul and Baxter said: "It is common on the Pentland burns where we found it nesting to above 1000 feet. It nests on the Water of Leith." David Hamilton told me that he had found it nesting at the Torduff waterfall for close on fifty years; he had also found nests along the Logan Burn.

During the 1948-49 traverse the Grey Wagtail was found only at the Clubbiedean outflow and at Torduff. In 1948 there was no record between 2nd May and 3rd October, and after 14th November there was again no further record until 28th March 1949.

G. L. Sandeman has these post war records:

1946	May 9th	Torduff — Breeding
1971	May 13th	Crossword Burn — Recorded
	June 9th	Clubbiedean — Adult feeding young
	September 16th	Cairns Castle — Recorded
1972	March 31st	Crosswood Burn — Recorded
	November 2nd	Cairns Castle — Recorded
1973	April 13th	Crosswood — Two or three
	May 1st	Crosswood — One
	July 9th	Harelaw Ravine — Two
	October 15th	Harperrig — One
	October 30th	Crosswood — One
1975	May 19th	Cairns Castle and Crosswood — Recorded
	May 26th	Bonaly Tower — Breeding
	July 3rd	Torduff Waterfall — Breeding
	July 18th	Crosswood Burn — Two
	September 3rd	Crosswood Burn — One
	September 3rd	Harperrig Dam — One
	September 9th	Crosswood Burn — One

He also found during walks in the Glencorse Valley (1946-49) that he saw Grey Wagtails there from early March to November, but not from December to February.

During the period 1981 to 1984 there were reports of pairs breeding at Glencorse Reservoir, North Esk Reservoir, Torduff, Bonaly and particularly in the Flotterstone/Loganlee valley where up to five sites were suspected.

In 1985 single pairs were seen at Loganlee and Flotterstone in the breeding season, but in 1986 the only breeding pair recorded was at Loganlee.

Pied Wagtail. *Motacilla alba.* Resident. Passage migrant spring and autumn.

The Pied Wagtail leaves many of its breeding areas during the winter months, and frequents farmyards low down on the hills, especially those which still have stackyards and dungheaps. It is also found along the Water of Leith at this time, and exceptionally at the reservoirs. Where dung spreading has taken place the species may sometimes be found in open country during the winter.

In spring the Pied Wagtail arrives at the reservoirs about the second half of March, sometimes in flocks exceeding the breeding numbers. Migration extends until May as a rule, when small flocks have been seen roosting in the willows at Bavelaw.

Holes in farm buildings and houses are common nesting sites, but it is also found breeding at reservoir dams and sluices, in dead trees, in rocky banks along the burns, under bridges and at weirs up to 1500 feet.

Family parties are much in evidence late in July along the lower burns and at the reservoirs. Some migration in a south-westerly direction takes place by the end of August. There are records of migrants roosting in the willows at Bavelaw at this time. This autumn migration extends until early October.

In 1889 Harold Raeburn found a nest in a decayed tree stump at Harelaw Reservoir, and another nest with young above the sluice door at the west end. William Evans records that the Pied Wagtail nested annually in the Redford ruin at Bavelaw Reservoir. J. Kirke Nash in his *Birds of Midlothian* said "that the species migrated in autumn but some remained. In winter it haunts the farmyards.''

Rintoul and Baxter found Pied Wagtails breeding in the Pentlands up to a little below 1500 feet. David Hamilton told me that he had found the species common and nesting freely. He had found nests on the Glencorse Burn both above and below the reservoir, beside the Water of Leith at the Lanark road, above Balerno away from water and along the road at Lothianburn. In 1899 he also found a nest similar to a Sand Martin's at the end of a tunnel at Torduff. In 1925 he found a nest (c5) in a hole in the wall of Howlet's House, Loganlee, and in 1929 a nest (c1) at the Torduff Waterfall.

The *Crosswood Migration Schedules* 1908-16 give the arrival dates between 12th March and 3rd April with the average falling during the last fortnight of March. The census notes of 1932-34 gave total numbers of Pied Wagtails seen as 89 in March, 72 in September and only three in December. In 1934 Rintoul and Baxter found the species on the Henshaw Burn almost to the top of the Bore Stane Pass, and at Crosswood, Torduff and Clubbiedean.

The results from the 1939 farms' and houses' enquiry show that Pied Wagtails were regarded as resident at Buteland Hill, Harelaw, and Bavelaw Castle; and as migrants at Medwin, Medwinbank, Shothead, Cairns Castle, Hillend, and Bonaly Tower. Arrival dates varied between 16th February and 15th May, with an indication that the second half of March was the norm. During the 1948-49 traverse the species was seen on every outing except those of 22nd August, 5th and 12th September, 7th November, 12th December, 30th January and 27th February. G. L. Sandeman told me that in the Flotterstone to Loganlee valley in the years 1946-1949 Pied Wagtails were summer visitors from mid-March to the end of July. There was then autumn passage from the end of August to the first week of October. In 1971 R. L. Swann said of Threipmuir: ''Recorded March to November in small numbers. One pair probably breeds.''

In 1981 some six to seven pairs were breeding at Flotterstone/Loganlee and in 1982 the estimate was between eight and nine pairs. During the years 1981 to 1984 Pied Wagtails nested at North Esk Reservoir and Threipmuir.

White Wagtail. *Motacilla alba.* Passage migrant in small numbers.

This race of the Pied Wagtail is not often recorded but does occur. On 29th April 1897 W. Eagle Clarke saw one at Comiston, and there is a very interesting note by David Hamilton for 14th May 1899. On that date he found a nest among grass on a ledge of rock on the Bonaly Burn. He caught the bird on the nest, and noticed that it had a light grey back, and was much lighter all over than the usual Pied Wagtail. He then let the bird away, and found on examining the nest that it contained five eggs different from the usual type of Pied Wagtail's eggs. Instead of being speckled with grey they were speckled with a distinct brown. In shape and size they were like Pied Wagtail's eggs.

In 1953 G. L. Sandeman saw a male at Loganlee Waterfall on 25th April, and on 3rd September 1971 saw six probables at Harperrig.

Single birds were seen on two occasions in the September 1932-34 census outings.

It would appear from the following recent records that the White Wagtail may be a migrant through the Pentlands in late April and early May, and again in September.

1981	April 20th	Loganlee Reservoir	One
1983	April 20th	Crosswood	One
1984	April 23rd	Threipmuir	One
	May 12th	Torduff	One
1985	April 27th	Glencorse Reservoir	One
	May 23rd	Bonaly Reservoir	One
	September 18th	Crosswood	One
1986	May 1st	Crosswood	Two
	May 4th	Loganlee Reservoir	One
	September 23rd	Harperrig	Two

WAXWINGS

Waxwing. *Bombycilla garrulus.* Occasional winter visitor.

Waxwings were recorded for Colinton Parish in 1845 when the *New Statistical Account* was published. In 1847 W. Evans noted that one had been seen quite recently for several days in the Bruces' garden at Kenleith Mill. J. Kirke Nash pointed out that none was recorded in the Pentlands during the great invasion of 1921. On 15th January 1933 David Hamilton saw one at Currie feeding on the hips of a wild rose. In 1937 Rintoul and Baxter recorded three at Balerno, and one was seen at Easting on the same day. On 4th December David Hamilton saw the species feeding on elderberries at Currie. I myself saw two at Kenleith Mill on 24th November 1946 hawking for flies, despite there being plenty of berries.

Other records are:

1959	November 2nd	Seven at Loganlee. *Scottish Birds* 1960
1961	November 18th	Reported at Hillend. *Edinburgh Evening News* 18.11.61
1962	January 11th	One at Swanston Avenue, Edinburgh. *Scottish Birds*
1964		Ten at Swanston. *Scottish Birds*

R. L. Swann saw one at Threipmuir on 13th November 1965 and six there on 20th November 1965.

In 1981 five were seen between Torduff and Clubbiedean on 7th November.

DIPPERS

Dipper. *Cinclus cinclus.* Resident. Breeding.

Although the Dipper is resident within the area it leaves the high breeding areas in winter. However it can still be found at that season along the Water of Leith and the lower burns such as Glencorse and Logan. It also occurs at Torduff, Clubbiedean, Glencorse and Loganlee Reservoirs at this time, where it often swims or dives near the shore.

The Dipper moves up the burns in spring, and may then be found at any of the rocky burns right up into the hills until such burns narrow to three feet or so. It commonly nests in bridges and walls, on banks and at caulds along the Water of Leith. A favourite site is near or under a waterfall, those at Torduff and along the Logan Burn being typical.

Harold Raeburn knew the Dipper in the Pentlands. There are records in his diary of his seeing one on the Bonaly Burn on 23rd March 1883 and on the Glencorse Burn on 19th December during hard frost. On 8th January 1888 he saw five on Glencorse Burn, and on 26th June 1890 he saw several on the Medwin. The census figures 1932-34 indicate that the Dipper leaves some areas during the winter. The figures were: twenty-eight in March, twenty-two in September and eight in December in total.

In 1932 the winter population of the Glencorse Burn was given as twenty-one (compared with the breeding population of seven pairs). Corresponding figures for the North Esk were (Harlawmins Burn to source): winter population sixteen, breeding seven pairs.

During the winter of 1938-39 I made a survey of the winter status of the Dipper on the Water of Leith from Colinton road bridge to its source.

Section I	Colinton road bridge to Balerno. Four miles. December 18th.
	This section is below the 500 feet contour and the river runs through wooded urban country for the most part. There was a certain amount of contamination from mill outflows. December 18th was a cold day of east wind and light powdery snow. Nine Dippers were present: two pairs and five single birds.
Section II	Balerno to Leithhead Mill. Five miles. 25th December. This section lies between the 500 and the 750 feet. Contour. The downstream half is thickly wooded in places, but the upper part lies amid open fields and sheep pasture, with a few willows and straggling trees along the banks. On the 25th December snow lay on the ground to a depth of some inches, with a thin frozen crust. The river was flecked with cakes, and in places sheets, of ice. Only two Dippers were seen and they were nearly two miles apart.

Section III	Leithhead Mill to Harperrig Reservoir. Three miles. 19th January 1939.

Lying between 750 and 900 feet the course lies amid desolate grass moorland with no cover on the banks, but it is clear, shallow and rapid flowing; an ideal Dipper habitat. 19th January was a mild day of bright sunshine. No Dippers were seen for the first one and a half miles, but between the Dean Burn junction and Harperrig three were recorded: these appeared not to have territorial claims, as all three were together at one point.

Section IV   East Cairns to the source of the West Burn. Three miles. 29th January 1939. This section lies between 900 and 1300 feet and differs little from Section III in character, but the water dwindles gradually to a small burn and climbs onto the bleak peat moorland above Crosswood. When this section was explored snow lay to a depth of three inches and a cutting east wind blew. No Dippers were seen.

To summarise these results:

A total of fourteen Dippers was found on a section of the Water of Leith of fifteen miles.

Nine were below 500 feet over a distance of four miles.

Five between 500 feet and 900 feet over a distance of eight miles.

None over 900 feet over a distance of three miles.

In 1971 R. L. Swann said of Threipmuir: "Very few winter records. One at outflow at east end of Reservoir on 14th November 1964."

There are many breeding records. David Hamilton found a nest at the Torduff Waterfall on 23rd April 1899; on 30th April of the same year he found two nests (c5 and 4) at the side of small burns running into Loganlee Reservoir, and on 6th May another nest (c5) at the side of a burn at the head of Loganlee Reservoir. In 1937 he told me that Dippers had nested for at least thirty years at the waterfall above Loganlee Reservoir, and had also nested under the Cockburn road bridge.

Rintoul and Baxter said: "It is common on all the Pentland burns, found on the Water of Leith from its source right to Edinburgh, and also on the North and South Esk." They had the following records in 1934:

May		
20th	North Esk	A pair at waterfall
		A pair at Fairliehope
May		
29th	Crosswood Burn	Three pairs
May		
30th	Torduff	One flying over. North Esk
		Reservoir one on a tiny burn

G. L. Sandeman has these breeding records:

Flotterstone to	
Loganlee	1932, 1947, 1948, 1949,
Reservoir	1971, 1972, 1975
Crosswood Burn	1935
Harperrig	
Reservoir	1974

During the 1948-49 traverse single birds were seen regularly in the Torduff to Clubbiedean district but not elsewhere.

Recent breeding records 1981-84 are Torduff one pair, North Esk Reservoir two pairs, and Flotterstone/Loganlee waterfall up to six or seven pairs, but in 1986 only two pairs were recorded from the Water of Leith from Colinton to Balerno.

WRENS

Wren. *Troglodites troglodites.* Common resident. Breeding.

The Wren is a common resident with a very wide distribution. It can be found in house gardens, shrubberies, coniferous woods with thick undergrowth, young plantations, long grass at the edge of reservoirs, moorland bracken, long heather among cleuchs, whins, etc. On 28th January 1934 one was even present at the Wolf Craigs, which is one of the most isolated spots in the Pentlands. The Wren is normally seen singly except during the breeding season.

Miss Rintoul recorded breeding up to at least 1500 feet, and David Hamilton found a nest in Howlet's House at Loganlee on 16th May 1920. This nest contained six eggs, and was lined entirely with Grouse feathers.

In 1934 Rintoul and Baxter found it up to the North Esk Wood. It was also common right to the top of the Carlops/Carnethy/Loganlee pass at 1400 feet, and everywhere from Carlops to the Bore Stane and at Torduff.

The total census figures (1932-34) gave twenty-five for March, thirty-one for September and forty-three for December. From 1946 to 1949 there was an increase in numbers in the Glencorse valley in June, July and August which could be due to the presence of young birds. During the 1948-49 traverse the species was noticeably less common in high areas in winter.

In 1971 R. L. Swann said of Threipmuir: "Very common. Seen all the year round. Several pairs breed."

ACCENTORS

Dunnock. *Prunella modularis.* Resident. Breeds.

There seems to be little change in distribution over the year, although the high woods are deserted in winter. It frequents gardens, farmyards, and hedgerows for the most part; but it also occurs among whins, in the younger plantations, at isolated patches of bushes, and even among the willows at Bavelaw Reservoir. Dunnocks are not normally found in isolated firwoods, except those with thick undergrowth. There is a record of quite a number being seen in the whins at Torduff on 27th November 1933 which may suggest a weather movement as the species is not normally found in flocks.

The Dunnock was common in all the 1932-34 census outings, the total figures being March 64, September 14 and December 53.

In May 1934 Rintoul and Baxter found that Dunnocks were fairly common from Carlops to the North Esk Reservoir. They were seen in Cap Law Wood and North Esk Wood. They also saw one at Loganlee Reservoir and found the species breeding up to 1250 feet.

In the 1948-49 traverse there was a noticeable increase on 17th April which suggested migration. In 1971 R. L. Swann said of

Threipmuir: "Common all the year round, several pairs breed especially in Redford Wood."

One was singing in the Scald Law Plantation on 20th April 1981.

WHEATEARS, ROBINS AND CHATS

Robin. *Erithacus rubecula.* Resident. Breeding. Migrant spring and
    autumn.

In winter Robins are mostly found where thick cover exists. It is then commonest in house gardens and shrubberies, particularly along the wooded portions of the Water of Leith, but it is also found at farmyards, rubbish tips and house gardens in the more isolated areas as well.

Robins are normally found singly at this season, as territory is observed in winter. While it is seldom recorded far from human habitation, there are regular records from the willows at Bavelaw even when the reservoir is icebound, and several other records of Robins being seen at least 400 yards from the nearest house. High woods are deserted in winter.

When spring comes the Robin extends its range to include the higher farms and woods, including coniferous woods at some distance from houses. The house association is still strong however, and this seems to be a greater attraction than thick cover. There are for example records from Crosswood, Cairns Castle, Harperrig waterkeeper's house, Listonshiels and Loganlee waterkeeper's house: all rather exposed and isolated places.

In 1905 David Hamilton saw a Robin at the summit between the Carlops road and Loganlee on 16th December. In May 1934 Rintoul and Baxter walking from Carlops to North Esk Reservoir saw Robins as far as the North Esk wood, where young were being fed. They also saw the species in the West Kip wood and found it common at Torduff.

The total census figures (1932-34) were 100 for March, 70 for September and 53 for December. Robins were very noticeable during the 1948-49 traverse in the first half of September, but by November they were becoming uncommon, and they were not back to the high woods until March.

In 1971 R. L. Swann said of Threipmuir. "Seen throughout the year, a few pairs breed."

Black Redstart. *Phoenicurus ochruros.* Rare vagrant.

There are two records in April 1939, one from Loganlee and the other from the public park at Balerno railway station.

In 1982 one was seen at Harperrig on 9th April and in 1984 there was one at Loganlee waterfall on 12th May.

Redstart. *Phoenicurus phoenicurus.* Summer visitor. Breeds.

The Redstart is a local and rather uncertain summer visitor, arriving early in May or late April as a rule and leaving during August, but these dates sometimes vary considerably. While the bird is most frequently recorded from well-timbered areas such as at Dreghorn, Woodhall House, Woodhouselee, and along the Water of Leith from Balerno to Boll-o-Bere, there are records from coniferous woods at Glendarroch, Baddinsgill House, Slipperfield and North Esk Reservoir. I have found the nest in the wall at Harelaw, and in the old curling house at Malleny. There are also some records from quite treeless country, such as in whins at Carlops and on a wall at Malleny shooting range.

As far back as 1835 Macgillivray found a male feeding a youngster perched on a whin bush at Swanston on 26th July, and this was apparently somewhat unusual, as in 1837 he said: "In the Lothians one scarcely meets with a pair in the course of a ramble of fifteen to twenty miles, although in gardens it may be the object of everyday observation." There was a record from Dreghorn on 27th April 1897.

David Hamilton saw a pair at Glencorse Reservoir on 3rd May 1903, and on the 24th June found a nest with young in the wall at the back of Logan House wood, and in 1907 a nest at Logan Cottage. He found a pair on the hill above Swanston on 28th August 1921. There was a record from Comiston on 2nd May 1917.

William Evans recorded a bird at Redford ruin on 2nd May 1924.

Only two Redstarts were seen during the 1932-34 census outings, both in early September, and there was only one record during the 1948-49 traverse, one being seen at Harelaw on

22nd August. G. L. Sandeman found Redstarts in the Glencorse/Loganlee Valley from mid-April to mid-September 1946-49.

J. K. Adams heard two males singing in Thrashie Dene on 11th May 1946, and Howden Glen Plantations on 9th May 1945. David Hamilton said in 1947 that he had found Redstarts at Bonaly Tower, Ravelrig, Balerno, and Redford Plantation. R. L. Swann said of Threipmuir in 1971: "Recorded May to September, one pair nests in the wood at Redford ruin, and another pair usually nests in the beech trees along the road north of the reservoir."

G. L. Sandeman said: "I have found it breeding at Flotterstone and Woodhouselee in 1946, 1947, 1949, 1971 and 1975." He also has the following records:

1935	August 24th	Harperrig Farm. Two
1951	May 19th	Dreghorn ranges. A pair
1952	June 7th	Dreghorn ranges. A pair feeding young
1954	May 26th	Silverburn. Two pairs
		T Wood — One singing
1966	August 11th	Hillend Park Wood. Four
1972	July 13th	Clubbiedean Wood. A family
1973	September 4th	Lothianburn. A male

Whinchat. *Saxicola rubetra.* Summer visitor. Breeds.

The Whinchat is a summer visitor, breeding (as Miss Rintoul says in *A Vertebrate Fauna of the Forth*) largely among the bracken and long grass of the Pentland Cleuchs, and up to 1250 feet at least.

It arrives towards the end of April or early in May, and stays until mid September. Favourite glens are Dens Cleuch, Boghall, Howden Glen, and the Logan Valley. It also frequented Harmeny and Redford Plantations before the trees grew too tall.

In 1837 Macgillivray said that Whinchats were plentiful along the base of the Pentland Hills and were not uncommon among whins there. There is a record from Linton on 1st May 1894, and another at Comiston on 4th May 1899. David Hamilton saw the species along the Lanark road between Balerno and Harperrig on 21st May 1905 and in later years. He had a record from

Clubbiedean on 31st July 1932, and of a pair at Threipmuir on 12th May 1935.

In 1934 Rintoul and Baxter saw Whinchats in May and early June along the road between Carlops and the North Esk Reservoir, and along the North Esk. They said that it was a common bird at Harelaw and Threipmuir, and also by the grassy burns between Saltersyke and Cap Law. Only five were recorded during the 1932-34 census outings, two on 9th September 1933, and three on 8th September 1934. During the 1948-49 traverse Whinchats were seen from 25th April to 12th September. Two were seen in Cap Law wood on 30th May at a height of 1400 feet.

G. L. Sandeman has these records:

1948-73		Breeding Glencorse glen. Flotterstone to Loganlee.
1946	June 24th	Howden Glen. Five to six pairs with young
1947	June 28th	Crosswood. A pair with young
	July 21st	Swanston Burn. A pair with young
1974	July 8th	Harperrig East Farm. Recorded
1975	May 1st	East Rig to West Rig. Three
	May 26th	Bonaly Reservoir shore. Seen

K. S. Macgregor saw an early cock at Balerno on 23rd April 1962, and H. A. Ford recorded a male at Glencorse Reservoir on 3rd May 1962. In 1964 H. A. Ford saw three at Hillend on 29th April.

R. L. Swann said of Threipmuir in 1972: "Recorded mid May to early September. Three pairs breed most years."

During the years 1981 to 1984 breeding sites were given as below: Black Hill six pairs; Swanston five pairs; Loganlee one pair; Bonaly one pair; Threipmuir four pairs, Quarrel Burn Reservoir three sites; and present Allermuir.

Breeding of four pairs was noted in 1985 at Swanston, and of a pair at Black Springs, Threipmuir. There was no change in 1986.

In 1985 there were spring records from Glencorse Reservoir, Bavelaw to Loganlee, Swanston and Threipmuir, and in the autumn from Crosswood, Harperrig and Threipmuir.

Stonechat. Saxicola torquata. Resident. Breeds.

The Stonechat is resident in very variable numbers, for a severe winter decimates the population and it may take years to recover. Although widely distributed it is rather local, frequenting whins, heather clad cleuchs and moors, and young coniferous plantations. Both Harmeny and Redford Plantations were used as nesting areas up to 1933 when the trees had grown too tall. Favourite areas before the 1939-45 war were in the whins at Torduff, in Den's Cleuch, and up the Logan Valley; but I also found birds at Bonaly Reservoir, Swanston, Nine Mile Burn, Boghall, Glencorse Reservoir, and at places as dissimilar as the Wolf Craigs and the rough ditch which used to exist west of the Convent in Woodhall Road, Colinton. A series of hard winters after the 1939-45 war led to Stonechats becoming rare in the Pentlands, and since then there have been several severe fluctuations in numbers.

David Hamilton had early records as below:

1915	January 24th	Loganlee to Bavelaw. Pair on heather slopes
	May 15th	Loganlee to Bavelaw. Nest (c6)
1921	April 10th	Torduff Reservoir. Recorded
1924	May 10th	Torduff Reservoir. Recorded
1925	September 4th	Torduff Reservoir. Recorded
1927	July 23rd	Torduff Reservoir. Recorded
1928	August 4th	Swanston. Nest with fully fledged young

The total numbers of Stonechats recorded in the 1932-34 census outings were: eleven in March, twelve in September, and two for December: but none were seen during the 1948-49 traverse.

Rintoul and Baxter in 1934 found Stonechats in small numbers in several other parts of the Pentlands, for example a female by the Grain Burn and a male at Glencorse Reservoir on 23rd May:

G. L. Sandeman has records going back over years, these are:

| 1934 | June 19th | Clubbiedean to Torduff | Two |

1935	May 24th	Torduff Falls	Three
1937	May 18th	Torduff	Two
1939	March 23rd	Howden Glen to Woodhouselee	Two pairs

Rintoul and Baxter said (*Scottish Naturalist* 1948) that "In Forth it was pretty widely spread . . . it was seen throughout the Lothians in small numbers, particularly in higher lying country with whins . . . and in 1941 was nesting sparingly in suitable localities. We have notes from a considerable number of observers in the Lothians, and with the exception of one male seen in Midlothian in the summer of 1947, not a single Stonechat is recorded." I have no records of the species in the Pentlands in either 1946 or 1947. However in 1949 G. L. Sandeman saw one at Kirkton Farm on 24th September. In 1950 R. G. Thin records that he saw two males and one female in the Howden Glen on 29th January and he commented that these were the first he had seen in Midlothian, or indeed in any south eastern county, for very many years. In the same year E. A. Blake found a pair along with a single male at the extreme east end of Threipmuir on 19th November. On 2nd December they were still there, and two males were present where Den's Cleuch comes out of Glencorse. In January 1951 however there was no trace of these birds.

On 14th November 1954 D. G. Andrew found a pair in extensive gorse cover at the foot of the Howden Glen, and later records show further evidence of a very slow return to the area. Other records are:

1959	October 7th	Glencorse Reservoir. Male
1961	March 9th	Threipmuir. Male, and a pair on 15th-16th April
1962	April 15th	Carnethy Hill. Recorded
1964	September 27th	Glencorse Reservoir. Male and immature
1964	October 9th	Threipmuir. Two
1973	March 14th	Colzium Plantation. Male
	September 4th	Torduff to Clubbiedean. Three
1974	July 1st	Torduff. Three pairs
	November 7th	Clubbiedean. Two

1975	March 31st	East Threipmuir. Two pairs
	May 26th	Torduff area. Two to three pairs
		Clubbiedean area. Three pairs
	June 27th	Hillend car park area. Pair with four young
	October 30th	Swanston. Two

In 1976 Lance Vick wrote in the *Edinburgh Ringing Group Report:* "It is clear from the records that Holyrood Park and the Pentlands are the strongholds of the Stonechat in Midlothian. Even when the population was low they were normally reported from one or other of these areas. . . . From the reports received by local recorders, one might guess at . . . a handful of pairs on the Pentlands . . . a similar population explosion occurred in the Pentlands in 1976. A few visits to certain areas in the north eastern end of the Pentlands revealed at least twelve breeding pairs. These figures suggest that the whole Pentland range could have had a breeding population in excess of fifty pairs, a figure well above any previous estimate." In 1977 however he reported that these figures were halved owing to the cold spell which lasted through most of December 1976 and January 1977. He also said that the nest was usually deep in low gorse, heather, or below a large grass tussock. Two pairs were found at Torduff on 31st October 1976 but none were seen there on 2nd December.

There was a marked decline in numbers after the 1978-79 winter, but in that year a pair bred at Threipmuir and one at Swanston. Another bad winter 1981-82 brought the comment from the *Lothian Bird Report* for 1982: "The species has been virtually wiped out." The only record for that year was of one or two pairs at Loganlee during the breeding season.

There was a slight recovery in 1983 when three or four pairs bred in the Loganlee valley; a male was seen at Harperrig on 14th March; and in autumn a pair was at Threipmuir. In 1984 there were only one or two pairs at Loganlee, but there was a female and six young in the nest at Swanston on 8th June.

1985 was a bad year with no breeding records but there was a male at Bonaly on 3rd November.

Wheatear. *Oenanthe oenanthe* Common summer visitor and passage migrant.

The Wheatear is a common summer visitor, normally arriving during the last week of March or early in April. It breeds freely on the hills, particularly where walls, heaps of stones, or rabbit burrows provide suitable nesting sites. As might be expected it is less common in arable areas, although a few pairs nest along the walls. It has been seen on the tops of the hills.

During August and until mid-September, the bird appears in small numbers at the reservoirs which are not normally frequented in spring. These may be post-breeding wanderers, but it seems more likely that they are autumn migrants passing through. The breeding areas are normally vacated by late July.

In 1837 Macgillivray recorded that a nest had been taken in a stone wall at the base of the Pentland Hills where the species was not uncommon.

In 1886 Harold Raeburn saw several in the T Wood area on 11th April. There are also old records by William Evans and from the *Annals of Scottish Natural History* 1892-1911.

1879	April 11th	Habbie's Howe	One
1886	March 28th	Torduff	Two
1893	March 19th	Torduff	Four
1896	March 19th	Torduff	Male
1897	April 1st	Torduff	Pair
1898	April 13th	Harelaw Moor	Seen
1899	April 4th	Comiston	Twenty-one in a field
1900	April 2nd	Torduff	Not seen
1902	March 25th	Swanston	Male
1903	March 24th	Lothianburn	Seen
1904	March 24th	Bavelaw Castle	One

The *Crosswood Migration Schedules* 1908-19 show arrival dates between 12th April and 3rd May, with the average date being 19th April.

David Hamilton saw a late bird on a walk from Silverburn to Balerno on 4th October 1914, and on 19th March 1916 one was seen at West Linton.

In the 1932-34 census work nine were seen late in March, and thirteen in the first weeks of September. During May and early June 1934, Rintoul and Baxter reported: "Carlops to North Esk Reservoir, pretty common by the Esk. One near Crosswood Reservoir. A good many Windy Gowl, and recorded Logan Burn."

Between 1946 and 1949 G. L. Sandeman found Wheatears from the end of March to the end of August in the Glencorse to Loganlee Glen.

Some early dates recorded in spring are:

1956	March 31st	Torduff	One seen
1957	March 16th	Carnethy Hill	One on scree
1964	March 28th	Black Hill	Male
1966	March 19th	Flotterstone	Male
1968	March 22nd	Hillend	One

In 1971 R. L. Swann said of Threipmuir: "Recorded April to September in small numbers, mainly at the foot of the Black Hill." In 1975 G. L. Sandeman found the species breeding in the broken wall on the summit ridge between Caerketton and Allermuir.

There is an exceptionally late date in 1978, when three were seen at the West Water Reservoir on 3rd November.

In 1986 there were records of twenty-four at Threipmuir on 4th May and twenty-one at Swanston on 8th May.

Greenland Wheatear. *Oenanthe oenanthe leucorrhoa.* Rare migrant.

There are two early records of the Greenland race. On 9th May 1911 William Evans saw a male at the cairn on the summit of the south Black Hill, and on 12th May 1962 W. Brotherston saw a male on the West Linton side of the Cauldstane Slap.

Ian J. Andrews (*The Birds of the Lothians*) says birds of the Greenland race *O.o.leucorrhoa* are undoubtedly under-recorded. He reports occurrences at Swanston between 23rd April and 22nd May during the years 1968-84.

Ring Ousel. *Turdus torquatus.* Rather local summer visitor.

In addition to being common in the Glencorse-Loganlee-Bavelaw valley with its side cleuchs, there are records of Ring

Ousels from the Wolf Craigs, Deerhope Rig, and from the burns above Baddinsgill. They normally arrive about the beginning of April and leave again at the end of August. Heathery ravines are their normal haunts, but are occasionally found at the outskirts of woods.

The history of the Ring Ousel in the Pentlands goes back a long way. John Fleming (*History of British Mammals* 1828) said: "The Ring Ousel is not rare in the Pentland Hills," and the species was recorded in the *New Statistical Report for Colinton Parish* in 1845. Other early records are:

1889	June 3rd	Den's Cleuch. Two singing from hillside
1890	June 26th	Medwin. Several
1894	April 2nd	Loganlee. Recorded
1899	March 30th	Clubbiedean. One
	April 30th	Loganlee. Nest (c4) on steep bank at side of Howlet's House
	May 21st	Loganlee. Nest at waterfall with four young
1901	April 12th	Torduff. Recorded
	May 4th	Loganlee. Two nests found
1902	September 16th	East Kip. David Hamilton found one right at the top, and remarked: "I thought they would have left the high ground by this time."
1903	May 9th	Listonshiels. Nest (c4) in heather
1912	May 12th	Listonshiels. A pair
1920	May 14th	Logan Valley. David Hamilton estimated that about six or seven pairs were present

In 1837 Macgillivray said: "A few individuals are found here and there among . . . the Pentland Hills, generally in the vicinity of masses of furze and juniper." He noted two pairs between Glencorse Reservoir and the Lover's Loup Waterfall, and said that Ring Ousels arrive about the middle of April and depart at the beginning of October. He said that the species was not uncommon in the Pentland Hills, especially in the Glencorse valley.

In 1920 James Ritchie wrote in *The Influence of Man on Animal Life in Scotland:* ''Perhaps the same vague influences (replacing of once universally distributed food plants by pasture and arable land, which led to the localisation of many species of insects) have to do with the gradual disappearance of the Ring Ousel on the Pentlands where it nested commonly in the seventies of last century according to Lt. Col. Wedderburn, but where it is now seldom to be seen.''

In *A Vertebrate Fauna of the Forth* 1935 Rintoul and Baxter said: ''It has long been known to breed in the Pentlands; Mr Hamilton characterises it as common on the Pentlands where he has seen over twenty nests, seven pairs in one valley.'' In 1934 Rintoul and Baxter had been agreeably surprised by the number of Ring Ousels they saw in the Pentlands. They heard the species singing in the heather at the West Kip, and found several pairs, again in heather, above 1200 feet, between Carlops and the Bore Stane. On Carnethy there were four pairs in the heather, again from 1200 feet up.

G. L. Sandeman has frequent records, for example:

1933	May 16th	Medwin. Nest with four young
1949	April 4th	Allermuir. A pair on the summit

He found ring Ousels breeding in the Logan Valley between 1941 and 1975. No Ring Ousel was seen either in the census outings 1932-34 nor during the traverse of 1948-49, which shows how local the species is in the Pentlands.

David Hamilton told me in 1947 that he had found the species nesting by the Bonaly Burn, at several places in the Logan Valley, on the Black Hill facing Threipmuir, on the Carlops path, near Listonshiels, and also on the Carlops Burn below the North Esk Reservoir.

In 1971 R. L. Swann said of Threipmuir: ''Seen occasionally at the foot of the Black Hill during summer where a pair may nest.'' Other records are:

1952	April 12th	Threipmuir. Recorded
1954	March 29th	Green Cleuch. At least five

1955	March 27th	Loganlee Reservoir. Male in heather
1956	April 6th	Loganlee. Pair
1957	March 24th	Loganlee Waterfall. Probably two
1961	November 10th	Glencorse. One feeding near a flock of Fieldfares
1966	March 26th	Loganlee Reservoir. Male
1967	March 25th	West Water. One
	March 30th	Loganlee. Two
1976	November 2nd	Glencorse. Ten

R. F. Durman in the *Edinburgh Ringing Group Report* for 1977 wrote: "From 1973 to 1977 the optimum habitat can be found in the locality of Habbie's Howe in the moorland valley between Glencorse Reservoir and Bavelaw Castle. In 1973-4 nine broods were ringed. In 1975-6-7 forty-three nests were found, forty of them in heather, two in bracken and one on a crag at the foot of a silver birch tree. All nests have been on a distinctive edge of vegetation and never within a uniform expanse of heather. I have evidence of the re-use of only one nest in the Pentlands. This was a successful one in 1976 which was relined and used again in 1977, the same colour ringed male being in attendance in both seasons.

"In my almost treeless study area ground nesting Mistle Thrushes and Blackbirds are common, and appear to fill similar ecological niches to Ring Ousels. There appears to be little aggression between Blackbirds and Ring Ousels (but) there is much more noticeable aggression between Ring Ousels and Mistle Thrushes."

A breeding survey taken in 1985 gave only five territories in the Pentlands.

Blackbird. *Turdus merula*. Common and well distributed resident and winter visitor.

The Blackbird is much commoner than the Song Thrush in the Pentlands, and unlike the Song Thrush usually remains at the high farms in winter, although it withdraws from some of the high plantations where it nests in summer. In winter it is commonest along the low ground, where shrubberies, house gardens and thick cover give it shelter; but I have found it feeding at the T Wood, in the Bavelaw willows and on the Kitchen Moss (28th February) at some distance from woods. More usual winter haunts are farmyards, stackyards where these still exist, along hedgerows, and on open grass fields or on plough along with other Turdidae.

A considerable immigration, mostly of males, takes place in February; and in autumn there is a large inflow, presumably from Scandinavia. On 24th November 1946 over a hundred were seen between Juniper Green and Kenleith Mill. Even the highest woods are used for nesting, and in some places the Blackbird breeds in treeless hill valleys.

The Blackbird was recorded for Mid Calder Parish in 1791, and almost a hundred years later Harold Raeburn found nests in the T Wood in the springs of 1882 and 1883. He recorded it in the woods on the lower reaches of the Medwin in 1890. On 10th May 1910 David Hamilton found a nest (c4) in the wall of an old house at the head of Loganlee Reservoir. J. Kirke Nash said in his *Birds of Midlothian* 1935: "Like the Song Thrush it also breeds in some of the hill valleys."

In May 1934 Rintoul and Baxter found Blackbirds common up to the North Esk Wood during a walk from Carlops, and also common from Logan House down the Glencorse valley when going by Carnethy and Loganlee to Flotterstone. Later they found a few in the highest wood between Carlops and the Bore Stane.

The total census figures for 1932-34 were 134 in March, 63 for September and 150 for December. During the 1948-49 traverse the species was seen in Braid Law Wood throughout the winter, but not in Cap Law Wood. There was an influx to the area on 17th October, and a considerable increase on 28th March. Then thirty-four were seen, of which thirteen were seen together in Fernilaw Avenue, Colinton, on fields.

Fieldfare. *Turdus pilaris.* Winter visitor in variable numbers.

In the Pentlands the Fieldfare usually arrives about the middle of October and leaves by the end of the first week of May. Fieldfares are to be found on pasture fields, on stubble, along hawthorn hedges, on plough, on manured fields and on golf

courses, especially where trees or hedgerows exist to which they
fly when disturbed. Favourite haunts have been near Bonaly
Tower, Bavelaw Moor, and the hedges and fields there.

The fields west of Clubbiedean are also used. A further influx,
often of large flocks, takes place rather later than the first
immigrants, usually in November. There are records of up to 500
coming in from the north east. These birds are often very wild,
seldom settling for long, and are possibly on passage further
south; they are often seen on hillsides and moors where the
normal winter visitors are seldom recorded. Such flocks
sometimes roost among the bushes at Bavelaw Reservoir.

Although Fieldfare flocks and parties are often recorded by
themselves, their usual companions on the fields are Redwings
and other Turdidae, Starlings, Chaffinches, Greenfinches, and
Lapwings.

Some early and late dates are:

1894	September 24th	Base of Pentlands
1895	October 24th	Comiston
	October 25th	Comiston. Flocks flying west
1896	October 28th	Threipmuir
1897	April 29th	Balerno
1899	May 13th	Dreghorn. Flock of 180
1903	February 28th	Harperrig. Flock of at least 200
	May 9th	Balerno
1905	October 11th	Balerno. Small flock going west
	October 14th	North Esk
1907	November 3rd	Glencorse. Arrived

The 1932-34 census figures were in total 131 in March, none in
September and 493 in December. In the 1948-49 traverse
Fieldfares were only recorded in March, November and January.

Between 1946 and 1949 G. L. Sandeman recorded Fieldfares in
the Flotterstone-Glencorse district from the third week of October
to the end of November.

Later records are:

1958	May 9th	Hillend Park. One
1959	November 7th	Glencorse. Unusual numbers settling in heather and rough grass, which is unusual too

| 1962 | November 2nd | Flotterstone. 200 in hedges |
| 1966 | April | Glencorse Reservoir. Large flock in pines |

In 1971 R. L. Swann said of Threipmuir: "Flocks of up to 100 recorded between October and April."

In 1973 G. L. Sandeman recorded the species at Glencorse Reservoir from mid-May to June, which suggests an attempt at breeding.

There are recent records of large flocks: in 1980 150 per hour passed south from Bavelaw on 14th October, and on 15th October 1981 some 200 plus were going north west from Bavelaw. In 1983 many were seen at Balerno and Crosswood on 29th October, and in 1984 there were 200 at Bavelaw on 9th November. In 1985 there was a flock of 100 at Harperrig on 18th December.

There are also records of numbers in spring.

1981	April 26th	Bavelaw	800 plus
1982	April 1st	Threipmuir	350
1984	March 22nd	Torphin	1000
	March 25th	Bavelaw	400
	April 4th	Nine Mile Burn	200

Song Thrush. *Turdus philomelos*. Resident. Breeds. Spring and autumn migrant.

Song Thrushes are not as common in the Pentlands as Blackbirds are. In winter they desert many of the higher nesting haunts at the high woods and farms, whereas the Blackbird is apparently able to remain at least at the farms. It seems possible that many of our Thrushes travel west and south for the winter.

Return migration takes place during February and March, when Thrushes can be seen in unusual surroundings. On 15th March 1936 for example, several were seen on grass moorland in the Tongue apparently on migration. Although the normal nesting habitat is in gardens and shrubberies on low ground, or in hedgerows and plantations, some nest in the high woods such as Redford Plantation, Crosswood, Bavelaw Castle, Fairliehope, North Esk Reservoir and the T Wood. Others may nest on the ground at some distance from trees.

In the houses' and farms' enquiry the Song Thrush was considered to be a summer visitor at some hill areas, and at these, dates of arrival were given as 13th February at West Bavelaw, 20th February at Spittal, mid-February at Cairns, and 6th March at North Esk. It was considered as resident at the other thirteen places surveyed.

The *Old Statistical Account* of 1791 notes the Song Thrush for Mid Calder Parish, and the *New Statistical Account* of 1845 for Colinton Parish says: "It is understood that the Mistle Thrush has here as elsewhere very much usurped the place of the common Thrush."

On 3rd June 1899 Harold Raeburn found a nest with two young on a ledge in the East Threipmuir quarry. A Song Thrush was singing at Crosswood on 25th February 1907, and first singing dates from the *Crosswood Migration Schedules* are:

1910	February 20th
1911	January 27th
1913	February 12th
1914	February 12th
1916	January 29th

J. Kirke Nash saw nests even in the quiet hill valleys (*Birds of Midlothian* 1935), and Rintoul and Baxter said (*A Vertebrate Fauna of the Forth* 1935) "Though commonest in the wooded parts, it also nests on some of the hills away from woodlands. We found it in the Pentland woods up to about 1250 feet, and Mr Hamilton tells us of a nest in the Pentlands on a ledge of rock within a yard of a Dipper's nest on 4th May 1901 . . . after the breeding season our Thrushes begin to move down towards the Firth." During their Pentland walks in May 1934, Rintoul and Baxter noted "Carlops to North Esk Reservoir, plentiful up to Fairliehope, and on the Carnethy-Loganlee-Flotterstone walk very common on Logan Burn and at Glencorse Reservoir." On the Carlops to Bore Stane journey they saw Thrushes up to the North Esk Wood.

The 1932-34 census figures were in total 81 in March, 48 in September, and 33 in December. G. L. Sandeman said that the Song Thrush was mainly seen from the third week of March to October in the Glencorse valley, 1946-49. R. L. Swann said of

Threipmuir (1971): "Seen throughout the year, a few pairs nest."

Redwing. *Turdus iliacus*. Regular winter visitor in variable numbers.

The Redwing is a sporadic winter visitor to the Pentlands, arriving in October and leaving in March or early April. Although often seen with Fieldfares or other Turdidae, the Redwing has a greater preference for sheltered feeding areas on low ground than other Turdidae species. Grass fields and paddocks are favourite haunts: those at Balerno, Fernilaw Avenue in Colinton, Torduff water filters, Harelaw, Lymphoy and Oxgangs are popular; but with the great spread of housing some of these fields are under threat.

Redwings are sometimes recorded from stubble, and I have seen them scratching among fallen leaves in the T Wood. The Redwing is not as a rule as numerous as the Fieldfare, flocks of up to twenty birds being normal. There are however records of larger flocks; including one of at least 100 on pasture at Balerno on 21st January 1934 and on 24th November 1946 one of 100 to 150 between Juniper Green and Kenleith.

Redwings are sometimes seen on high ground, presumably on migration. On 11th October 1893 flocks were seen flying west high up, and in later years there are records as below:

1895	October 24th	Comiston
1897	October 4th	Bonaly and Loganlee. Several
1898	October 6th	Boghall. A few
1903	October 12th	West Linton

The total census figures 1932-34 were 233 in March, none in September and one in December. Redwings were first seen at Balerno in 1944 on 23rd October. G. L. Sandeman found the species as winter visitors to the Flotterstone-Glencorse valley between early October and December (1946-49).

On the 1948-49 traverse Redwings were seen only once when they were on the thorn trees at Threipmuir on 21st November 1948. In 1971 R. L. Swann gave the status of the Redwing at that date as "Seen October to March at Threipmuir in small flocks".

Mistle Thrush. *Turdus viscivorus* Resident. Spring and autumn migrant.

Mistle Thrushes are apparently resident in the area, but there are indications that some migration through the Pentlands takes place. Although breeding for the most part in the pine plantations and deciduous trees, some nest on the ground well away from cover in Ring Ousel habitats.

Mistle Thrushes nest even in the highest woods at 1300 feet. Small flocks may be seen from July to October, usually on the lower ground. These are possibly composed of several families collecting where food is plentiful, or perhaps of migrants. In winter such groups are observed less often, as the species is usually seen singly or in small numbers of up to four or five birds. They often consort with Fieldfares.

In winter moorland and high woods are normally deserted when pasture fields, gardens, plough, stubble, coniferous woods and deciduous woods are favoured. In spring Mistle Thrushes sometimes start singing as early as the end of January, when the country name of "Storm Cock" is often appropriate.

In 1837 Macgillivray wrote: "At Colinton . . . and generally in the wooded parts of this division, they are seen here and there in pairs during summer, and in winter occur in flocks in the fields." The *New Statistical Account* of 1845 adds: "It is understood that the Mistle Thrush has here as elsewhere, very much usurped the place of the common Thrush."

In 1889 Harold Raeburn found a nest in a pine at Harelaw on 3rd June, and in the same year David Hamilton found a nest (c4) in a wood at Glencorse on 9th April. He is quoted (*A Vertebrate Fauna of the Forth*) as saying that numbers nest in the Pentlands quite away from woodland; in 1947 however he told me that only odd pairs nest away from woods. On 10th April 1904 he found a bird sitting on a nest at Bonaly Tower and heard one singing there on 11th February 1911.

In 1934 Rintoul and Baxter made the following observations: "Fairliehope common in wood; Glencorse Reservoir several; recorded North Esk Wood."

The monthly totals of Mistle Thrushes seen during the 1932-34 census outings were 33 in March, 58 in September and 24 in

December. G. L. Sandeman said of Flotterstone to Glencorse 1946-1949: "A peak in September suggests passage."

During the traverse 1948-49 the species was heard singing in Redford Wood on 15th February, but it was the 14th March before birds were singing in Braid Law and Cap Law Woods. By 27th June a small party including immatures was seen at Torduff Reservoir. August was a very dead month, Mistle Thrushes only being recorded twice in four visits; and none was seen on 26th September or 17th October. On 30th January however one was heard singing on the Kitchen Moss.

In 1971 R. L. Swann gave the status of the Mistle Thrush at Threipmuir at that date as being "Seen throughout the year. One pair usually breeds." In 1977 R. F. Durman wrote: (*Edinburgh Ringing Group Reports*) "Loganlee area: In my almost treeless study area nesting Mistle Thrushes and Blackbirds are common, and fill similar ecological niches to Ring Ousels, choosing similar nest sites and probably similar food."

In the *Scottish Bird Report* for 1978 it was recorded that forty-five had been seen in the Pentlands on 19th June of that year.

In 1982 five pairs were breeding from Flotterstone to Loganlee, and in 1986 there were two to three territories at Threipmuir and two at Loganlee.

WARBLERS AND GOLDCREST

Grasshopper Warbler. *Locustella naevia*. Uncommon summer
   visitor. Probably breeds.

On 19th May 1889 William Evans heard one singing in a field at Comiston Farm. On 23rd June of the same year he heard one singing from a grass field beyond Hillend, and on 1st July in the same year one sang from a hayfield at Fairmilehead.

In 1904 one was singing in Bavelaw Moss on 20th May, and in June 1904 one sang nightly in a strip running north from the keeper's house at Dreghorn.

David Hamilton however had never recorded the species in a lifetime of Pentland birdwatching. There are quite a number of more recent records:

1956	June 9th to 22nd	Threipmuir. One singing near car park
1966	May 14th	Threipmuir. One

1971	April 30th	Dreghorn. One
1972	June 16th	East Rig-West Rig railings
	July 20th	Middle Threipmuir
1978	April 22nd	Threipmuir

In 1980 between one and three pairs were present at Threipmuir during the breeding season, and one bird was at Glencorse on 13th May. In 1981 however, the Threipmuir breeding area was ploughed up.

Sedge Warbler. *Acrocephalus schoenobaenus.* Local summer visitor. Breeds.

The Sedge Warbler is a very local summer visitor in small numbers, arriving about the beginning of May, and leaving by the end of the first week of September. Bavelaw is the main breeding area, but there are records during the breeding season from East Threipmuir, Middle Threipmuir, Malleny Curling Pond, Slipperfield, Kenleith Curling Pond and Cairns Castle. There are also some records near Swanston and Colinton, where the species appeared to be nesting in ditches at the edge of cornfields, and in a plantation at Hunter's Tryst.

The earliest record is of one at Comiston on 10th May 1899. During the 1932-34 census work three were recorded at Threipmuir on 9th September 1933 where there was one on 8th September 1934. Rintoul and Baxter found several at Bavelaw on 22nd May 1934. David Hamilton writing in 1947 said that it nested regularly at Bavelaw, but was not common elsewhere. He had recorded it by the Water of Leith.

On the 1948-49 traverse one was singing in Bavelaw Marsh from 6th June to 18th July 1948. One was recorded at West Linton on 13th May 1962.

In 1971 R. L. Swann said of Threipmuir: "Recorded May to September. Several pairs nest." G. L. Sandeman saw one at Crosswood on 22nd May.

The species seems to have become commoner in recent years as the following records show:

1979	Threipmuir	Eight plus territories
1980	Bavelaw	Twenty plus territories
1982	Bavelaw	Sixteen singing

1984	Threipmuir/	
	Bavelaw	Nine to ten territories
1985	Threipmuir/	
	Bavelaw	Twenty-four to twenty-seven territories

Lesser Whitethroat. *Sylvia curruca.* Seldom recorded but possibly overlooked.

On 10th June 1967 M. A. Macdonald heard one singing at Threipmuir, and for some weeks in the spring of 1980 a Lesser Whitethroat sang in West Carnethy Avenue, Colinton.

Whitethroat. *Sylvia communis.* Summer visitor in small numbers. Breeds.

The Whitethroat is a summer visitor to low ground in small numbers, and has not been recorded above 1000 feet. Its numbers are very subject to world population swings, but despite these the species is widely distributed where suitable tangled cover exists. Many of the records are from the valley of the Water of Leith, but the species occurred in the Redford Plantation when the trees were small; in bracken at Threipmuir East Marsh; at Mansfield Farm; at Carlops; in whins at Torduff; and in nettle patches at Balerno.

The only old record is from Comiston on 8th May 1899. Whitethroats were not found in the 1932-34 census work, but in 1934 Rintoul and Baxter saw several in May — in a garden at Carlops, at Glencorse Reservoir, and several at Torduff.

G. L. Sandeman has these records:

1935	August 24th	Harperrig Farm
1937	June 22nd	Dreghorn nest (c5)
1947	August 23rd	Threipmuir. Breeding

During 1946-49 he recorded Whitethroats in the Flotterstone to Glencorse area from 1st May to 10th September. In 1972 they were breeding at Dreghorn on 27th June, but from 1973 onwards he had no records from either Glencorse or Threipmuir.

1948-49 were good years for Whitethroats, for on the traverse they were recorded from late June to 11th July at Middle Threipmuir, on the sandy track leading south from the top of Currie Brae, and at Clubbiedean and Torduff.

Garden Warbler. *Sylvia borin* Summer visitor in small numbers. Breeds.

Macgillivray did not record the species in the Pentlands, but he heard of it occurring at Currie. Between 1889 and 1904 William Evans heard and saw one in Dreghorn Avenue, Colinton, heard one singing in a plantation behind Hillend, and found a nest with newly hatched young in a wood at Larch Grove House, Balerno. There is a record from Dreghorn on 30th April 1905. In 1935 Iain Ogilvie of Bonaly Tower said that he only once found a nest at Bonaly Tower, but had seen young birds there on a number of occasions.

W. T. Blackwood in his *History of Peeblesshire* 1925 said: "It has been known to nest in the West Linton district." In 1947 David Hamilton said that the Garden Warbler was rather irregular, but in May 1914 he found two birds singing at Ravelrig, and found a nest (c4) there in a privet bush. In 1915 he heard one at Cockburnhill Farm. On 23rd June 1946 one was heard singing at Lynedale.

The species was not recorded on either the 1932-34 census or on the 1948-49 traverse. G. L. Sandeman has these later records:

1970	June 26th	Dreghorn. Two pairs
	July 16th	Flotterstone. Young being fed
1972	June 16th	Harelaw Ravine. Recorded
	June 26th	Dreghorn. Breeding
1974	April 30th	Dreghorn. Recorded
	July 1st	Dreghorn. Recorded
1975	June 13th	Dreghorn. Breeding

The species was reported from Flotterstone during the breeding season in 1980.

Blackcap. *Sylvia atricapilla.* Uncommon summer visitor. Breeds. A few winter.

W. Evans heard one singing in Dreghorn Avenue, Colinton, on 21st June 1904. David Hamilton told me in 1947 that he had not recorded it during his many years of birdwatching in the Pentlands. It may be that Blackcaps have become commoner in recent years, but of course so have birdwatchers.

There have been some interesting winter records as below:

1959	November 22nd	West Linton. A pair
1968	January 3rd and 6th	Carlops. Recorded
	January 1st	Juniper Green. Recorded
	February 10th-12th	Colinton. Male

G. L. Sandeman has a number of records as below:

1970	June 3rd	Dreghorn. Two
	June 26th	Dreghorn. Two
1971	June 9th	Dreghorn. Two
	June 30th	Dreghorn. Two
	June 30th	Flotterstone. Male
	July 7th	Flotterstone. Recorded
1972	June 8th	Logan Tower. Male
1975	June 12th	East Rig Wood. Two
	June 26th	Flotterstone. Two
	July 8th	Flotterstone. Recorded
	September 30th	East Rig Wood. Female

He also has records from Dreghorn for each year from 1972 to 1975 between May and July.

In 1984 there were winter records from Bonaly from 14th February to 22nd March, and a spring observation from Dreghorn on 25th April. In 1986 breeding was reported at Dreghorn, Glencorse, Marchbank Hotel and Threipmuir.

Wood Warbler. *Phylloscopus sibilatrix.* Summer visitor in small numbers. Breeds.

In the Pentlands the Wood Warbler is largely confined to areas where there are beech trees. There are records from Balerno, Redford Plantation, Bavelaw, Slipperfield, Bavelaw Castle policies and Avenue, Woodhouselee, Dreghorn and Flotterstone.

W. Macgillivray in his list of the *Summer Birds of the Lothians* (1839) said: "Not very rare Colinton." David Hamilton found it nesting in the beech wood west of Ravelrig on 9th May 1914, and Rintoul and Baxter heard it singing at Flotterstone on 23rd May and 3rd June 1934. J. Kirke Nash (*Birds of Midlothian* 1935) said that he had seen the nest at Balcrno. J. K. Adams heard one singing at Bavelaw on 9th June 1945.

G. L. Sandeman has these records:

1934	June 2nd	Cairns Castle. One
1947	July 15th	Bavelaw Avenue. One
	September 6th	Flotterstone. One
1948	May 15th	Glencorse Ravine. Singing
1949	May 31st	Glencorse Ravine. Breeding
1950	June 10th	Glencorse Ravine. Three
1970	May 25th	Glencorse Ravine. One
1971	May 31st	Glencorse Ravine. Singing

He had no further records from Glencorse Ravine between 1971 and 1974 but on 23rd May 1972 he recorded one at Ravelrig.

Wood Warblers were not found during the census work 1932-34, but on the 1948-49 traverse there are these records:

1948	May 30th	Bavelaw Castle. Singing
	June 6th	Redford Wood. Singing
	June 20th	Bavelaw Castle and Malleny Curling Pond. Singing

On 29th April 1952 the species was first recorded at Glencorse.

In 1983 Wood Warblers were heard singing at Bavelaw Castle and Marchbank, and in 1984 one sang at Bavelaw Castle on 6th June. In 1985 one was seen at Threipmuir on 18th June.

Chiffchaff. *Phylloscopus collybita.* Summer visitor in small numbers. Breeds.

The Chiffchaff is very local in the Pentlands and there are very few records. Dreghorn Woods appears to be the most likely place to see them. In 1899 Eagle Clarke heard one in Dreghorn Woods on 30th May, and many years later there is another record there on 14th June 1939.

There are some later records:

1952	April 23rd	Dreghorn
1956	April 1st	Threipmuir. Two seen and heard

M

1958	May 25th	Dreghorn. One possibly two singing
1970	June 3rd	Dreghorn. Recorded
	June 26th	Bavelaw. Family with four young
1971	June 9th	Dreghorn. Four

There are breeding season records as below:

1980		Swanston, Flotterstone, Bavelaw, Bonaly
1981		Balerno. Three or four sites
1982		Dreghorn. Two sites
1983		Dreghorn. Four singing. Young seen
		Threipmuir. One
1984		Bavelaw Castle, Crosswood
1985		Dreghorn, Bonaly Tower, Threipmuir

There is also an exceptionally early record of one at Dreghorn on 18th February 1983.

Willow Warbler. *Phylloscopus trochilus.* Common summer visitor. Breeds.

Willow Warblers may be expected from the middle of April onwards. At first only a few are noticed, but in a day or two they seem to be singing everywhere. The birds then settle down in their territories, and numbers drop somewhat. The species is still very common however, and may be found in deciduous woods, gardens, coniferous woods and plantations, whin, birch plantations: in fact anywhere where thick cover exists, right up to the highest wood at 1500 feet. Beechwoods are not chosen as often as other woods.

The species nests freely on the ground wherever trees or bushes are found, but not normally away from these. The nest has however been seen under long heather near trees. By July many of the higher nesting areas are deserted, and the autumn migration has started in August. Numbers then dwindle and by the end of September the species has normally completely deserted the area.

In 1897 Macgillivray said on 14th June: "I first fell in with a male at Swanston as it shifted and fluttered about among the whin bushes . . . and entering Swanston wood I came upon another perched on the summit of a tall tree. On 1st May 1839 great numbers were seen by me . . . along the Water of Leith from Currie to Slateford . . . as well as in the woods on the southern side of the Pentland Hills. (The species is) plentiful along the base of the Pentland Hills." There are records in the *Annals of Scottish Natural History* from Dreghorn and Balerno between 22nd and 30th April from 1897 to 1915.

W. Evans said that it was recorded from Redford Wood from bushes and undergrowth prior to 1919-20 when the wood was cut. J. Kirke Nash notes (1935) that the species usually arrives in Midlothian about the third week in April. Rintoul and Baxter said in 1934 that they found Willow Warblers in May that year in woods up to 1500 feet, and said that it was common between Carlops and North Esk, even in the North Esk Wood. They also found it at Harelaw, Threipmuir, Torduff, Clubbiedean and Cap Law Wood.

During the 1932-34 census outings only twelve were recorded, all in the three September ones. On the 1948-49 traverse Willow Warblers were well distributed on 25th April 1948, even in Braid Law and Cap Law Woods. None was recorded on 26th September, and on 24th April 1949 the species was once again back in its breeding numbers.

Some arrival dates given in *Scottish Birds* are:

1962	April 21st	Threipmuir
1964	April 16th	Fairmilehead
	April 18th	Dolphinton
1968	April 21st	Threipmuir. Many

In 1971 R. L. Swann said of Threipmuir: "Recorded late April to September. A few pairs breed."

Recent records (1980-84) show that up to twenty pairs breed annually at Bavelaw/Threipmuir, and Willow Warblers are also particularly common at Flotterstone.

Goldcrest. *Regulus regulus*. Resident. Breeds. Winter visitor. Passage migrant.

A large influx of Goldcrests takes place early in October, and sometimes near the end of September. The species is then present in numbers, mostly in pine plantations and woods, but also among whins at Torduff and Swanston and in hedgerows and deciduous strips elsewhere.

By the end of October, however, the species is not so noticeable, and some birds perhaps move further south and west. In winter Goldcrests are widely distributed, mostly in coniferous woods except for high woods above about 1000 feet. However, owing to its retiring habits and the fact that it normally feeds high up in the trees, the species can easily be overlooked.

In spring it extends its range to include the highest woods. There is some indication of passage in August and September.

The *Old Statistical Account* of 1791 records the Goldcrest in Linton Parish, and the *New Statistical Account* of 1845 records the species in Colinton Parish. In 1837 Macgillivray notes that there was no accession of numbers at the period of the arrival of the Woodcock and Fieldfare.

In 1924 William Evans said of Redford Wood: "Recorded prior to this being cut in 1919-20." David Hamilton wrote in the *Scottish Naturalist* of 1933 that: "Since the severe winter of 1916-17 which almost decimated the Goldcrest, this species has gradually been filling up its depleted ranks, and at present seems to be well up to the normal, and in some localities to have actually increased. . . . During . . . 1932 . . . they were abundant in all the woods near the Pentland Hills, in one of which we found five nests in a very small area, and there would certainly be others which we passed. Most of the woods are very narrow, but extend for long distances, and while searching through them the song of the Goldcrest could be heard as we worked along the entire length. . . . May seemed to be the best nesting time, as we found them in all stages during that month. On the first of the month they were seen building; some had eggs on the 7th, others were observed pairing on the 17th, and on the 29th, we found others just laying. On 3rd September we saw newly fledged young being fed. All the nests were in Spruce and Fir. Most of the nests were from 12 to 18 feet from the ground."

The total census figures 1932-34 were: 23 in March, 85 plus in September and 31 plus in December.

In May 1934 Rintoul and Baxter found Goldcrests nesting up

to 1250 feet in the wood at North Esk, and also at Glencorse Reservoir.

David Hamilton remarked to me in 1947 that Goldcrests did not seem to be as common then as they had been in earlier years.

During the 1948-49 traverse the species was very noticeable at the end of August and during September, but was seldom seen in November or December. G. L. Sandeman found Goldcrests breeding at Glencorse Reservoir in 1949 and 1976 and commented that in the Flotterstone to Glencorse Valley the numbers rose in the period from August to October.

In 1971 R. L. Swann said of Threipmuir (Redford Wood): "Seen throughout the year when large flocks are often present. Many pairs also breed."

FLYCATCHERS

Spotted Flycatcher. *Muscicapa striata.* Summer visitor. Breeds.

The Spotted Flycatcher is a summer visitor between the middle of May and late September. It is locally common where thick cover exists, and breeds freely along the Water of Leith, particularly west of Balerno. The Glencorse Valley is another favourite haunt. Other nesting localities are at Bonaly Tower, Poet's Glen, Woodhall, Bavelaw Castle, Crosswood, Dreghorn, Harperrig, Woodhouselee and Glencorse Ravine.

William Evans said in 1924 that the species frequented the immediate vicinity of the Redford ruin at Threipmuir. J. Kirke Nash said in 1935 that it was "seldom seen before the third week in May. Well distributed in all river valleys and even resorts to the woods in the lower hills. The first nest I ever found was . . . in a rock cleft on the bank of a small hill stream in the heart of the Pentlands."

A total of six birds was seen during the three September outings of the 1932-34 census.

Iain H. Ogilvie told that before the 1939-45 war he saw the species at Bonaly Tower nearly every near. In 1947 David Hamilton described it as not uncommon in the Pentland Woods. During the 1948-49 traverse Spotted Flycatchers were seen between 30th May and 26th September at Nine Mile Burn, Westside, Bavelaw Castle, and at Cap Law Wood where a family was seen.

In 1971 R. L. Swann said of Threipmuir: "Summer visitor. One pair probably breeds."

Pied Flycatcher. *Ficedula hypoleuca.* Uncommon summer visitor. May breed.

David Hamilton had no records, but there have been a few since the 1939-45 war. From 9th May to 21st June 1945 J. K. Adams found a male singing in the Howden Glen Plantation. He also found a singing male in Thrashie Dene on 11th May 1946. The Howden Glen tradition continued in 1955 when a brown male was watched singing on 23rd May.

Ian Balfour Paul saw a cock at Bavelaw on 10th May 1958.

TITS AND TREECREEPER

Long-tailed Tit. *Aegithalos caudatus.* Irregular visitor in small numbers. Has bred.

Long-tailed Tits are not often seen in the area, although a few pairs breed. The places where one is most likely to see them are birch plantations such as those at John's Smithy at Balerno, Marchbank, Bavelaw Bridge, and along the Water of Leith in its wooded and urban reaches. Small flocks are present in winter.

The *New Statistical Account* of 1845 records the species in Colinton Parish, and Rintoul and Baxter said that David Hamilton also observed the species there. The Long-tailed Tit was not recorded either on the 1932-34 census or the 1948-49 traverse. In 1946 about twelve were seen at Logan Cottage on 26th October, and D. G. Andrew records that on 24th August 1954 a flock of twenty-six passed through his garden in Colinton. He said that such numbers were most unusual there.

G. L. Sandeman has these notes:

1970	December 8th	Glencorse	Fourteen
1971	March 12th	Glencorse	Two
	April 28th	Glencorse	One
	November 5th	Logan Cottage	One
1972	May 30th	Dreghorn	Breeding
1973	April 18th	Dreghorn	Breeding
1975	January 1st	Bavelaw	Ten

In 1971 R. L. Swann said of Threlpmuir: "One pair breeds in most years. Flocks of up to ten are recorded in winter."

On 5th October 1974 there were twenty-five at Bavelaw.

Willow Tit. *Parus montanus*. Rare straggler.

In 1926 Walter Stewart (*Scottish Naturalist* 1926) said: "In the Symington and Biggar districts it appears sporadically in winter and so also in the Medwin Water districts." In his *Pentland Walks,* R. A. Cochrane recorded the species (under the name Marsh Tit) breeding in 1918.

W. Evans found Willow Tits in mixed woods at Cockburnhill in September 1905, and W. T. Blackwood in the *History of Peeblesshire* (1925) said that Evans also saw the species in the West Linton district.

In 1934 Miss Rintoul saw one in the pine trees at Glencorse Reservoir on 23rd May. David Hamilton (1947) had never recorded it in the Pentlands.

Coal Tit. *Parus ater*. Resident. Breeds.

In winter the Coal Tit is normally found in coniferous woods, but it also occurs in mixed woods, beech and other deciduous trees as well as among whins. As many of the pinewoods are shelter belts on the hill slopes, Coal Tits are commoner on the high ground than the other Tits. They are less commonly found along the Water of Leith and in hedgerows. Some of the high woods are deserted in winter. After the breeding season local wandering takes place, when parties extend their habitat. At this time they are often seen among the willows at Bavelaw.

William Evans knew of Coal Tits in Redford Wood prior to its being felled in 1919-20.

The total 1932-34 census figures were: 17 in March, 56 plus in September and 65 plus in December. During the 1948-49 traverse Coal Tits vacated some high woods early in October and did not return until late March.

In 1971 R. L. Swann said of Threipmuir: "Seen in good numbers throughout the year, mainly in Redford Wood. Numerous pairs breed."

G. L. Sandeman has breeding records at Harelaw on 7th May 1974 and East Rig Wood on 12th June 1975. He found at that time also that at the Glencorse Valley numbers rose in early August and dropped again at the end of September.

Blue Tit. *Parus caeruleus.* Common resident. Breeds.

The Blue Tit is considerably commoner than the Great Tit, with a wider distribution. It normally deserts the high ground in winter, and is then found at low level plantations, along road and field hedges, in treerows, in gardens, along the Water of Leith, at stackyards, in whins, among the willows at Bavelaw, and at rubbish tips. Its range is more restricted during the breeding season, and after breeding it roams in family parties, often with Great Tits and other passerines. There seems little indication of migration.

The total 1932-34 census figures were: 48 in March, 45 in September and 90 plus in December. There were no significant changes in numbers during the 1948-49 traverse.

In 1971 R. L. Swann said of Threipmuir: "Seen throughout the year with maximum numbers in winter. A few pairs probably breed."

On 16th September 1985 there were thirty-nine at Threipmuir.

Great Tit. *Parus major.* Common resident. Breeds.

In winter the Great Tit is usually found low down in the hills where thick cover exists: in house gardens, low woods (both coniferous and deciduous), hedges, along the Water of Leith, and at low lying farmyards. The species also nests in such places, but exceptionally also in high woods. After the nesting season families wander and may then be found in places where the species does not nest, for example in the willows at Bavelaw, and in young plantations. There is no evidence of migration.

In May 1934 Rintoul and Baxter saw Great Tits in a garden at Carlops, and in birch trees at the North Esk Reservoir. In 1947 David Hamilton said: "The Great Tit nests in most woods on lower ground. I have seen the nest in the wall round Glencorse Reservoir."

The 1932-34 census records were March 17, September 56 and December 65.

In 1971 R. L. Swann said of Threipmuir: "Seen throughout the year in small numbers. Probably breeds."

There is a record of no fewer than seventy having been seen between Juniper Green and Balerno on 29th December 1982.

Treecreeper. *Certhia familiaris.* Resident. Breeds.

The Treecreeper can be found wherever there are trees, either coniferous or deciduous, and even on the willows at Bavelaw; but it is nowhere numerous and can easily be overlooked.

The total 1932-34 census results were none in March, four in September and four in December. In 1947 David Hamilton said: "The species breeds in many of the Pentland woods on lower ground." He had seen a nest in a tree at Glencorse Reservoir, and one creeping on a wall at Bonaly Tower. During the 1948-49 traverse the species was found as high as the Cap Law and Braid Law woods even in winter.

G. L. Sandeman has seen Treecreepers with young in 1949 and 1970 in the Glencorse valley. On 1st July 1975 he found breeding birds at Bavelaw Castle and Redford Plantation. He said of the Glencorse Valley: "One or two seen throughout the year, probably resident" (from 1946 to 1949).

ORIOLES

Golden Oriole. *Oriolus oriolus.* Very rare.

There are two early records. On 11th April 1937 Mr W. Short said of a bird at Carlops: "I was able to obtain a splendid view of the bird as it sat on a dyke on the opposite side of the road . . . a visit to the Royal Scottish Museum proved it undoubtedly to be the Golden Oriole." In 1951 there was another record from Hillend Public Park (*Edinburgh Bird Bulletin*): "A male with such a passion for biscuit crumbs that it almost allowed itself to be caught by hand . . . all this in the presence of a large crowd. . . . The bird's previous history appears extremely doubtful."

SHRIKES

Red-backed Shrike. *Lanius collurio.* Very rare.

The *Old Statistical Account for Colinton Parish* (1791) records it as the Butcher Bird without being more specific.

Great Grey Shrike. *Lanius excubitor.* Rare vagrant.
There are some old records from W. Evans:

1885	February 21st	One shot about the middle of January
1886	October 30th	One seen near Colzium by Peter Adair
1888	November 21st	One seen at Glencorse kennels by Wood the Gamekeeper

More recent records are:

1966	November 26th	Den's Cleuch	One
	December 4th	Threipmuir	One
1967	January 4th and 5th	Glencorse	One

CROWS AND THEIR ALLIES

Jay. *Garrulus garrulus.* Rare visitor.

In the *Scottish Naturalist* of 1875-76 Lumsden wrote: "Lt.-Col. Wedderburn in his list of the birds found at Rosslyn and neighbourhood marks the Jay as a common species. But it is rather rare in other districts. . . . In Linlithgowshire it has very much decreased in numbers during the last 20 or 25 years: for at one time I am informed, it was a comparatively common bird in the county, and now is rarely seen. In the upper ward of Lanarkshire the Jay is decidedly local, and in Peeblesshire the Jay is and has been for some time very rare in this county." In the Midlothian parish of West Calder two or three pairs were still nesting in 1886.

Writing of the Jay in the Forth area, W. Evans remarks: "Once a well known resident in every County in the area the Jay is now through persecution only a rare and uncertain straggler" (*Birds of Midlothian*).

A pair was shot at Baddinsgill in April 1932, and another pair at the same place on 20th April 1933, which looks as though Jays were attempting to re-establish themselves (Rintoul and Baxter 1935).

David Hamilton never saw the Jay in the Pentlands during his many years of birdwatching there.

Magpie *Pica pica.* Resident. Breeds.

The Magpie is still rather commoner on the north slopes of the Pentlands than on the south. It is apparently sedentary, there being no marked difference in distribution between winter and summer, except that in winter it tends to keep closer to the shelter of woods and hedgerows, and the higher plantations on the hill slopes, and also in the deciduous wooded lowland country. It is also present in hedgerows, isolated woods, and on both heather and grass moorland. Here it is sometimes seen at some distance from trees, or in fact any sort of cover. I have seen a Magpie at the Bore Stane at a height of 1300 feet.

During the winter the species is often recorded in groups, and occasionally in flocks of over twenty birds. Where undisturbed it nests freely in the woods and plantations, both coniferous and deciduous, and also along the treerows. While the Magpie is a well known Pentland bird, the total population cannot be great, as it is frequently shot, trapped or poisoned as vermin.

In 1882 Harold Raeburn found a nest in the T Wood and on 23rd April found three nests in Scots pine beside the road at Harperrig. He also notes on the same day that there were a great many Magpies about. In 1891 Evans described the status in Peeblesshire as decreasing throughout the district where it was formerly common. He said: "It still occasionally breeds with us." In 1928 Stewart, writing of Lanarkshire, records that "The higher grounds of . . . Carnwath have a few scattered pairs." In 1938 Mr Blackwood writes: "Practically unknown in Peeblesshire. An odd bird was occasionally seen in the Broughton-Biggar area."

The total census figures of 1932-34 were five in March, four in September and nine in December.

In 1935 Rintoul and Baxter said: "The Magpie has for long been a common bird in Midlothian and West Lothian." John Prentice, gamekeeper at Baddinsgill, said that in 1934 Magpies were common in low woods there, and in 1935 we find the species described by Rintoul and Baxter as: "Fairly common round Edinburgh at Colinton and Balerno. Gatherings of over a dozen are often seen."

In 1947 David Hamilton said that Magpies were common along the west side of the Pentlands from Bonaly to Crosswood.

During the 1948-49 traverse Magpies were seen on all but seven occasions out of forty-eight outings. They were not present in the high woods, but on five occasions parties of more than ten were seen on low ground.

Chough. *Pyrrhocorax pyrrhocorax.* One record.

A Chough was shot about 1872 by James Culloch on Leadlaw Hill near Stoneypath and given to Mr Porteous, late landlord of Townhead Hotel, Peebles, who got it stuffed in Penicuik.

Jackdaw. *Corvus monedula.* Resident. Possibly winter visitor.

The Jackdaw is largely sedentary in the area, with no noticeable migration taking place. In winter the species frequents the hamlets and low lying agricultural ground, often in small flocks, being particularly common along the urban stretches of the Water of Leith, but is not normally found on the hills or high ground. At this season it roosts socially with Rooks outside the area. In the breeding season the Jackdaw may be found nesting; either as single pairs on houses, on ruined buildings and in holes in trees; or in small colonies, often at a rookery. The railway embankment at Juniper Green Station is a favourite place. Jackdaws do not normally breed at the high farms and houses, but several colonies have been found in rabbit burrows and in holes in the ground on Mendick hill at a height of about 1200 feet.

In May and June Jackdaws often frequent grassy hill slopes, in company with Rooks. After breeding they leave the high colonies, and occur more often in open agricultural country. Jackdaws are frequently seen on stubble in company with Rooks. The species has been recorded on the reservoir mudflats in September.

In 1934 Rintoul and Baxter said: "They are distributed over every different kind of country, being numerous and on the hillsides in the Pentlands." Miss Rintoul, again in 1934, considered that Jackdaws were nesting in burrows at Braid Law Wood on 25th May, while Walter Stewart (*Scottish Naturalist* 1927) notes Dunsyre Hill, and several small colonies round Dolphinton in burrows.

The total 1932-34 census records indicate that in March the species is uncommon away from villages. Only seven were seen in March. In September nineteen were seen and in December eighty-two, which suggests that there may be winter visitors then, but flocks are much more frequent in winter and this can give a wrong impression of relative abundance.

During the 1948-49 traverse the species was not recorded from high up in the hills.

In 1971 David Hamilton said that the Jackdaw "Is a common bird breeding freely especially along the Water of Leith, but also all round the foot of the Pentlands, in ruins, trees, railway embankments, etc."

John Prentice, gamekeeper at Baddinsgill, told me that he did not see Jackdaws very often on the hills there.

There are some recent records of autumn flocks as below:

1982	August 16th	Castlelaw	100
1983	September 9th	Flotterstone	266
1984	October 30th	Threipmuir	90

Torphin Quarry is now (1985) a favourite nesting site with eighty-five birds present there on 13th March.

Rook. *Corvus frugilegus.* Common resident. Breeds.

During the winter months the Rook may be seen in flocks of up to 1000 or more birds, often associated with Jackdaws, on all types of agricultural land. The species is very sociable at this season, and therefore there are not many flocks present, indeed the Rook may be absent from considerable areas of apparently suitable feeding grounds. The reason is that these flocks may start moving towards their winter roost as early as mid morning, and as the main roosts are outside the Pentland area, it is not uncommon to search in vain for Rooks in the afternoon. During most of the winter rookeries are visited daily, but when darkness falls, all the Pentland Rooks are safely gathered at the winter roosts.

The roosts in use in 1970/71 were as below:

Lanarkshire	Carstairs House, Spittal Farm, Biggar
Midlothian	Borthwick Church, Dalmahoy Hill
Peeblesshire	Burnhead Farm, Eddleston, Felton Farm, Dolphinton

Early in March the birds normally begin sleeping at their rookeries.

After the breeding season, from about June to September, the Rooks wander in small parties, and have been recorded from ground not visited at any other season. There are moorland records of birds feeding high up on Carnethy, at the Wolf Craigs, and even on the summit of King Seat at 1500 feet. The reservoirs too are visited more often at this time than during the rest of the year. Apart from the West Linton rookery which is in pines at a height of about 850 feet, the rookeries lie below 650 feet above sea level. The Water of Leith valley is a favourite breeding area.

The Rook has been numerous in the Lothians and Peeblesshire for many years as this extract from the *Agricultural Survey of Peeblesshire* published in 1802 shows: "Crows which everyone is allowed to destroy at pleasure, occasion much more damage to the crops than the whole tribe of game animals put together." In 1837 Macgillivray commented: "The vicinity of Edinburgh seems specially favourable to Rooks, for go where you will at all seasons of the year and in all sorts of weather, you will find them scattered over the fields. They shun the barren moorland and hill districts. . . . The nests are mostly placed in deciduous trees, those most favoured in Midlothian being Oak, Elm, and Beech, and many colonies are found in clumps of trees close to human dwellings. When the young are fledged they resort to the neighbouring fields with their parents, who for some time continue to feed them".

The 1932-34 census figures were 22 in March, 328 in September, and 546 in December. All these figures are totals. In 1934 the status of the Rook at Baddinsgill was given by John Prentice the gamekeeper as "Abundant on low ground. When Rook shooting starts the birds move out of harm's way onto the hills."

During the 1948-49 traverse there was an interesting extension of habitat on 30th May; parties of twenty to thirty were seen on grass fields as usual, but some also on hillsides. On 30th June such parties were present on hillsides, even as high as 1600 to 1700 feet. By the 18th July the habit had ceased and no Rooks were seen on the higher hills.

During the period 1981-1984 the number of nests in the

Castlelaw rookery varied from 153 to 203, but in 1986 the Castlelaw figures for breeding pairs were given as 1984, 211; 1985, 236 and 1986, 251. In 1981 a count of the Rooks and Jackdaws at the Dalmahoy winter roost gave a figure of 15500.

Carrion Crow. *Corvus corone.* Resident. Breeding.

The Carrion Crow is a common resident in the Pentlands. While occasional small flocks are present on high ground in winter, the species is more restricted both in numbers and range at this season. It tends to be more often seen on cultivated ground, and among the lower wood strips where food is no doubt more easily obtained. In 1947 there was a winter roost in the wood strips above Woodhouselee, which housed over 150 birds. This roost appeared to serve an area lying to the north and east, but it seemed likely that Pentland Carrions also used it.

During the breeding season the species is well distributed from the Water of Leith and cultivated ground, to the highest woods, and despite constant persecution it breeds freely and successfully. In autumn family parties or small flocks are often to be seen foraging, and at this season the species is occasionally found in company with Rooks, especially on the verges of the reservoirs, but, for the most part, it is not gregarious.

In the *Zoologist* of 1894 Harold Raeburn said: "Far from being scarce the Carrion Crow is quite a common bird in all the Southern Scottish Counties . . . Edinburgh, Linlithgow . . . Peebles. It is a curious fact, and one that almost leads to the idea that the black Crow is pushing northwards, and that the real Hooded Crow was once the prevalent form in the Scottish lowlands, that by gamekeepers, shepherds, and country people generally in that district the black Crow *Corvus corone* is invariably called a 'Hoodie'."

Later observers agree that the species remains common. In 1933 J. Kirke Nash wrote: "Resident and to some extent migratory it is by no means rare in Midlothian, breeding in many of the small plantations on the moorland slopes of the Pentlands." The total census figures for 1932-34 were 55 in March, 66 in September and 44 in December. Rintoul and Baxter said that the species nested in considerable numbers in the woods about the Pentlands. They saw a pair or two nesting in high patches of wood in the hills between Carlops and the North Esk Reservoir in 1934, and saw the species in the highest wood between Carlops and the Bore Stane at 1500 feet. In the same year John Prentice, gamekeeper at Baddinsgill, said of the Baddinsgill area: "The species is abundant. Sometimes seen in packs."

During the 1948-49 traverse a flock of sixty plus was seen on a hillside above Westside on 21st November, and G. L. Sandeman noted that there was normally an increase in the Flotterstone numbers from October to mid March.

Hooded Crow. *Corvus cornix*. Once common. Now rare.

There was at one time a large influx of wintering Hoodies but this has practically ceased. While occasional hybrids can still be seen, particularly in low lying areas, there is no doubt that the Hoodie is now rarer in the Pentlands than the Raven. Single birds are most frequently seen, and hybrids showing varying amounts of grey are as often seen as pure grey individuals. The Hoodie is of course considered to be conspecific with the Carrion.

The earliest record of the Hoodie in the Pentlands appears to be in the late 1880s. Mr Stewart wrote in the *Scottish Naturalist* of 1928: "About the same period (late 1880s) in the Cairns Castle, Causewayend, and Crosswoodhill districts we saw newly shot Grey Crows in July . . . in more recent times we have heard of Grey Crows nesting in the Dolphinton district, and the shooting of young Grey Crows in August is vouched for, but when the matter came to be thoroughly sifted we could find no authentic instance of these Crows nesting, indeed we have not seen a pure Grey Crow in the County (Lanarkshire) between the dates of 1st April and 1st October. A winter visitor to Lanarkshire, remnants of two geographical sections of the Grey Crow meet within the county's borders. From North West Europe comes the larger or main section, the route of penetration being along the Pentland Hills into Dunsyre, Carnwath, Walston and Biggar." In 1894 Harold Raeburn followed on saying: "In all the southern counties with which I am acquainted . . . Edinburgh, Linlithgow . . . Peebles . . . the Hooded Crow is merely occasional and sporadic. . . . I have seen hybrids killed at the nest in the County of Edinburgh, but the gamekeeper considered them very uncommon." In 1898 a Carrion/Hoodie hybrid was shot from the nest near Listonshiels. Its mate appeared typical Carrion.

No Hoodies were seen during the 1932-34 census outings.

Iain Ogilvie found about six in Windy Gowl on 2nd November 1935.

In 1946 G. L. Sandeman saw three at Dreghorn on 30th April, and D. G. Andrew noted in the *Edinburgh Bird Bulletin:* "In the Colinton area I doubt if as much as a quarter of the breeding stock are pure Carrion Crows. The remainder vary from several apparently pure bred Hoodies through a whole range of intermediate plumages. Odd birds (Hybrids) certainly occur throughout the Pentlands."

All of David Hamilton's records between 1910 and 1947 fall between October and February, the maximum number being six on the Black Hill-Logan Valley area on 16th February 1913, and he had no knowledge of the Hoodie breeding.

No Hoodies were seen during the 1948-49 traverse. One was seen at Dreghorn Mains on 3rd February 1985.

Raven. *Corvus corax.* Occasional, usually in winter. Has bred.

It is tempting to assume that because the Raven was common in the streets of Edinburgh in the late 16th century, it nested among the Pentlands at that time. Indeed the several Raven's Cleuchs and Corby Hill lend support to that assumption, but there appear to be no early historical records of nesting, and the lack of suitable cliffs and trees makes it probable that Ravens did not nest regularly in late historical times.

In 1837 Macgillivray notes that: "In the middle part of Scotland it is of much rarer occurrence . . . although I have seen it in many places," and he mentions the Pentlands as one of these.

There is a record from the 1932-34 census of two Ravens having been seen on 10th September. In 1934 John Prentice, gamekeeper at Baddinsgill, said: "A pair may be seen all the year round on the Pentlands, usually on ground south-west of the Bore Stane Pass." He mentioned that none nested to his knowledge, but that Mr Smith, the Bavelaw gamekeeper, had told him that a nest was found about 1924 on the ruin of a shooting box south of Listonshiels.

David Hamilton told me in 1947 that his records over the previous sixty years show that he had normally seen the Raven only during the winter months, and as single birds or in pairs.

On the traverse of 1948-49 Ravens were seen on five occasions. There were two pairs on Cap Law on 22nd February; and the other sightings were on 29th February, 25th April, 24th October and 26th December 1948.

After the prolonged heavy snow of spring 1947 there was evidence that Ravens attempted to nest in that year. Two large nests were found above Loganlea Reservoir, and the shepherd there told me that a pair of Ravens was seen about the ravine in which one of the nests was present. On the same day (11th May) two Ravens were seen in Den's Cleuch, in much the same district. Both nests were unfortunately incomplete, and it is possible that the birds were disturbed.

In 1966 A. Ramsay recorded (*Edinburgh Natural History Newsletter* 1966): "For the first time for a number of years a pair of Ravens have built a nest and by 13th March one bird was sitting on six eggs. Sadly these disappeared between 19th and 26th March."

In 1970 G. L. Sandeman saw a Raven at Castlelaw on 18th November. Ravens are sometimes seen between April and September. No doubt the Peeblesshire breeding birds visit the Pentlands at this time when carrion may be expected during the lambing season. It is possible also that some of these records refer to a post-breeding movement of Ravens nesting outside the area. A young Raven ringed in Dumfriesshire on 15th April 1932 was recovered at West Linton on 17th November 1932.

One was seen at Bavelaw on 15th March 1981, and in the same year two were recorded at Harperrig on 14th September. Two Ravens were seen on the Pentlands on 19th April 1986 and the *Scottish Bird Report* for that year recorded that this was the first Lothian sighting since 1981.

STARLINGS

Starling. *Sturnus vulgaris*. Resident. Summer visitor. Breeds.
　　Winter visitor. Migrant.

In winter the Starling deserts some high farms and may then be found in small numbers in hamlets and at low lying farms and isolated houses. However it is also often seen in flocks of up to some hundreds wherever a concentration of food exists in more open country. Some of these flocks may be composed of winter visitors from outside the area. Pasture fields are a favourite feeding ground, but dunged fields, topped turnip fields, and even hill slopes are visited. In such places the Starling is often associated with other species, of which Redwing, Fieldfare, Golden Plover, Lapwing, Chaffinches and Greenfinches are the commonest.

Such winter flocks may continue until early April when other Starlings are already nesting. There are also records of flocks after the breeding season.

The Starling breeds freely at the farms and houses in the area, in holes in trees, under bridges and in ruins; and it is particularly common along the Water of Leith. Many high nesting sites are deserted after the young have flown; and the species may then be found in parties, not only in normal winter habitats but also on the reservoir shores, on stubble fields, cut hay, bracken, and even bare hillsides. Some post-breeding parties may be composed almost entirely of young birds. In 1977 for example a flock of about 7000 was seen at West Water Reservoir on 10th July and was mostly composed of juveniles.

At the beginning of the nineteenth century the Starling was absent or very rare in the Pentlands. Mr Evans found the first pair to breed at Oxgangs Farm in 1846 when one was shot and considered a rarity, but he added that they were common there in the 1860s, and also at Comiston, Buckstone, and elsewhere in this neighbourhood.

In 1895 Dr Harvie Brown mentioned the great increase of the Starling in Midlothian within his time. By 1928 J. Kirke Nash described the species as being: "A familiar bird from the hills to the coast . . . after the nesting period Starlings young and old betake themselves to the open fields and pastures joining in flocks which are greatly augmented during the winter months through the influx of migrating birds."

In 1931 David Hamilton, writing of Listonshiels on 7th June said: "Considerable numbers observed. The flocks consisted of adult birds and also great numbers of this year's young birds — one flock we estimated to comprise over 300 birds, and there were several groups. The ground they were confining their attention to was a large tract of rough grass, very marshy, with numerous patches of reeds, moss and heather. That the Starling is now too numerous is generally acknowledged, and something will soon have to be done to reduce their numbers, if only to save other species.''

The 1932-34 census numbers were 542 in March, 318 in September and 481 in December. In 1934 John Prentice said of Baddinsgill: "sometimes seen in huge packs, but not on the hills".

In 1939 the date of return to the hill farms and isolated houses where the species was considered as a summer visitor only, varied from 11th February at West Bavelaw and Medwinbank to mid-April at Fairliehope and Middle Kenleith.

In 1947 David Hamilton described its status as common, breeding everywhere. During the 1948-49 traverse the nesting pair at West Bavelaw did not return until 25th March. On 18th July there was a pack of fifty to sixty on heather at the Hare Hill summit path. Starlings were then not seen at all from 15th August to the end of September except in Colinton, the hills being deserted. In 1949 there was an increase on 28th March and 3rd April which suggested passage.

On 17th July 1983 there was a huge flock at the West Water Reservoir estimated as 11500 plus birds.

SPARROWS

House Sparrow. *Passer domesticus.* Resident. Summer visitor. Breeds.

The House Sparrow is such a well-known bird about houses and farms that it seems curious at first to find it absent from some of the more remote buildings on the Pentlands. I have no records for example from Craigenterrie, West Bavelaw, or Westside. The presence of House Sparrows particularly in winter appears to depend on food supply. Some of the higher farms and isolated houses where the species breeds are deserted in winter; but wherever stackyards or other sources of food exist, the Sparrow winters. It finds shelter during rough weather in barns, stables or other farm buildings, and may then easily be overlooked, as is also the case when it travels a short distance from habitations to feed. A pair of House Sparrows which used to nest at the Glencorse waterkeeper's house and roost in the thick ivy on the house wall, were not always to be seen during daylight hours near the house.

There is a record of Sparrows roosting under the Harperrig Reservoir outflow bridge during September. After the breeding season flocks visit the cornfields, feeding among the standing grain and stubble, often with flocks of Finches, or move a short distance along hedgerows to nearby plantations or to rubbish tips.

The 1932-34 census figures were 118 in March, 157 in September and 165 in December.

Now that modern farming methods have considerably reduced the number of hay and grain stacks at farms House Sparrows are becoming fewer, and now seem absent from East Rig and other farms on the north side of the hills.

Tree Sparrow. *Passer montanus.* Resident in small numbers.

Within recent times Tree Sparrows were most frequent along the Water of Leith and in the Swanston area. I have records from East Kenleith, Woodhall, Middle Kenleith, John's Burn, Upper Dene Park, Bonaly Tower, Oxgangs, and at the outskirts of Colinton, but its status appears to vary considerably from year to year.

Neither Macgillivray nor Jardine recorded the Tree Sparrow near Edinburgh. In 1895 W. Eagle Clarke saw a small flock feeding with Greenfinches in stubble at Comiston, and noted that the species had not hitherto been recorded from the county. J. Kirke Nash however put the date of the first Tree Sparrow in Midlothian at 1882, and went on to say: "Since this time (1912) I have been familiar with it . . . in the valley of the Water of Leith." The Misses Rintoul and Baxter recorded: "About 1918 it began to increase," and quoted David Hamilton as having found it nesting in the grounds at Dreghorn Castle. David Hamilton wrote: "Although recorded in the vicinity over thirty years ago the Tree Sparrow up to 1912 was by no means a familiar bird near Edinburgh. . . . During the last ten years it has gradually become more numerous and at the present time (1928) it can be met with almost any day. . . . On the road from Braid Hills to Carlops birds have been observed at Comiston House, Lothian

Burn, Hillend and at farms out to Flotterstone. They occur on the Water of Leith and on farms out to Balerno and beyond.''

David Hamilton had these notes:

1915	May 15th	Nested at Dreghorn and Harelaw Farm
1928	August 4th	Nested at Dreghorn
1931	February 28th	Recorded Juniper Green
1932	January 24th	Recorded Currie and Colinton
	November 17th	Recorded Currie Kirk

Tree Sparrows were only seen once on the nine census outings 1932-34 on 25th March. During the traverse of 1948-49 again there was only one record, one being seen on 30th May in Fernilaw Avenue, Colinton.

G. L. Sandeman has these records:

1949	July 5th	Glencorse valley. Recorded
1968	June 13th	Nine Mile Burn to North Esk Reservoir. Nest with young in beech tree
1971	March 18th	East Rig and West Rig. Recorded
	April 1st	East Rig and West Rig. Eight
	April 15th	Castlelaw Farm. Breeding
1972	October 5th	Harperrig Water House. One
1973	September 4th	Lothianburn. Twenty plus
1974	February 18th	Swanston Burn. Ten to twenty
	March 19th	Leithhead Farm. About twenty
1975	April 18th	Lothianburn. Twelve
	June 5th	Glencorse valley. One

In 1971 R. L. Swann said of Threipmuir: ''Only a few winter records.''

There are the following recent records:

1980	February 10th	Threipmuir. Fifteen
1981	November 28th	Flotterstone. Seventeen
1982	January 13th	Swanston. Twelve

FINCHES

Chaffinch. *Fringilla coelebs*. Resident. Breeds. Winter visitor. Passage migrant.

In winter the Chaffinch can be found between October and March in flocks of up to several hundred on top dressed fields, stubble, or places where there are concentrations of food. Here its usual companions are Greenfinches, and a few Yellowhammers and Bramblings. Farmyards and rubbish tips are other favourite haunts, but here the flocks are usually smaller. Although flocks sometimes occur in open fields, it is more usual to find them close to trees, bushes or hedges, to which they fly if disturbed.

The winter flocks usually arrive towards the end of October or early November, and leave at the end of March or early in April. The status is complicated by flocks in September and April. These may well be composed of birds on passage, or in the autumn by resident families forming loose flocks where food is plentiful. Such flocks are smaller as a rule than the winter ones.

Many of the high woods and shelter belts are completely deserted in winter. In low breeding areas song restarts about the middle of February, but it is fully a month later before the high woods are colonised. When the full breeding population is present the Chaffinch is widely distributed, breeding freely even in small high isolated woods, but I have not found it at the Bore Stane Wood.

In 1881 Harold Raeburn found a nest in the T Wood, and in 1935 J. Kirke Nash said: "It is well distributed and common in Midlothian. . . . In winter it associates largely with Bramblings in the top dressed fields. It is also a frequent visitor to the farmyard during hard weather."

The 1932-34 census figures were 327 in March, 135 in September and 573 in December in total. In 1934 Rintoul and Baxter found Chaffinches common in all woods between Carlops and North Esk Reservoir, and plentiful wherever there were trees up to 1386 ft.

During the 1948-49 traverse the fluctuating status of the Chaffinch was plainly shown: on 15th February there was a little short song in Braid Law Wood, but none there on 29th February, nor was there any song in Cap Law Wood up to 14th March. By 28th March however woods were fully colonised, and on 30th

May the Chaffinch was the commonest bird in all the woods, singing freely in all the highest woods.

By 10th October the autumn withdrawal was in full swing, and the species was almost absent from the high woods. There was a flock of 100 plus at Bavelaw Mill. On 13th February in the following year Chaffinches were much more noticeable even in Braid Law Wood, but a cold spell then arrived and on 27th February there had been a setback to colonisation. On 24th April breeding areas were well occupied, but there was a flock at Middle Threipmuir, possibly of migrants.

G. L. Sandeman's notes up to 1975 gave the status of the Chaffinch in the Glencorse Valley as: "Noted throughout the year. Territories were occupied about the beginning of March, with a decrease after mid August, and there were very few Chaffinches in September and October. Winter flocks were present from November to January, with very few birds present in February due to the normal hard weather."

Brambling. *Fringilla montifringilla.* Winter visitor in varying numbers.

The Brambling is a regular winter visitor to the Pentlands, but numbers vary greatly from year to year. It is not normally found in large flocks, but as it often joins the mixed winter flocks of Chaffinches and Greenfinches, it is sometimes difficult to count the precise number in each flock. Fifty Bramblings would count as a large flock. The normal feeding grounds are on stubble, plough, manured fields, and other arable ground where food may be found. It also occurs in stackyards and under beech trees where the fallen beech mast provides food. A favourite feeding ground lies to the north of Bavelaw Reservoir, where hedges fringe the fields, and to which the finch flocks fly if disturbed. Another much frequented place is at the beech strip at Marchbank.

Bramblings normally arrive in October and leave by the third week of March, although there are some April records. The total number of Bramblings in the Pentlands in any year is probably not great.

In 1837 Macgillivray mentioned that he only once saw the species in the Edinburgh district, which suggests that the Brambling was not common at that time. In 1845 the *New*

Statistical Account for Scotland mentions Bramblings on the list of birds for Colinton Parish.

One was seen at Swanston on 13th October 1898, and on 8th March 1899 there is another record from Fairmilehead. William Evans recorded that Bramblings were numerous in the vicinity of Edinburgh during the severe winters of 1860-61 and 1874-75. Among other Pentland records, he saw a flock of 30-40 in trees and stubble on the north side of Clubbiedean on 15th November 1907, and another flock of fifty to sixty at the Water of Leith above Ravelrig in March 1909. He also saw a male at Oxgangs Farm in April 1908.

J. Kirke Nash wrote (1935): "Large flocks are occasionally seen in the Lothians, but it is not a species that comes much under observation. The bird may be looked for in the vicinity of beech trees bordering the fields." He also noted that Bramblings were plentiful in Midlothian during the winter of 1928-29.

David Hamilton in addition to winter records over the period from 1908 to 1947, saw twenty birds at Listonshiels as late as 3rd April 1932. Only one Brambling was seen during the nine census outings 1932-34.

G. L. Sandeman saw Bramblings in the Glencorse valley during the years 1946-49. His records ranged between 20th March and 22nd April in spring, and the earliest and latest winter records were 10th October and 15th December. He tells me that in some winters he has seen large flocks at Harperrig. He saw a party of twenty plus at East Rig road on 1st April 1971, and a large flock of 300-400 at Leithhead Farm on 19th March 1974.

In 1971 R. L. Swann said of Threipmuir: "An occasional winter visitor, flocks of up to ten birds present."

In 1986 there was a flock of 220 birds at Threipmuir on 4th January, and on 22nd January 1987, 220 were seen at Threipmuir.

Greenfinch. *Carduelis chloris.* Resident. Breeding. Winter visitor.

Owing perhaps to the lack of suitable shrubberies, gardens and hedges, the Greenfinch is not an abundant breeding bird, but it is common locally, particularly along the Water of Leith. After breeding they often frequent grainfields where they have been seen attacking the standing ears.

Both J. Kirke Nash (1935) and Rintoul and Baxter (1935) described the Greenfinch as being a common bird in the Lothians, but made no specific mention of its status in the Pentlands. Our 1932-34 census figures were 61 in March, 84 in September and 729 plus in December. During the 1948-49 traverse it was 14th March before a Greenfinch appeared in Braid Law Wood, and 25th April before the species was well distributed, but even then not in Cap Law Wood. None was seen on either 15th or 22nd August, and by 12th September there was a flock of fifty to a hundred at Bavelaw Mill. Then from 23rd January to 27th February no Greenfinch was seen, but on 17th April my note was that they were astonishingly common.

In the 1970s G. L. Sandeman found that in the Glencorse Valley the breeding birds came in about the third week of March in a flock and were singing by mid April. There seemed to be a post-breeding influx in the middle of July, and Greenfinches were not seen after August until the wintering birds arrived in November and stayed until February.

We have found in general that wintering flocks normally appear towards the end of October in numbers of up to several hundred birds. At this time they frequent arable land (particularly stubble), stackyards, manured fields, or where livestock feeding pens have been set up. They are often in company with Chaffinches, Bramblings, Yellowhammers, Reedbuntings and House Sparrows. Such flocks may contain up to a hundred or more Greenfinches, and are often close to trees or hedgerows to which they fly on being disturbed. At this time of year the species is also found in smaller numbers in house gardens, bushes, hedgerows, and deciduous woods. It seems likely that in these places resident birds remain in winter. Winter visitors leave about the beginning of April.

Goldfinch. *Carduelis carduelis.* Resident in small numbers.
   Breeding.
   In the past the population has varied greatly.
   The *Old Statistical Account for Scotland* of 1791 recorded the Goldfinch as being present in Mid Calder Parish, but in 1837 Macgillivray describes it as being "very rare in the neighbourhood of Edinburgh in which I have never met with

more than a single flock". The first Pentland record appears to have been in 1897 when a pair was seen by Adair and Campbell in the plantations at Hunter's Tryst near Dreghorn. In 1905 one was caught by a birdcatcher near the Hillend-Carlops road.

Goldfinches were not seen during the 1932-34 census outings.

J. Kirke Nash said in 1935: "High farming has long made the bird scarce in the Lothians." David Hamilton (1947) had never seen the Goldfinch in the Pentlands over many years of birdwatching.

The species however showed signs of increase immediately before the 1939-45 war. Single birds were recorded at Glencorse Reservoir on 12th April 1939, and at Newmills, Balerno, on 23rd April 1939. There was a marked increase since that war as the following records show:

1946	February 24th	Harperrig. Three
	May 19th	Flotterstone. Two or three
	August 24th	Crosswood. Three
	September 21st	Dunsyre. Two
	November 10th	East Kenleith. Two

G. L. Sandeman has these records:

1947	December 6th	Glencorse Reservoir. Three
1948	April 3rd	Glencorse Ravine. Two
	July	Glencorse Ravine. Juvenile seen
	October 2nd	Kirkton. Two
1949	March 5th	Glencorse Ravine. Eight
	July 22nd	Glencorse Ravine. Two

Goldfinches were seen on five occasions during the 1948-49 traverse, at Harelaw and Nine Mile Burn in April, June, September, and January.

G. L. Sandeman commented that some Goldfinches were seen in the Glencorse valley between January and March 1946-49, and occasionally at other dates. R. L. Swann has these records from Threipmuir:

| 1965 | April 15th | Nine |
| | December 30th | Seven |

G. L. Sandeman has these further records:

1970	June 30th	Clubbiedean. Four probably nesting
1970 and 1971		Breeding at Glencorse Reservoir house
1971	April 1st	Bavelaw. Twelve
	March 11th	Harperrig. One
1972	November 22nd	Torduff. Nine
1973	June 21st	Clubbiedean and Dreghorn. Breeding
1974	January 3rd	Crosswood. Two
	February 1st	Harperrig. Seven
	March 4th	Harperrig Farm. Twelve
	September 27th	Harperrig. Eight
	October 14th	Harperrig. Three
	November 8th	Harperrig. One
	November 18th	Harperrig. Six
1975	December 15th	Harperrig Old Schoolhouse. Twelve
	January 20th	Dreghorn Polo Ground. Twenty
	October 30th	Dreghorn Polo Ground. Sixteen

Flocks were seen near Harperrig and Clubbiedean in October 1981.

It would appear that the Goldfinch is now largely a winter visitor to the Pentlands as the above and recent records shown below indicate:

1980	November 22nd	Crosswood. Thirty-six
1981	October 21st	Clubbiedean. One hundred
	October 30th	Wester Causewayend Farm. One hundred plus

Siskin. *Carduelis spinus.* Winter visitor. Possibly resident. Breeds.

It seems possible that a few Siskins may be resident in the Pentlands but there is little evidence to support this view. There are over the years a good many winter records and a few definite breeding records.

On 10th December 1905 Mr Evans reported a flock of five or

six at the lower end of Glencorse Reservoir, and on the 30th of the same month a flock of eight passing over Hillend in the direction of Roslin. He mentioned that a birdcatcher near Hillend said that Siskins had been very common that autumn. They appeared about the second week of November, and he had caught nearly fifty during the last two months there.

In 1935 J. Kirke Nash said: "The Siskin is an occasional winter visitor in Midlothian." However David Hamilton never saw the species.

On 22nd November 1936 six were seen on alder trees at Mansfield Farm, and one was seen also near the farm in the copse on the west side of the road on 25th November 1944. On 3rd November 1946 a flock of eight to ten was seen between Dolphinton and Garvald House. During the summer of 1946 Siskins were found in small numbers at Lynedale, and in the Glencorse Reservoir ravine under conditions that suggested breeding. Here at least one pair was seen in July, September, October, November, and in April and May of the following year, but no nests or young birds were found. The waterkeeper at Glencorse Reservoir said in 1946 that they bred there.

Breeding was recorded from Bonaly Tower in 1976.

During the 1948-49 traverse the species was recorded in both Braid Law and Cap Law Woods from April to August, and was probably breeding. On 12th November 1950 R. A. Blake saw a flock of about 100, with Lesser Redpolls, Goldfinches, and Bullfinches, at Buteland.

G. L. Sandeman has these records at about this time:

1948	March 26th	Glencorse Ravine. Recorded until end of July
	May 8th	Glencorse Ravine. Six
1949	March 19th to 17th September	Recorded

In 1964 during June, July and September, Siskins were singing at Harelaw Reservoir and at Hillend. In 1967 five were seen between Flotterstone and Glencorse Reservoir on 27th September, and seven on 24th December.

G. L. Sandeman has these further records:

1971	February 1st	Logan Cottage. Thirty plus
	January 13th	Logan Cottage. Thirty-forty
	April 1st	East Rig Plantation. Twenty
1972	April 21st	Logan Cottage. Fourteen
1974	November 13th	Redford Plantation. Thirteen

There are some records of breeding between 1980 and 1984 as below:

1980	Bonaly. One pair
1982	Flotterstone/Glencorse. Two pairs
	Bonaly. Four pairs
1983	Harelaw. Noted as breeding
1984	Threipmuir/Harelaw. Three birds on 15th July

The species was described as widespread in the Pentlands between the end of March and May 1982.

In 1985 a marked midsummer movement was noted all over Britain. In the Pentlands seven were seen at Bavelaw on 7th July. In 1986 singing males were recorded at Glencorse Reservoir, Loganlee and Threipmuir.

Linnet. *Carduelis cannabina.* Resident. Breeds. Winter visitor.

Despite the Linnet being abundant on the Braid Hills, it is distinctly local in the Pentlands. During October to March the species may be seen in flocks, usually small, but occasionally containing up to at least a hundred birds. In dry winters the muddy exposed reservoir beds are a favourite feeding ground, but Linnets are also seen on stubble (often with other Finches), on waste ground, along hedges and ditches, among the whins at Torduff and Swanston, and sometimes at farmyards. Its range becomes wider from April to June, but (probably owing to lack of suitable whin areas) it is nowhere common. From time to time disastrous fires reduce the whin growths, and those, with destruction for farming particularly in the Glencorse Valley, reduce nesting areas. It seems curious however that many apparently suitable whin patches are not occupied for nesting. During a walk from Woodhouselee to Castlelaw in 1936, a distance of about a mile, only three pairs were found in fairly extensive areas of whin 3-4 feet high.

Some favourite nesting areas are in the plantation at the top of Currie Kirk Brae, Hunter's Tryst Plantation, Swanston district, Howden Glen, Threipmuir Boathouse, Flotterstone to Glencorse whins, among the whins in the higher reaches of the Water of Leith, and rather thinly at some places on the south slopes of the hills.

The higher nesting areas are usually deserted between July and September but small flocks may be seen at the lower nesting places. There is at this time an extension of distribution, the birds being often seen in grainfields with other Finches, and dry reservoir beds are also much frequented.

There is no indication of migration either in spring or autumn.

In 1791 the *Old Statistical Account for Mid Calder Parish* mentions the Linnet. In 1837 Macgillivray records that a Linnet shot in the Pentlands on 23rd June had a bright red forehead (some individuals have rose red foreheads). David Hamilton saw the species at Hillend in December 1905, and found several nests at Torduff in 1921. He also saw numbers at Clubbiedean on 31st July 1932, and found a nest with young at Malleny in June 1935.

The total number of Linnets seen in the 1932-34 census was none in March, twelve in September and forty-six in December. In May 1934 Miss Rintoul found the Linnet common in the whins at Torduff, but in the *Fauna of the Forth* the Misses Rintoul and Baxter commented: "We were struck by the absence in the spring of 1934 from many apparently suitable nesting places round Carlops and about the Pentlands. Gorse patches which were, as far as we could see, entirely suitable, did not hold a single Linnet." In 1947 David Hamilton gave the Linnet's status as "Not very common. Small flocks during the winter months."

Linnets were recorded on every traverse outing in 1948-49 except that of 29th August. In 1971 R. L. Swann said of Threipmuir: "Seen throughout the year in small numbers."

G. L. Sandeman has these notes:

1971	January 26th	Bavelaw Mill	Fifty
1975	June 27th	Hillend Car Park	Breeding
	June 11th	Threipmuir Whins	Breeding

In 1984 there were several occasions where Linnets were seen in late summer, these were:

July 30th	Harperrig	Fifty plus
August 16th	Crosswood	Fifty plus
September 24th	Threipmuir	Sixty-eight

A count of seventy-four was made at Harperrig on 13th April 1985.

Twite. *Carduelis flavirostris.* Formerly rare winter visitor. A few
recent records.

It seems that last century the Twite was a rare winter visitor to the Pentlands. William Evans recorded that nine or ten were caught at Hillend in October 1884; Forty were seen on stubble above Comiston in November 1899, and a flock of twelve to eighteen flew over Bavelaw Moss in a westerly direction on 14th October 1904. The only other early record for the Pentlands comes from Harold Raeburn, who recorded Twites in the Medwyn district on 26th June 1890.

Rintoul and Baxter (*Vertebrate Fauna of the Forth* 1935) quoted Mr Serle as writing: "I have looked in vain for the Twite . . . on the Pentlands, but am told they are breeding birds there," and Mr Gunn as writing: "I have spent a considerable number of evenings in May and June every year for some time back bird hunting in the Pentlands, but I don't seem to have seen the Twite at all." J. Kirke Nash had no experience of the bird in Midlothian, and in the spring of 1934 Rintoul and Baxter did not see a Twite on the hills, nor had David Hamilton seen the species there.

In 1931 however P. L. E. Wood saw one at the Cauldstane Slap on 5th January, and on 10th April 1932 Donald Watson saw two at Bonaly Reservoir.

In 1980 there were two records, one at Glencorse on 15th April, and the other at Threipmuir on 28th November.

Redpoll. *Carduelis flammea.* The British race is resident in small
numbers. It is also a winter visitor.

The Redpoll can be seen in small numbers in winter, often close to its breeding area, which suggests that it is sedentary to some extent. However flocks of up to thirty birds have been seen at this season, so it is possible that some of these were migrants. The birds are often seen feeding on the ground, or on low growing plants. The willows and birches at Bavelaw are favourite places.

A marked extension of breeding range was noticed during the ten years prior to the 1939-45 war. The species was recorded under conditions that suggested breeding, at Redford Plantation, Bavelaw (in birch), Malleny Curling Pond (in birch), Hunter's Tryst Plantation (in pine), Crosswood, Slipperfield (in birch), Woodhouselee, Glencorse Reservoir, and Bonaly Plantation (in pine). Numbers have declined somewhat since the war, but Redpolls still breed in small numbers, where birches or young coniferous plantations exist. The age of such plantations affects their attractiveness as breeding areas, for the birds readily colonise any young coniferous plantations when the trees have grown above the undergrowth, and are less common as such plantations mature.

Early records from William Evans show that the species was breeding at Hillend in 1889, at Marchbank in 1900, and probably at Malleny Dam in 1906. In September 1884 thirteen were caught near Glencorse Reservoir. J. Kirke Nash observed it in Midlothian chiefly during the winter, and usually in small numbers (*Birds of Midlothian* 1935).

David Hamilton saw flocks on the lower slopes of the Pentlands in winter and by the Water of Leith. He found it nesting at Malleny Curling Pond in 1933 and 1936.

The total census figures of 1932-34 were none in March, one in September and twenty-one in December.

The *Scottish Naturalist* of 1935 records several nests in young birch at Balerno in 1933 and 1934. In 1935 nests were seen in several woods on the hills. During the 1948-49 traverse Redpolls were seen in Redford Wood, Harelaw Ravine, and Bavelaw Castle garden more or less throughout the year. On 12th November 1950 the species was seen at Buteland. R. L. Swann said of Threipmuir in 1971: "Seen all the year round. About five pairs nest in birches opposite Redford Wood." In 1973 G. L. Sandeman saw twenty at Harperrig on 30th October. In the *Edinburgh Ringing Group Report* of 1977, Derek Langslow said: "Observation and ringing evidence suggests that virtually all our

Redpolls winter in southern Britain or continental Europe. They return to the Lothians mainly in late April and early May, and depart again between mid-September and mid-October."

In 1981 between five and seven pairs bred between Flotterstone and Glencorse, and the following year there were many pairs at Bonaly. In 1984 between four and five pairs bred at Threipmuir/Harelaw, and some at Crosswood.

Breeding territories were noted in 1985 at Threipmuir and Flotterstone, and in 1986 there were three such territories at Threipmuir.

Mealy Redpoll. *Carduelis flammea.* Irregular winter visitor.

In the past the Mealy Redpoll was irregular as a winter visitor to the Lothians, although the flocks were sometimes large. In 1910 for example, William Evans said: "So far as the records show, it would appear that the invasion of 1910 has had few equals; if indeed it has not surpassed all others in magnitude at any rate in Scotland. . . . The number that came into the Forth area was quite phenomenal. . . . The movement was probably at its height in this district during the closing days of October . . . others took south westerly or inland courses, following roughly the valley of . . . the Water of Leith, but records from the south and west of Edinburgh are scanty. . . . Hillend at the eastern termination of the Pentlands (on several dates in November flocks of as many as thirty to seventy seen) . . . West Linton (reports of Redpolls about here in November probably refer to this species). . . . Fresh captures continued to come in plentifully till about the middle of November when they rapidly fell off, and by the end of the month had ceased entirely." David Hamilton told me in 1947 that he had never seen the species in his many years of walking over the Pentlands.

Derek Langslow in the *Edinburgh Ringing Group Report* for 1977 said: "The few Redpolls present in the Lothians in winter are mainly Mealy Redpolls, with a tiny proportion of the Lesser Redpolls from Scotland."

Crossbill. *Loxia curvirostra.* Sporadic visitor.

William Evans did not record the Crossbill from the Pentlands during the 1909 influx. P. W. Gunn however saw a number in a

fir wood at the north-east end of Harelaw Reservoir on 23rd
August 1930

David Hamilton had not seen Crossbills in the Pentlands over
many years up to 1947. R. L. Swann had two records from
Harelaw up to 1971: one on 13th June 1950, and the other of
about twenty on 16th May 1953.

In 1958 I. Balfour Paul, again at Harelaw, saw at least one on
13th June and a party of at least 20 on 19th July. On 3rd April
1966 two were seen at Glencorse Reservoir, and on 11th March
1973 some eight to ten were there also.

There were two records in 1983, both at Crosswood: six on 9th
January and one on 26th December.

There was an influx in 1985 and 1986 as the following records
show:

1985	March 25th	Crosswood	Four to six
	August 20th	Crosswood	Twenty
	October 30th	Crosswood	One
	November 18th	Bavelaw	Four
	December 18th	Crosswood	Twenty-two
		Harperrig	Six

G. L. Sandeman saw flocks of up to 100 at the Lang Whang
from December 1985 to March 1986, and in numbers between
eight and thirty-eight at Crosswood from May to September
1986. There were other 1986 records:

May 24th	Crosswood	A pair with three juveniles
January 26th	Harperrig	Seven
March 30th	Bavelaw	Four
April 9th	Bavelaw	One
July 12th	Bavelaw	Six

There was a maximum of 150 at Crosswood between 5th
January and 28th March 1986.

Bullfinch. *Pyrrhula pyrrhula*. Resident. Breeds.
The Bullfinch has a restricted range at all seasons because of
lack of suitable thick hedges, shrubberies, or young plantations,

but the species although local is by no means rare. In winter it is often seen in small parties of up to six, possibly family groups, but occasionally as many as twelve to fifteen birds may be seen together. While the species normally frequents the habitats mentioned above, it is often seen in birches, heather, larches, pinewoods, roadside ditches and indeed anywhere that seeds and buds are available. When Bullfinches are feeding on heather buds they may be seen at some distance from cover or at high woods. There is a record for example from the East Kip Plantation at 1400 feet where the birds were feeding on the heather on 24th March 1946.

Summer records are less numerous, but the species is rather secretive at this season. Bullfinches nest in small numbers at, for example, Kirk Loan, Currie, West Kenleith, Logan Cottage, Glencorse Ravine, Bonaly Park, Torduff and Threipmuir. There are also records from shrubberies at Slipperfield and along the Water of Leith during the breeding season.

There is no indication of migration either in spring or autumn, but there is considerable evidence that Bullfinches are much commoner now than even ten years ago.

The *Old Statistical Account of Scotland* 1791 describes the status in Mid Calder Parish as: "In Calder Wood the Bullfinches are pretty numerous; and this is all the more remarkable as they are not common in the neighbourhood," while in Linton Parish we are told that: "The Bullfinches . . . are but lately come." No doubt the lack of suitable cover in the Pentlands at that time would have limited the distribution.

J. Kirke Nash said in 1935: "Mr Evans' notes are sufficiently sparse to indicate that even up to 1917 the bird was not common in the area." One of these notes quotes the gamekeeper at Cockburnhill as saying: "There are a pair or two about the woods but they are very scarce now."

J. Kirke Nash himself said that the Bullfinch was rare in Midlothian (1935), while in the same year Rintoul and Baxter (*A Vertebrate Fauna of the Forth*) recorded that Bullfinches were reported as being seen on the Pentlands every winter and it was possible that they had bred in the woods there, but they had no record of their doing so. On the other hand David Hamilton told me in 1947 that during this century he had found Bullfinches common at Balerno, Currie, and Crosswood, and had seen nests or young at Malleny Curling Pond and in the Balerno district.

In the 1932-34 census outings the total figures were none in March, none in September and twenty-one in December. In 1934 John Prentice, gamekeeper at Baddinsgill, wrote saying that in 1933 Bullfinches were very numerous in November in the Baddinsgill area. J. K. Adams told me that he heard a Bullfinch at Bonaly Tower on 15th February 1945, and that a pair were resident in a thicket at the west end of Threipmuir from 1944 to 1946.

During the 1948-49 traverse when Bullfinches were seen or heard pretty regularly, the species was recorded in Cap Law Wood as early as 29th February, and Braid Law Wood on 28th March. It was usually to be seen at Malleny Curling Pond and Middle Threipmuir where a very young bird was seen in the willows on 26th September.

G. L. Sandeman has many records. He found Bullfinches breeding near Flotterstone in 1948 and 1949. In the 1950 *Edinburgh Bird Bulletin* there was a record from Buteland on 12th November, and in 1957 there was a flock of twelve feeding on heather at Loganlee Reservoir on 2nd January.

G. L. Sandeman recorded Bullfinches at Crosswood during the breeding seasons of 1970 to 1975 inclusive. Some of his other records are:

1970	October 23rd	Glencorse Ravine	Ten
1972	November 2nd	Cairns Castle	Male
1973	July 9th	Dreghorn	Breeding
	September 13th	Kirkton	A juvenile
1974	May 29th	Dreghorn	Breeding

In 1971 R. L. Swann said of Threipmuir: "One pair nests. Up to twenty have been recorded in winter."

The preponderance of winter records continued in 1981 and 1983 as the following sightings show:

1981	February 1st	Loganlee	Nine
	December 11th		
	January 7th	Bavelaw	Eleven
	January 9th	Red Moss	Nine
1983	November 2nd	Dreghorn	Six

There was another record from Bonaly on 2nd March 1983, and seven were seen at Threipmuir on 31st December 1986.

BUNTINGS

Snow Bunting. *Plectrophenax nivalis.* Winter visitor in variable numbers.

The Snow Bunting can be expected any time from the middle of October to the middle of March, and visits are often associated with snowy weather. Numbers are very variable, for in some years none are present while in others there are records ranging from one bird to several hundreds.

Habitats visited vary from barren hillsides, heather moors, stubble, the island on Harperrig, manured fields, and other places where seeds are available. We have no records of association with other species.

In 1845 the Snow Bunting was recorded as a winter visitor to Colinton Parish (*New Statistical Account for Scotland*), and on 27th October 1892 W. Evans saw one at Fairmilehead. On 30th October 1893 he recorded a flock near Rullion Green, and on 13th November 1897 a flock was seen on Swanston Hill. David Hamilton saw a few at the West Kip on 18th December 1910, and on 31st December 1928 a number at the Water of Leith near Balerno, and also at Threipmuir. He commented in his diary that Snow Buntings were very plentiful everywhere that year.

The 1932-34 total census figures were none in March, none in September and twenty in December. In 1935 Iain Ogilvie told me that he saw small numbers on Cap Law, Mount Maw, and Craigengar between 16th October and 16th November in that year.

During the period 1935-39 Snow Buntings were common in winter on football grounds in Edinburgh. They even alighted to feed on the International Rugby Football Ground at Murrayfield while an international game was in progress.

During the 1948-49 traverse Snow Buntings were first seen on 7th March and again on 21st March. In the autumn the first record was on 10th October and the species continued to be seen throughout the winter until 27th February. A flock of 300 was seen at Harelaw Reservoir on 2nd January 1949.

Some later notes are:

1954	March 2nd	Clubbiedean	Five
1957	January 2nd	Threipmuir	Fifty
1958	January 19th	Threipmuir	Two flocks of thirteen each
	December 7th	Glencorse	Seventy-five
1962	January 11th	Swanston	One hundred and fifty
	December 24th	Swanston	Over two hundred
1967	January 2nd	Threipmuir	Fifteen
1973	October 30th	Crosswood	One
1974	December 12th	Threipmuir	Two hundred
1975	January 1st	Threipmuir	Thirty
	March 4th	Threipmuir	Two
	December 15th	Harperrig	Nineteen

Recent records are:

1975	December 23rd	Harperrig	One hundred
1979	February 4th	Threipmuir	Seventy-six
1981	January 7th	Threipmuir	Two
1984	January 15th	Glencorse	Fifty

The species was scarce in 1985 with only two records both at Threipmuir on 2nd January and 5th February. In 1986, however, there were records:

January 4th and 16th	Threipmuir	One hundred and twenty
February 11th	Threipmuir	Two hundred
February 2nd	East Rig	Twenty
December 3rd	East Kip	Eight

Yellowhammer. *Emberiza citrinella.* Resident. Breeds. Summer visitor. Winter visitor.

In winter the Yellowhammer frequents the low ground feeding at farmyards, stackyards, livestock feeding pens, and to a lesser extent along the hedgerows. Here it consorts with winter finch flocks, usually in small numbers of up to ten birds, but there are occasional records of larger flocks, which suggest that the winter population may be augmented from outside the area. In 1933 for example, fifty to one hundred were seen on 24th December at Upper Dene Park with Reed Buntings; and on 24th February 1935 thirty to forty were seen at Middle Kenleith along with Greenfinches. Breeding birds move into their nesting areas about the end of February or early in March. The species is then well distributed along hedges and young plantations, and especially in areas of whin on the lower slopes. No marked immigration of breeding birds or spring passage migrants is noticeable, and late in March small groups can still be seen feeding as in winter.

Many breeding birds appear to leave the area during August, while winter immigrants arrive in October as a rule. The total numbers seen in the 1932-34 census outings were 45 in March, 12 in September and 39 in December. In May 1934 Rintoul and Baxter found the species common in whins. During the 1948-49 traverse Yellowhammers were well distributed, particularly on low ground, and were not seen in high woods. R. L. Swann said of Threipmuir in 1971: "Seen in small numbers throughout the year. One pair probably breeds in the area along the road leading to the reservoir."

G. L. Sandeman has the following notes of flocks:

1974	February 18th	Swanston Burn	Thirty-six to forty
1975	October 30th	Lothianburn to Swanston	Twenty plus

There were three to six breeding sites in the Flotterstone to Glencorse district between 1981 and 1984 and records of flocks as below:

1981	January 10th	Balerno	Seventeen
	February 10th	Clubbiedean	Fifty
	December 8th	Clubbiedean	Twenty

| 1982 | January 21st | Swanston | Sixty |
| 1984 | February 26th | Currie | Forty-five |

In both 1985 and 1986 the species was breeding at Threipmuir.

Reed Bunting. *Emberiza schoeniclus.* Resident. Breeds. Winter visitor. Summer visitor.

In winter the Reed Bunting frequents the reedy parts of the lower reservoirs, pools, marshy areas in fields, and so on; but it is more often seen in stackyards and along hedges, often at some distance from water. There are also records from birches at Malleny Curling Pond, in the willows at Bavelaw, among bracken at East Threipmuir Marsh, and on arable land with finch flocks.

The Reed Bunting is not normally found in large numbers, but occasionally flocks occur. For example fifty to a hundred were seen at Upper Dene Park on 24th December 1933 along with Yellowhammers. Such flocks are no doubt composed of winter visitors.

Reed Buntings breed freely at Bavelaw and to a lesser extent at the other reservoirs with suitable cover, for example Harperrig, Crosswood, Torduff, Clubbiedean, West Water, North Esk and Baddinsgill. They also breed at ponds such as Malleny Curling Pond, Malleny Mills Pond, and along lowland burns.

In 1837 Macgillivray found a nest at Ravelrig bog, and in 1889 Harold Raeburn found nests at Harelaw and Threipmuir Reservoirs.

The total 1932-34 census figures were 32 in March, 20 in September and 24 in December. In the *Vertebrate Fauna of Forth* Rintoul and Baxter said that the Reed Bunting was not uncommon in the Pentlands, and in May 1934 they found it nesting freely at Bavelaw.

In 1947 David Hamilton told me that he had seen nests beside the Water of Leith above Balerno, along the Lanark road there, and at Bavelaw. He noted a number at Threipmuir on 20th January 1935.

During the 1948-49 traverse there were no records on 22nd August, 5th September, and 19th and 26th December; but Reed Buntings were seen surprisingly high up on the hills on the

Kitchen Moss, Scroggy Hill, Pillar Knowe, and at both Braid Law and Cap Law.

G. L. Sandeman said of the Glencorse valley: "Odd birds mostly in March to June," and in 1971 R. L. Swann said of Threipmuir: "Several pairs breed, the largest numbers being seen in spring when up to thirty may be present."

The number of breeding territories given for the Bavelaw/Threipmuir area for the years 1980-84 varied between fifteen and twenty-four.

Corn Bunting. *Miliaria calandra.* Formerly resident and breeding, also summer visitor, but present status doubtful.

Before the 1939-45 war the species occurred in the fields at Clubbiedean and principally in the Swanston Oxgangs area when it was farmland. Now hedges have been removed, the new ring road gashes through the fields, and there has been considerable housing development, which is increasing. As a result it is doubtful if a viable breeding population of Corn Buntings remains.

It appears however that the Corn Bunting was never common in the Pentlands. David Hamilton's only record up to 1947 was of several being seen at Lothianburn on 31st January 1903.

No Corn Buntings were seen on either the 1932-34 census or the 1948-49 traverse. There are however the following records:

1937	May 18th	Hunter's Tryst	One
1939	May 6th	Threipmuir	Song heard
1948	July 27th	Lothianburn	One
1949	May 2nd, 16th and 31st	Lothianburn	Recorded
	May 2nd	Kirkton Farm	One
1952	June 25th	Lothianburn	Recorded
1954	May 17th and 26th	Lothianburn	Recorded
1970	June 3rd	Lothianburn	Recorded
	June 29th	Swanston	One
1971	June 30th	Swanston	One
1974	February 18th	Swanston Burn	Five

SUMMARY OF CENSUS WORK 1932-1934

C ENSUSES were carried out by members of the Inverleith Field Club and the Midlothian Ornithological Club on nine occasions, in spring, autumn and midwinter of each of the three years. We even managed to have outings on Christmas Eve in 1932 and on Christmas Day in 1933.

Census dates were:

	1932	1933	1934
March	19th	25th	24th
September	10th	9th	8th
December	24th	25th	22nd

It was not easily possible to conduct a census during the breeding season due to holiday and other commitments, so we do not know how populations changed over a complete year.

The number of observers varied from five to twelve. The mileage covered on each census was never less than thirty, and on 12th March 1933 an astonishing distance of nearly seventy miles was walked. In all we walked a total of four hundred and ten miles.

With a team of keen young and knowledgeable observers a very good indication of the variation in the bird population was obtained for a series of traverses in the Pentlands. We normally tried to start each census as soon as convenient each day, but except on Christmas Day 1933 when we got away soon after breakfast, we started about midday and continued until dark. An indication of the places checked is given below. Each visit is marked thus +

	1932			1933			1934		
	Mar.	Sept.	Dec.	Mar.	Sept.	Dec.	Mar.	Sept.	Dec.
Torduff	+	+	+	+	+	+	+	+	+
Clubbiedean	+	+	+	+	+	+	+	+	+
Bonaly	+	+	+	+	+	+	−	+	−
Glencorse	+	+	+	+	+	+	+	+	+
Loganlea	+	−	+	+	+	+	+	+	−

| | 1932 | | | 1933 | | | 1934 | | |
	Mar.	Sept.	Dec.	Mar.	Sept.	Dec.	Mar.	Sept.	Dec.
Harelaw	+	+	+	+	+	+	+	+	+
Threipmuir	+	+	+	+	+	+	+	+	+
North Esk	+	+	+	+	+	−	+	−	+
Harperrig	+	+	+	+	+	+	+	+	+
Crosswood	+	+	+	+	+	+	+	+	+
Crane Loch	+	+	−	+	+	−	−	+	−
Kersew Pond	+	+	−	−	−	−	−	−	−
Slipperfield	+	+	+	−	+	−	−	+	−
Baddinsgill	+	+	+	+	+	−	+	−	−

In addition twenty crossings of the Pentlands were made using the hill passes and drove roads to give a taste of what was happening on the high ground. The weather of course varied considerably from census to census and this affected our results to some extent.

The number of species seen during the nine censuses was:

March	Sixty-eight
September	Seventy-three
December	Sixty-five

BIBLIOGRAPHY

Agricultural Survey of Peeblesshire, 1802.

ANDERSON, W. *The Pentland Hills,* 1926.

ANDREWS, Ian J. *The Birds of the Lothians,* 1986.

Annals of Scottish Natural History, 1892-1911.

BAXTER, EVELYN, V. and RINTOUL, LEONARA J.
 Reports on Scottish Ornithology, separate edition, 1911-13.
 Some Scottish Breeding Duck, 1922.
 The Geographical Distribution and Status of Birds in Scotland, 1928.
 A Vertebrate Fauna of the Forth, 1935.
 The Birds of Scotland, 1953.

BERRY, DR JOHN. *The Status and Distribution of Wild Geese and Wild Duck in Scotland,* 1939.

Bird Study, 1953 et seq.

B.T.O. News.

BLACKWOOD, W. T. *History of Peeblesshire,* 1925.

BOECE, HECTOR. *Scotorum Historiae a prima gentis origina,* 1526; Bellendens translation; Hollinshed's translation. 1805 ed.

BOOTH, E. T. Rough Notes, 1881-87.

British Birds, 1907 et seq.

BROWN, J. A. HARVIE. *The Capercaillie in Scotland,* 1879.

CADELL, H. M. *The Story of the Forth,* 1913.

COCHRANE, R. *Pentland Walks,* 1908.

COLQUHOUN, JOHN. *Sporting Days,* 1866.

COWAN, CHARLES. *Reminiscences.*

Crosswood Migration Schedules, 1908-19.

Edinburgh Bird Bulletins.

Edinburgh Natural History Newsletter, 1966.

Edinburgh Naturalist Field Club Transactions.

Edinburgh Ringing Group Reports.

EVANS, A. H. *A Fauna of the Tweed Area,* 1911.

Field, 1853 et seq.

FLEMING, JOHN. *History of British Mammals,* 1828.

FORDUN, JOHN of Scotichronicon 1447, edited and enlarged by W. Bower; Goodall's edition, 1959.

GRAY, ROBERT. *Birds of the West of Scotland,* 1871.

HALDANE, ELIZABETH S. *Scots Gardens in Old Times.*

Ibis, The. 1859 et seq.

INNES, PROFESSOR COSMO. *Scotland in the Middle Ages,* 1860.

JARDINE, SIR WILLIAM. *Birds of Great Britain and Ireland,* Naturalists' Library 1838-42.

LESLIE, JOHN. *De Origine Moribus, et Rebus gestis Scotorum,* 1578.
LINDSAY, ROBERT OF PITSCOTTIE. *The Chronicles of Scotland,* 1814 edition.
Lothian Bird Reports.
MACGILLIVRAY, WILLIAM,
    Descriptions of the Rapacious Birds of Great Britain, 1836.
    History of British Birds, 1837-52.
Memoirs of the Wernerian Natural History Society, 1808-37.
Migration Reports of the Committee of the British Association, 1880-88.
NASH, J. KIRKE. *The Birds of Midlothian,* 1935.
New Statistical Account of Scotland, The, 1834-45.
Proceedings of the Royal Physical Society of Edinburgh, 1854 et seq.
Proceedings of the Royal Society of Edinburgh, 1832 et seq.
RITCHIE, PROFESSOR JAMES. *The Influence of Man on Animal Life in Scotland,* 1920.
Scottish Bird Reports.
Scottish Birds.
Scottish Naturalist, The, 1871-91, 1912-39 and 1948-50.
Smith, Charles J. *Historic South Edinburgh,* 1979.
Statistical Account of Scotland, 1791-99.
TURNBULL, W. P. *Birds of East Lothian,* 1867.
WITHERBY, H. F. *The Handbook of British Birds,* 1938-41.
YOC/ENHS. *Water of Leith Survey,* 1978.
Zoologist, 1894.

    Also articles and notes published in *The Scotsman* and *Evening News.*

SPECIES INDEX

	Page		Page		Page
Auk		Duck		Great Crested	20
Little	100	Long-tailed	43	Little	22
		Tufted	42	Red-necked	21
Bittern	26	Dunlin	75	Slavonian	21
Blackbird	149	Dunnock	137	Greenshank	84
Blackcap	159			Grouse	
Brambling	184	Eagle		Black	56
Bullfinch	195	Golden	50	Red	54
Bunting		White-tailed	46	Gull	
Corn	202			Black-headed	89
Reed	201	Fieldfare	150	Common	94
Snow	198	Finch		Glaucous	97
Buzzard	48	Gold	186	Great Black-	
Honey	46	Green	185	backed	97
Rough-legged	49	Flycatcher		Herring	96
		Pied	166	Lesser Black-	
Capercaillie	58	Spotted	165	backed	95
Chaffinch	183	Fulmar	22	Little	89
Chiffchaff	161				
Chough	172	Gannet	24	Harrier	
Coot	63	Gadwall	35	Hen	46
Cormorant	24	Garganey	39	Marsh	46
Corncrake	61	Godwit		Heron	
Crossbill	194	Bar-tailed	80	Grey	24
Crow		Black-tailed	80	Hoopoe	113
Carrion	175	Goldcrest	163		
Hooded	176	Goldeneye	43	Jackdaw	172
Cuckoo	104	Goosander	45	Jay	170
Curlew	80	Goose			
		Barnacle	33	Kestrel	51
Dipper	133	Bean	28	Kingfisher	111
Diver		Brent	33	Kittiwake	98
Black-throated	20	Canada	32	Knot	73
Great Northern	20	Greylag	29		
Red-throated	20	Pink-footed	29	Lapwing	69
Dotterel	72	Snow	32	Lark	
Dove		White-fronted	29	Shore	117
Collared	103	Goshawk	48	Sky	115
Stock	100	Grebe		Linnet	190
Turtle	104	Black-necked	21		

	Page		*Page*		*Page*
Magpie	171	Redshank	83	Whooper	27
Mallard	37	Spotted	82	Swift	110
Martin		Redstart	139		
House	121	Black	139	Teal	35
Sand	117	Redwing	154	Tern	
Merganser		Robin	138	Arctic	100
Red-breasted	44	Roller	113	Black	100
Merlin	52	Rook	173	Common	98
Moorhen	62	Ruff	76	Sandwich	98
				Thrush	
Nightjar	110			Mistle	155
		Sanderling	73	Song	152
Oriole		Sandgrouse		Tit	
Golden	169	Pallas's	100	Blue	168
Osprey	50	Sandpiper		Coal	167
Ousel		Common	86	Great	168
Ring	146	Curlew	74	Long-tailed	166
Owl		Green	85	Willow	167
Barn	105	Wood	86	Treecreeper	169
Long-eared	107	Scaup	43	Turnstone	88
Short-eared	108	Scoter		Twite	192
Tawny	106	Common	43		
Oystercatcher	65	Shearwater		Wagtail	
		Manx	23	Grey	128
Partridge		Shelduck	33	Pied/White	130/132
Grey	58	Shoveler	39	Yellow	127
Red-legged	58	Shrike		Warbler	
Peregrine	53	Great Grey	170	Garden	159
Petrel		Red-backed	169	Grasshopper	156
Storm	23	Siskin	188	Sedge	157
Pheasant	60	Skua		Willow	162
Pintail	39	Arctic	89	Wood	160
Pipit		Smew	44	Waxwing	132
Meadow	124	Snipe	77	Wheatear	145
Rock	127	Jack	77	Greenland	146
Tree	123	Sparrow		Whimbrel	80
Plover		House	180	Whinchat	140
Golden	68	Tree	181	Whitethroat	158
Grey	69	Sparrowhawk	47	Lesser	158
Ringed	66	Starling	178	Wigeon	33
Pochard	40	Stint		Woodcock	78
		Little	74	Woodpecker	
Quail	59	Temminck's	74	Great Spotted	114
		Stonechat	142	Green	114
Rail		Stone Curlew	66	Woodpigeon	102
Water	60	Swallow	119	Wren	136
Raven	177	Swan		Wryneck	113
Redpoll	192	Bewick's	26		
Mealy	194	Mute	26	Yellowhammer	200

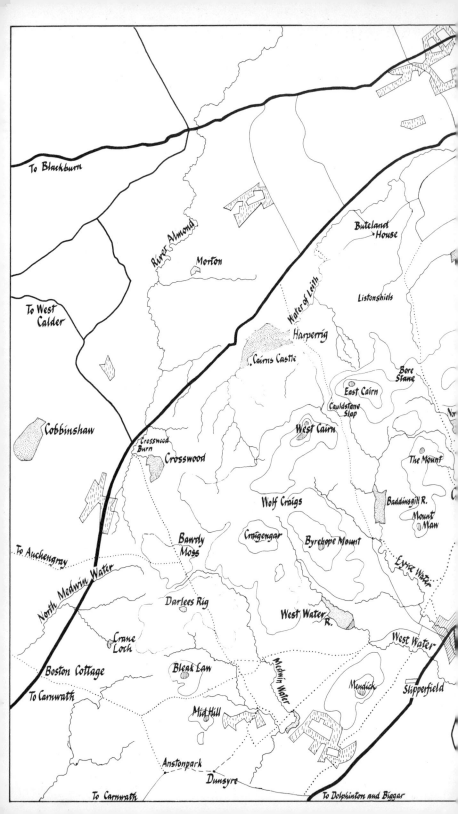

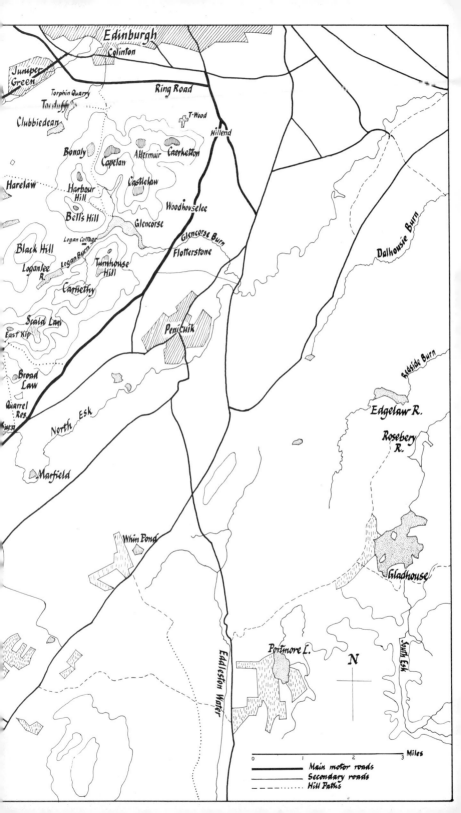